Rethinking
Working-Class
History

Dipesh Chakrabarty

•

Rethinking Working-Class History

BENGAL 1890–1940

PRINCETON
UNIVERSITY PRESS

Published by Princeton University Press, 41 William Street,
Princeton, New Jersey 08540
In the United Kingdom: Princeton University Press, Guildford, Surrey

Publication of this book has been aided by grants from the
Paul Mellon Fund of Princeton University Press and from the University of Melbourne

This book has been composed in Linotron Sabon

Clothbound editions of Princeton University Press books
are printed on acid-free paper, and binding materials are
chosen for strength and durability. Paperbacks, although satisfactory
for personal collections, are not usually suitable for library rebinding

Printed in the United States of America by Princeton University Press,
Princeton, New Jersey

Library of Congress Cataloging-in-Publication Data

Chakrabarty, Dipesh.
Rethinking working-class history: Bengal, 1890–1940 / Dipesh Chakrabarty.
p. cm.   Bibliography: p.   Includes index.
ISBN 0-691-05548-3 (alk. paper)
1. Jute industry workers—India—Calcutta—History—19th century.
2. Jute industry workers—India—Calcutta—History—20th century.
I. Title.
HD8039.J82I483 1989   331.7'6713'09541—dc19   88-19954

TO MY PARENTS
AND TO
KAVERI AND ARKO

CONTENTS

LIST OF TABLES

PREFACE

> There is a difference between the rule of master over
> slave and the rule of a statesman.
>
> ARISTOTLE, *The Politics*

There cannot be any capitalist production without a working class. But there can be, as Marxists have often pointed out in the recent past, capitalism that subsumes precapitalist relationships. Under certain conditions, the most feudal system of authority can survive at the heart of the most modern of factories. There is nothing in the logic of the market or profit that guarantees an automatic transformation of individuals into citizens. This poses interesting problems of narrative strategy for historical accounts of working classes in countries where the struggle to achieve a certain degree of "liberal" practice in everyday life comes long after the beginning of industrialization. In these contexts, the master-slave dialectic reproduces itself far more often than does the phenomenon of the rule of the citizen.

The problem of choosing an appropriate narrative strategy, in these cases, is even more complicated for the Marxist historian, since Marx's own ideas on the capital-labor relationship often take a hegemonic bourgeois culture for granted. This is the problem that this book addresses by examining in detail the history of a specific labor force—the jute-mill workers of Bengal under British rule. These workers constituted an important section of the Indian working class. The choice of this particular history is admittedly somewhat arbitrary, being contingent on the accidents of my intellectual evolution. In looking at this history in terms of Marx's categories, however, my objective is to develop a critical understanding of these categories themselves and of their use in the construction of historical narratives. I argue that there is an assumption regarding "culture" built into Marx's category of "capital," and much of what I have to say on Indian labor history, and labor history in general, follows from this reading of Marx.

This starting point allows me to develop and sustain two positions throughout the book. First, it helps me to isolate questions of culture and consciousness when looking at a working class that grows in a society where the assumption of a hegemonic bourgeois culture does not apply. Issues relating to working-class consciousness and organization in India are commonly explained by liberal nationalist or Marxist historians as factors following from the nature of Indian economic and technological development, the structure of the labor market, and machinations of the colonial (and the postcolonial) state. While not denying the validity of Marxian political economy as a way of explaining working-class history, I seek to demonstrate that the logic of a particular culture (or consciousness) cannot be explained by the methods of political economy, which often fail to make a distinction between "function" and "reason." Political-economic analysis of culture, however, constitutes the prevalent "common sense" of Marxist labor history in India and this book is an extended polemic against the reductionism inherent in that approach. Culture, one might say, is the "unthought" of Indian Marxism.

Focusing on Marx's assumption regarding culture also helps me to raise another set of questions. These are questions about the way power and authority operate in institutional and interpersonal arrangements in India. Everyday life in India, as all students of Indian anthropology will know, is marked by the relative absence of bourgeois notions of "equality" or individualism." These notions were introduced by the British and have since become significant parts of political rhetoric and formal political ideologies in India. But hierarchy and the violence that sustains it still remain the dominant organizing principles in everyday life.[1] Power, therefore, seldom takes the form of the disciplinary grid that Foucault writes about in his histories of the prison, the clinic, and the mental asylum in the Western context. Of course, these institutions have been grafted onto India along with capitalism, industrialization and a certain form of representative government. But one only has to scratch the surface to find power assuming forms typical of "sovereignty" and doing so in active and mocking defiance of all the requirements of a "disciplinary formation." This is a feature that I trace through the history of protest, organization, and factory rules in the case of the mill hands of Calcutta.

Hierarchy, lack of egalitarianism or individualism in everyday life, the often undemocratic nature of our practices and institutions—these will not surprise observers of Indian society. Yet Marxist historical writings in India show little regard for developing a critical understanding of the quotidian "experience," of the relations that go into its making. Instead the reigning assumption seems to be that inequalities and conflicts handed down from our past persist only because of the

---

[1] Though this book does not follow Louis Dumont's notion of "hierarchy," the importance of his contribution to this field can hardly be overlooked. Louis Dumont, *Homo Hierarchicus: The Caste System and Its Implications* (Chicago and London, 1980). For a discussion of the place physical and verbal violence occupies in Indian relationships of power, see Ranajit Guha, *Elementary Aspects of Peasant Insurgency in Colonial India* (Delhi, 1983), chapter 2.

economic ailments of the country—underdevelopment, unequal distribution of wealth, (neo)imperialist domination, and so forth. Remove them, runs the prescription, and we would move from precapitalist inequalities to capitalist ones.

This is in many ways a strange argument and its economism has always been employed by Indian liberalism (and its finest variety, Marxism) to protect itself from having to confront and criticize the culture of its own practice, which is deeply influenced by the inherent inegalitarianism of Indian society. But the argument has some obvious holes in it. No one needs to be told that the pursuit of equality, in today's world, neither begins nor ends with capitalism. Although there may have been points in human history when the logical connection between bourgeois notions of "equality" and the development of "capital" could be empirically observed, such coincidence has on the whole been atypical of capitalist development. Capitalist production—whether resulting in development or underdevelopment—has thrived in a variety of cultures, ranging from the hierarchical to the most democratic one. Perhaps we have long overestimated capitalism's need or capacity to homogenize the cultural conditions necessary for its own reproduction.

What happens, then, when we have a "working class" born into a culture characterized by the persistence of precapitalist relationships (or by the absence of notions of "citizenship," "individualism," "equality before the law," and so on)? How does this condition affect its capacity for class and revolutionary action? I try to answer these questions in the book. But in raising these questions I obviously take up a political-philosophical position in favor of the struggle to achieve "equality" and this will no doubt leave me open to criticism from several angles. Some of these issues I address in the final chapter. But let me briefly explain here the position that the notion of "equality" (and by implication the notion of "modernity") occupies within the theoretical judgment that informs my effort. The bourgeois idea of "equality," incorporating as it does concepts of "individual rights," "contract," and "possessive individualism," has extremely serious and grave limitations that are necessarily inimical to the construction of any socialist, communitarian ethic and order.[2] Living currently in a liberal-capitalist society, I am only too aware of the bankruptcy of bourgeois individualism. In many respects, it represents a cul-de-sac in

[2] I have taken the term *possessive individualism* from C. B. Macpherson's classic study, *The Political Theory of Possessive Individualism: Hobbes to Locke* (London, 1962).

human history. Yet Marxism shares in some of the premises of bourgeois egalitarianism (while being critical of it), and the task for classi-
cal Marxism was always one of transcending (in the Hegelian sense of
the word) its shortcomings.[3] The "concept of citizen," as Gramsci once
put it, was to "give way to the concept of comrade."[4] But the struggle
for "citizenship" and "equality" was not to be rejected out of hand.
Even the most radical, postmodernist program of challenging bourgeois individualism grounds itself in a principle of opposition to hierarchy. "Do not demand of politics that it restore the "rights" of the
individual, as philosophy has defined them," writes Foucault, trying to
define some "essential principles" of an "art of living" that runs
"counter to all forms of fascism":

> The individual is the product of power. What is needed is to "de-
> individualize" by means of multiplication and displacement,
> diverse combinations. The group must not be the organic bond
> uniting hierarchized individuals, but a constant generator of de-
> individualization.[5]

The question is this: Can we bypass all these dilemmas in third-
world countries like India and build democratic, communitarian institutions on the basis of the nonindividualistic, but hierarchical and illiberal, precapitalist bonds that have survived and sometimes resisted—
or even flourished under—the onslaught of capital? I have written my
book on the assumption that in countries such as ours, several contradictory struggles have to fuse into one. The struggle to be a "citizen"
must be part of the struggle to be a "comrade." We have to fight for
"equality" at the same time as we try to criticize and transcend the
bourgeois version of it. Giving up these battles means embracing an
illiberal, authoritarian, hierarchical social order in the name of socialism.

The ultimate provocation for raising these issues—such as culture,
hierarchy, equality, individualism, and citizenship, in short, the question of the everyday experience—lies in an area that stretches beyond
the purely theoretical. I must not presume to claim a complete objec-
tivity either for my theoretical concerns or for the history that I have

---

[3] See Michel Henry's outstanding work *Marx: A Philosophy of Human Reality*, trans.
Kathleen McLaughlin (Bloomington, 1983). See also Steven Lukes, *Individualism* (Oxford, 1979), and D. F. B. Tucker, *Marxism and Individualism* (Oxford, 1980).

[4] Antonio Gramsci, "Unions and Councils," in his *Selections from Political Writings
1910–1920*, ed. Quintin Hoare and trans. John Matthews (New York, 1977), p. 100.

[5] Michel Foucault, "Preface" to Gilles Deleuze and Felix Guattari, *Anti-Oedipus:
Capitalism and Schizophrenia* (Minneapolis, 1983), p. xiv.

written. Surely one's theoretical choices are completely rational; behind them lurk passions, anger, obsessions, and prejudices. An "Indian" by birth and upbringing, I have seen enough "medieval" spectacles of wealth and poverty to want to situate the "problems" of that culture within a struggle for "modernity." Though aware of the critiques of the Enlightenment now being launched in the name of postmodernism, I simply do not see how any definition or practice of "politics" in present-day India can altogether escape this "struggle."

> The extreme inequality of our ways of life, the excess of idleness among some and the excess of toil among others ... the over-elaborate foods of the rich, which inflame and overwhelm them with indigestion, the bad food of the poor, which they often go without altogether ... those late nights, excesses of all kinds ... the innumerable sorrows and anxieties that people in all classes suffer, and by which the human soul is constantly tormented: these are the fatal proofs that most of our ills are of our own making.[6]

These words, written in a different context more than two centuries ago, still speak to me with force. They remind me of the loudness with which power and wealth (or the lack of either) proclaim their presence in Indian society. They call to mind the contradiction that inhabits the disjuncture in our everyday life between our political ideologies and an undemocratic, hierarchical culture in which the politics of the left are no less caught than those of the right. This book arises, ultimately, from that unhappy consciousness.

Melbourne
February 1988

[6] Jean-Jacques Rousseau, *A Discourse on Inequality* (1755), trans. M. Cranston (Harmondsworth, 1984), p. 84.

ACKNOWLEDGMENTS

My debts are varied and many: to Barun De, my teacher in Calcutta, who gave me my first lessons in history and under whose tutelage this work was first conceived; to Anthony Low, my supervisor in Canberra, for his generosity with time, advise, criticism, and encouragement: to Partha Chatterjee and Ranajit Guha for their intellectual comradeship. My thanks also to those who—either as friends or as dissertation examiners, and in some cases as both—read the manuscript at the different stages of its evolution and offered helpful comments and encouragement: Shahid Amin, David Arnold, Gautam Bhadra, Raghabendra Chattopadhyay, Bernard Cohn, David Hardiman, Eric Hobsbawm, Ahmed Kamal, Sushil Khanna, Gyan Pandey, Peter Reeves, Sumit Sarkar, and Tanika Sarkar. In Australia, Jonathan Bader, David Bennett, Meredith Borthwick, Charles Coppel, Stephen Henningham, Sally Hone, Robin Jeffrey, Brij Lal, Pauline Rule, Julie Stephens, and Roger Stuart have kindly been a captive but responsive audience. In India, Amiya Bagchi, Sabyasachi Bhattacharya, Rajat Ray, and Asok Sen have often performed a similar function. To Ranajit Das Gupta I am specially grateful for a friendship that has survived some strong intellectual disagreements.

I also wish to thank the following for help in collecting source material: Nabaneeta Deb Sen and Basudha Chakraborty for access to the papers of K. C. Roy Chowdhury; J. G. Smith, secretary, Thomas Duff and Company, Dundee, for permission to consult their archives; Sarit Roy and S. K. Chatterjee of the Indian Jute Mills Association, for permission to use their documents; Nirmalya Acharya, for help with procuring some rare books; Raghab Banerjee, Narayanee Banerjee, Rudrangshu Mukherjee, and Lakshmisree Sinha for assistance with archival and field research; the staffs of the West Bengal State Archives, Calcutta, the National Archives of India, Delhi, the India Office Library, London, the Centre for South Asian Studies, Cambridge, the Dundee Central Library, the Dundee University Library Archives, the Dundee and District Union of Jute and Flax Workers, the Archives of Thomas Duff and Company, Dundee, the Menzies Library, and the former South Asian History Section, Australian National University, Canberra.

My friends Rosemary Smith and Leona Jorgensen have typed the manuscript at various stages. Thanks to both of them for their enthusiasm and the many helpful editorial comments they have kindly cared to make.

This study has received institutional support from the Australian National University, Canberra, the University of Melbourne, and the Centre for Studies in Social Sciences, Calcutta. To the authorities of these institutions, my grateful thanks. I also owe thanks to Margaret Case, editor, Princeton University Press, for her interest in this work and her patience toward its author, and for nominating referees whose comments I found extremely useful.

Earlier versions of parts of this book have appeared in different places: chapters 3 and 4 in Ranajit Guha, ed., *Subaltern Studies*, volumes 2 and 3 (Delhi: Oxford University Press, 1983–84), and chapter 5 and a part of chapter 6 in *Past and Present*, numbers 91 and 100, May 1981 and August 1983, respectively. I am grateful to the editors and publishers of these volumes for making it possible for me to reproduce here material previously published.

I must, finally, express my gratitude to my hosts whose hospitality I have enjoyed while engaged in fieldwork: Sayandev Mukherjee and Catherine Daniels in London; Henry and Barbara Daniels in Cambridge; Udaytapan and Krishna Das Gupta in Delhi. I have received invaluable support from my parents and sister in India and from Kaveri in Australia. But to thank them formally would be to behave like a "westernized Indian!"

ABBREVIATIONS

B.P.	Benthall Papers
C.S.A.S.	Centre for South Asian Studies, Cambridge
Com.	Commerce
CPI	Communist Party of India
DYB	*Dundee Year Book*
Ed.	Education
Genl.	General
IESHR	*The Indian Economic and Social History Review*
IJMA	Indian Jute Mills Association
IJMA, Report	*Report of the Indian Jute Mills Association*
IOL	India Office Library, London
IUC	Industrial Unrest Committee (1921)
JMB	*The Jute Mills of Bengal* (1880)
K.C.R.P.	Papers of K. C. Roy Chowdhury
NAI	National Archives of India, New Delhi
NMML	Nehru Memorial Museum and Library, New Delhi
Misc.	Miscellaneous
Poll.	Political
RCLI	*Report of the Royal Commission on Labour in India* (London, 1931)
RNPB	*Report on Native Press (Bengal)*
TDA	Archives of Thomas Duff and Company, Dundee
W.B.S.A.	West Bengal State Archives, Calcutta

Rethinking
Working-Class
History

· 1 ·

INTRODUCTION

If Marx gave the working class a special place and mission in history, it is also clear that he situated this class within a framework of bourgeois relationships. The figure of the worker invoked in his exposition of the category of "capital" was that of a person who belonged to a society where the bourgeois notion of equality was ingrained in culture. Thus Marx considered labor to be a "moment" (i.e. a constituent element) of capital, and capital, according to him, "is a *bourgeois production relation*, a production relation of bourgeois society."[1] The laborer of Marx's assumption had internalized and enjoyed "formal freedom," the freedom of the contract (which brought legal and market relations together), and he enjoyed this not just in abstraction but as "the individual, real person."[2] Until this was ensured and so long as precapitalist, particularistic ties made up and characterized the relations of production, capital, as Marx understood it, was "not yet *capital as such*."[3] This is why Marx thought that the logic of capital could be best deciphered only in a society where "the notion of human equality has already acquired the fixity of a popular prejudice."[4] Hence he chose the historical case of England as the one most illustrative of his argument. Indeed, as we now know from historians in our times, the "notion of equality before the law" was an essential ingredient of the culture with which the English working class handled its experience of

[1] Marx quoted in Roman Rosdolsky, *The Making of Marx's "Capital"* (London, 1980), p. 184, n. 3. Emphasis in original. For Marx's conception of labor as a "moment of capital," see his *Grundrisse: Foundations of the Critique of Political Economy*, trans. Martin Nicolaus (Harmondsworth, 1974), pp. 293–301. *Capital*, vol. 1 (Moscow, n.d.), p. 333, sees labor as "a mode of existence of capital." Hegel's *Logic*, trans. W. Wallace (London, 1975), pp. 79, 113, uses *moment* to mean both "stage" as well as a (constituent) "factor." Jindrich Zelený, *The Logic of Marx* (Oxford, 1980), p. xi, defines *moment* as "one of the elements of a complex conceptual entity."

[2] Marx, *Grundrisse*, p. 464. I should mention that the word *he*, whenever it occurs in an impersonal context in this book, is used in a generic sense.

[3] Ibid., pp. 296–297. Emphasis in original.

[4] Marx, *Capital*, vol. 1, p. 60. Admittedly, Marx made this statement with reference to the problem of deciphering the "secret of the expression of value." But then one has to remember that for Marx capital is self-expanding value and labor a moment of capital. For these and related points see also I.I. Rubin, *Essays on Marx's Theory of Value* (Montreal, 1975).

3

the Industrial Revolution.[5] This of course does not mean that everything about the culture of the English working class was bourgeois. Bourgeois society, Marx said, was "itself a contradictory development" where "relations derived from earlier [social] forms" were still to be found in "stunted" or "travestied" conditions.[6] Clearly, however, to Marx's mind, there were enough empirical instances in English history to allow him to identify and study the structure of bourgeois relations in separation from the prebourgeois ones.

Marx's discussion of the labor-capital relationship as it operated within the capitalist organization of work thus cannot be placed outside his assumption of a hegemonic bourgeois culture. This assumption, it will be shown in later chapters of this work, is a crucial one in Marx's understanding of the working class. On it rests his notions of "industrial discipline," "capitalist authority," and similar ideas that he used in analyzing the labor process in a capitalist factory. In other words, it is a key assumption in Marx's discussion of the power relationship between labor and capital, and since "power" or "authority" cannot be thought of without linking it to "consciousness," it can also be argued that a hegemonic bourgeois culture is an indispensable aspect of the social framework within which Marx locates his idea of working class consciousness.[7]

I propose to illustrate this argument here by looking at the issues of "discipline," "authority," "protest," "solidarity," and "organization" in the case of a particular working class—the jute-mill workers of Calcutta—that was *not* born into a "bourgeois society," but belonged rather to a culture that was largely precapitalist.[8] I shall seek to demonstrate how the predominance of prebourgeois relationships seriously affected these workers in respect of their capacity to constitute themselves into a class by developing the necessary kinds of solidarity, organization, and consciousness.

To maintain a nonreductionist view of "culture," however, is to risk being labeled a culturalist, especially by those Marxists who advocate the "primacy of the economic" thesis.[9] Indeed, to go against that thesis

[5] The classic statement is E. P. Thompson's *The Making of the English Working Class* (Harmondsworth, 1968).
[6] Marx, *Grundrisse*, pp. 105–106.
[7] The association between power and consciousness is discussed in chapters 3 and 5, below.
[8] Here and elsewhere in this work, the expression *working class* is used in a designative manner, that is, without any connotations of class consciousness.
[9] The term *culturalist* has gained currency in English historigraphy in the recent debate around E. P. Thompson's work. See the essays organized under the general heading "Culturalism" in Raphael Samuel, ed., *People's History and Socialist Theory* (London,

is also to invite nationalist criticism, since problems of Indian political
culture and democracy have for long been blamed on the "economic"
and material conditions created by colonialism and the resulting underdevelopment.[10] In labor history, as I have said before, this takes the
form of a certain kind of "economistic" understanding of issues of
"class" and "class consciousness." Obviously, at the core of this outlook is a deep-seated, crude materialism of the "matter over mind"
variety.

This book, as I have indicated in the Preface, is in the main a refusal
to accept this "materialism" and the conclusions that arise within it.
To do that, however, is not to revert back to seeing "culture" in a
casual, determining relationship with "history"; I do not wish simply
to reverse the dichotomous hierarchy that has been erected between
"material conditions" and "culture/consciousness." To me, this assumed dichotomy seems invalid and unnecessary to the project(s) of
Marxism.[11] As several recent commentators on Marx have cogently
argued, an acceptance of the centrality of categories like "mode of production," "labor," and "praxis" to Marxian social analysis, or of
Marx's famous statement about "social being" determining "consciousness," in no way entails the positing of a distinction between
"matter" and "spirit."[12] Having to interpret, as Gadamer has recently

---

1981), pp. 375–408. That my argument is not the same as Thompson's will be clear to
any careful reader.

[10] The typical figure in this respect is Jawaharlal Nehru, whose "Marxism" of the
1930s seems to provide the framework for many Marxist Indian historians even today.
See my "Invitation to a Dialogue," in Ranajit Guha, ed., *Subaltern Studies IV: Writings
on South Asian History and Society* (Delhi, 1985), pp. 364–375. Gyanendra Pandey's
forthcoming book, "Community Consciousness and Communal Strife in Colonial
North India," should further enlighten us on this question. See also Partha Chatterjee,
Nationalist Thought and the Colonial World: A Derivative Discourse? (London, 1986).

[11] I realize that this position would be contrary to many familiar readings of Marxism,
the writings of Marx and Engels being themselves open to contradictory interpretations.
G. A. Cohen's *Karl Marx's Theory of History: A Defense* (Princeton, 1978) provides a
sophisticated reading entirely opposed to the ones that I find acceptable. The status of
the question of "determination" in history remains a contested one within Marxian theory. Alvin Gouldner's *The Two Marxisms: Contradictions and Anomalies in the Development of Theory* (London, 1980) is a useful contribution to the subject.

[12] The literature bearing on this question is vast and a proper discussion must include
Marx's own texts. The following is a limited and arbitrary sample: Shlomo Avineri, *The
Social and Political Thought of Karl Marx* (Cambridge, 1970), pp. 65–77; Terrell
Carver, "Marxism as Method," in Terrence Ball and James Farr, eds., *After Marx* (Cam-
bridge, 1984), pp. 261–279; Georges Labica, *Marxism and the Status of Philosophy*
(Brighton, 1980), pp. 277–287; Michael Ryan, *Marxism and Deconstruction: A Critical
Articulation* (Baltimore and London, 1982), pp. 82–102; A. Pažanin, "Overcoming the
Opposition between Idealism and Materialism in Husserl and Marx," in B. Waldenfels

put it, is a "primordial givenness" of our world orientation.[13] Culture,
the practico-discursive field that exists in history and where this her-
meneutic activity is carried out, is therefore not subject to any rules
originating "outside" itself and constituting, as it were, such an "outside."

It follows then that the "universal" categories of Marx's thought,
such as "capital" and "labor," considered in their interrelationship,
offer us no master narrative of the history of "consciousness" or "culture" (and, by extension, of "politics"). To write "history" using these
categories is to assume a double stance, for it is also to interrogate the
nature of these categories themselves, to question the project that
stamps itself on their usage. There is thus no "working class" or
"working-class consciousness" that, to speak with Foucault, "is either
transcendental in relation to the field of events or runs in its empty
sameness throughout the course of history."[14] An analytic strategy that
seeks to establish a "working class" as the "subject" of its history must
also engage in the discursive formation that makes the emergence of
such a subject-category possible.

The conclusions that follow when the history of a working class in
a country such as India is read with these theoretical considerations in
mind are set out in the rest of this book. For the remaining part of this
chapter and until the end of chapter 2, I shall be mainly engaged in
developing the empirical context of the particular history at hand—the
jute-mill workers of Calcutta between 1890 and 1940—before returning again to theoretical issues in subsequent portions of the book. A
word needs to be said about the terminal dates selected for this study,
1890 and 1940. They refer mainly to the period for which I have examined the available historical documents. But the argument, I hope,
is not too circumscribed by the particular history in which it is
grounded.

THERE WAS a stage in the history of Calcutta when the city owed its
economic importance and fame to the jute mills that—thanks to British
enterprise in India—lined the two sides of the river Hooghly both

---

et al., eds. *Phenomenology and Marxism*, trans. J. Claude Evans, Jr. (London, 1984),
pp. 82–101. Bertell Ollman's *Alienation: Marx's Conception of Man in Capitalist Society* (Cambridge, 1977) has an interesting discussion of the ambiguities inherent in the
term *determination* as used by Marx.

[13] Hans-Georg Gadamer, "The Hermeneutics of Suspicion," in J. N. Mohanty, ed.,
Phenomenology and the Human Sciences (Dordrecht, 1985), pp. 73–83.

[14] Michael Foucault, "Truth and Power," in his *Power/Knowledge: Selected Interviews and Other Writings 1972–1977*, trans. Colin Gordon et al., ed. Colin Gordon
(Brighton, 1980), p. 117.

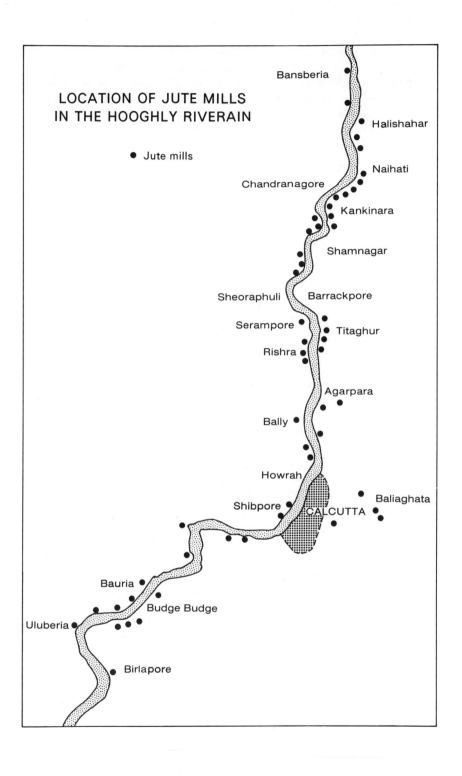

LOCATION OF JUTE MILLS
IN THE HOOGHLY RIVERAIN

● Jute mills

Bansberia

Halishahar

Naihati

Chandranagore

Kankinara

Shamnagar

Sheoraphuli   Barrackpore

Serampore   Titaghur

Rishra

Agarpara

Bally

Howrah

Shibpore   CALCUTTA   Baliaghata

Bauria

Budge Budge

Uluberia

Birlapore

north and south of the city. "To write about Calcutta without saying a word about jute," said a tourist guide to the city in 1906, "would be as bad as to deprive the lamb of its mint sauce."[15] Started in 1855, this industry by the 1910s was the most important jute industry in the world, consuming more raw jute than the "rest of the world" put together.[16] The chief advantage that the industry had over its rivals in other countries was its proximity to the source of its raw material. India, and Bengal in particular, had a virtual monopoly in the production of raw jute. In 1945–46 India produced 97 percent of the total world supply of raw jute and by far the greater part of it was produced in Bengal, eastern Bengal alone accounting for "nearly 60 percent of the total production of jute in the whole of India."[17] According to one estimate, Bengal produced more than 88 percent of the jute grown in India between 1922 and 1931.[18] Bengal was thus the main producer of jute; and jute manufactures—mainly cheap packing and wrapping material—being largely meant for overseas markets, most of the Indian jute mills came to be set up within a very narrow geographical region around the port city of Calcutta. "In 1940," writes T. R. Sharma, "95.5 per cent. of the jute looms in India were located in Bengal and all the jute factories containing these looms were situated in a small strip of land about 60 miles long and two miles broad, along both the banks of the Hooghly, above and below Calcutta."[19] The main centers of the Calcutta industry are shown in the map provided here.

The Indian jute industry was thus much more localized, geographically speaking, than the other important industry of India, the cotton textile industry. Moreover, individual jute mills employed a larger number of workers than did individual cotton mills. "While the average number of workers employed in the cotton industry [was] about 1,150 per establishment in 1929, the average number employed in the jute industry per establishment [was] nearly 3,635 in the same year."[20] The jute industry therefore brought together a very large number of people and put them all within a narrow geographical area under broadly similar conditions of life and labor. At the peak of the prosperity of the industry, in the 1920s, this was a labor force well over 300,000 in number. Even in the 1930s, when the industry suffered a

[15] W. K. Firminger, *Thacker's Guide to Calcutta* (Calcutta, 1906), p. 237.

[16] See D. R. Wallace, *The Romance of Jute* (London, 1928), p. 106.

[17] Tulsi Ram Sharma, *Location of Industries in India* (Bombay, 1954), p. 89.

[18] H. K. Chaturvedi, "On Jute Industry in Bengal," *Marxist Miscellany*, vol. 7, April 1946, pp. 94–143. I owe this reference to Stephen Gourlay.

[19] Sharma, *Location*, p. 89.

[20] P. S. Lokanathan, *Industrial Organization in India* (London, 1935), p. 112.

depression, the number of people employed by it remained substantially greater than 250,000 (Table 1.1).

Most of the jute laborers were adult males, women on an average forming about 16 percent of the labor force between 1921 and 1930 and about 13 percent in the decade that followed. Ranajit Das Gupta, who has made a detailed study of the supply of labor to the Calcutta jute mills, notes that before the 1890s most of the laborers were Bengalis.[21] Before long, however, streams of migration flowed in from other provinces of India—mainly the United Provinces (U.P.), Bihar, Orissa, Madras, and the Central Provinces—and the majority of the jute workers in the twentieth century belonged to the category of "migrants." A census was taken of the jute-mill laborers in 1921. By this time, according to Das Gupta, "the formation of the jute labour force [had been] completed." In 1921, of the approximately 280,000 jute-mill workers in Bengal, only 24 percent were Bengalis; 33 percent came from Bihar, 10 percent from Orissa, 23 percent from U.P., 4 percent from Madras, and less than 3 percent from other parts of India or outside India.[22]

The Indian censuses for 1911 and 1921 also gave some information regarding the caste backgrounds of the workers. The details have been reproduced in Das Gupta's study. His analysis shows that most of the laborers were low-caste people and "untouchables," "cultivators with little or no land, members of traditional laboring and service categories and artisans from the declining crafts" of northern India.[23] The western districts of Bihar (Gaya, Patna, Shababad, Saran, and Muzaffarpur), the eastern districts of U.P. (Azamgarh, Ballia, Ghazipur, Benares, and Jaunpur), Cuttack and Balasore in Orissa, and Ganjam in the Madras Presidency were the main supply areas for jute labor in Bengal.[24] In terms of their religious composition, about 30 percent of the jute workers were Muslims in 1929 and a little more than 69 percent Hindus.[25]

Though one of the largest working classes in the country, the jute-mill workers were also among the lowest paid of the industrial workers in India.[26] This was reflected in their dismal poverty and in their prob-

---

[21] Ranajit Das Gupta, "Factory Labour in Eastern India: Sources of Supply, 1855–1946: Some Preliminary Findings," IESHR, vol. 8, no. 3, 1976.

[22] Ibid., p. 281 and table 7, p. 298.

[23] Ibid., p. 315.

[24] Ibid., p. 292.

[25] W.B.S.A., Com. Dept. Com. Br., April 1930, A 19–20.

[26] The average monthly wage for workers in Calcutta jute mills between 1900 and 1939 was Rs. 15.61. The corresponding figures for the textile-mill workers in Bombay

TABLE 1.1.
Number of people employed in the jute industry of Bengal, 1912–44.

Year	No. of factories	No. of adult males	No. of adult females	No. of children
1912	61	145,389	31,329	23,007
1913	64	158,261	34,010	24,106
1914	69	167,858	36,800	25,909
1915	70	181,445	40,674	26,646
1916	70	191,036	42,145	27,603
1917	71	192,667	41,395	27,320
1918	72	199,977	43,278	27,709
1919	72	201,009	43,112	28,628
1920	73	207,255	44,545	28,521
1921	77	207,908	44,705	29,235
1922	80	239,660	49,257	28,267
1923	83	242,652	51,495	28,400
1924	85	252,107	54,801	27,823
1925	83	256,312	55,511	26,474
1926	86	253,935	52,827	20,785
1927	85	253,681	52,935	19,249
1928	86	260,342	53,678	17,879
1929	90	267,717	54,670	17,278
1930	91	264,417	52,114	11,646
1931	93	222,573	42,254	3,462
1932	94	212,505	40,294	1,515
1933	92	208,246	37,337	1,134
1934	93	213,894	36,932	915
1935	95	225,372	37,749	278
1936	94	233,481	38,261	4
1937	96	249,737	37,997	9
1938	97	242,342	36,683	9
1939	101	243,496	37,699	34
1940	101	248,046	36,640	34
1941	101	251,388	35,255	38
1942	101	252,799	35,083	32
1943	101	245,125	34,759	35
1944	101	231,121	36,005	67

SOURCE: S. R. Deshpande, *Report on an Enquiry into Conditions of Labour in the Jute Mill Industry in India* (Delhi, 1946), p. 6.

10

lems of housing, health, and chronic indebtedness. Their wages were often not enough to support their families and most jute workers—it is difficult to say just how many—left their families at "home" in the countryside and took long leaves to visit them when their means permitted.[27] The "majority of the [jute] workers" then, as a government report put it in 1946, "[had] some connection with lands in their villages." This, however, did not "always mean that they own[ed] the land." More often than not, "instead of receiving income from agriculture, they have to meet certain incidental expenses regarding farming being done in the villages by their relatives," apart from having to provide money "for certain conventional, although nonetheless obligatory expenses, such as marriages and funerals," when the workers had "no option except to borrow money to meet these obligations."[28]

In the slums around the jute mills of Calcutta there thus lived thousands of unfortunate human beings whose cheap labor served well the needs of the mill owners but whose capacity for bargaining a better deal out of the latter always remained low. The history of these people may therefore appear to provide an excellent subject for political-economic analysis. What was the labor market like? What were the "needs" of "capital"? What was the role of the colonial state? These and other similar questions have usually engaged the attention of scholars who have studied this particular group of laborers. These concerns are understandable, for factors usually classified as political and economic are of undoubted importance in the history of any working class. But problems arise when they are seen, in some sense, as the "primary" determinants of the state of workers' organization and consciousness. There is, of course, the most obvious humanist objection that such a point of view leaves us no clues to what role the workers themselves, as the willing subjects of their own history, played in it; or what role the bosses played, as human beings endowed with particular kinds of mentalities, in determining the nature of that history. More important, there is also the question of insisting on a place for a non-reductive view of "culture" or "consciousness" within Marxist theory itself. It is true that for Marxist historians of working-class consciousness, humanism always presents a "danger" of reducing the relations of productions to "mere human relations," as Althusser remarks in *Reading Capital*. Yet the solution offered by Balibar in the same

---

and Ahmedabad were Rs. 23.71 and Rs. 23.21, respectively. See A. K. Bagchi, *Private Investment in India 1900–1939* (Cambridge, 1972), p. 126.

[27] See Radhakamal Mukherjee, *The Indian Working Class* (Bombay, 1948), p. 10.

[28] S. R. Deshpande, *Report on an Enquiry into Conditions of Labour in the Jute Mill Industry in India* (Delhi, 1946), p. 28.

book—one that reduces the "humanness" of the worker on the shop floor to "a set of physical and intellectual qualities, a sum of cultural habits (an empirical knowledge of the materials, of the tricks of the trade, up to and including the crafts secrets, etc.)"—completely slurs over the question of the role that "consciousness" or "culture" might play in the structuring of the relations of production.[29] Production relations are relations after all, and relations, as Marx once said, can become manifest only through the mediation of ideas.[30] Ideas, that is, "consciousness," must therefore be central to any understanding of "relations of production."

Even at a less abstract level, it may be said that the so-called economic, technical, or political factors, on their part, do not operate outside culture. Behind the jute industry's demand for cheap unskilled labor, its problems of industrial discipline, or its choice of technology, lay the culture of the "bosses"—a deeply entrenched mercantilist outlook and the cultural milieu of the British Raj in India. This culture did not always act in the best "economic" interests of the industry. The same may be said of the jute-mill laborers. Their notions of authority, their modes of protest, the problems of their organizations, and the weakness of their solidarity all reveal, on inspection, the existence of a prebourgeois culture and consciousness that in combination with and acting through the so-called economic and political factors, impaired their capacity to act as a class. This is what eventually leads us to emphasize the importance, in Marx's discussion of labor-capital relationship, of his assumption regarding a hegemonic bourgeois culture.

The subsequent chapters of this study will develop these points. Chapter 2 takes a long view of the history of the industry. Its polemical target is the widespread practice of explaining workers' organization and "consciousness" in terms of something like the "needs of capital" or, in more common-sense language, the "nature" of the industry they work for. These "needs" in turn are seen as arising from a rational, economic calculus universal to "capital." By documenting the entrenched mercantilist spirit of the industry, chapter 2 aims to demonstrate that even such apparently "rational" "needs" as those relating to technology, for instance, are discursively produced in particular historical conjunctures and their invocation, therefore, does not necessarily win the day against the proponents of "culture." I carry forward this argument in chapters that come next. Chapter 3 describes the

[29] Louis Althusser and Étienne Balibar, *Reading Capital*, trans. Ben Brewster (London, 1977), pp. 139–140, 238.

[30] Cf. Marx: "Relations can be expressed, of course, only in ideas . . ." in *Grundrisse*, p. 164.

working and living conditions of the workers, conditions that are usually seen as having a determining influence on working-class consciousness. I, on the contrary, argue that questions relating to "culture" are built into the very structure of our knowledge of these
conditions. The following three chapters, 4, 5, and 6, look at the problems of organization, protest, and solidarity, respectively, in the jute
workers' history and attempt to relate these to the issue of consciousness. I close the discussion in a concluding chapter by returning to the
questions that inform the enterprise that this book represents, and end
by pulling together the elements of a possible auto-critique that, I
hope, runs throughout the book.

· 2 ·

JUTE: THE NATURE OF
THE INDUSTRY

A trader's mentality characterized entrepreneurship in the jute industry of Calcutta. "In the working of a jute mill there [were] three distinct operations," said the *Indian Investors' Year Book* in 1911: "the buying of raw jute, its manufacture into fabrics, and the sale of those fabrics." Of these three operations, buying and selling were considered "the most important," requiring "the exercise of much judgement and foresight," much more than the process of manufacturing did.[1] The main products of the industry—jute bags called hessian and sacking—had remained the same for years and were to continue unchanged in the years to come. Crude and simple in their structure, these bags were produced by a technology that was essentially mechanical in nature and easy to operate. The industry was guided by the belief that a "good" management of costs and prices was the key to economic success. So long as they kept their products cheap, exploited successfully the virtual monopoly of Bengal in the production of raw jute, procured cheap labor, and captured foreign markets—reasoned the leaders of the industry—their profits would remain assured. To help maintain the level of profits, the industry also developed a cartel-type combination in the Indian Jute Manufactures (later Mills) Association (IJMA), which frequently arranged for restriction of output by the members of the industry in order to match demand. IJMA thus represented the unity of the industry, on which its restrictive trade practices were based.

The very founding of IJMA in 1884 marked the end of a period in the history of the industry. Between 1855, when the first jute mill in Bengal was started, and the 1890s, the industry has stumbled from one crisis to another, crises that were caused by a small and uncertain market. After the 1890s and up to the end of the First World War, the quasi-monopolistic policies of IJMA and the opening of distant markets brought unprecedented prosperity to the Calcutta jute mills. After 1920, however, the policies of the industry ran into trouble as advances in the chemical sciences and textile technologies made it possi-

[1] *Indian Investors' Year Book 1911*, p. 68, quoted in A. K. Bagchi, *Private Investment in India 1900–1939* (Cambridge, 1972), p. 271, n. 33.

ble to produce more economic and better-quality substitutes for jute. Unfortunately for the Calcutta industry, its mercantilist economic philosophy had by then turned into a dogma. The leaders of the industry refused to see the problem in terms of technology or quality of output and clung more ferociously than ever to their age-old policies of price manipulation through restriction of output. This created further problems as new companies, owned and managed mainly by Indians, entered the industry in the late 1920s and refused to join hands with IJMA. This in turn severely affected the internal unity of the latter, making any cartellike arrangement harder to implement.

The details of this history are set out below in terms of the three phases mentioned above: the initial uncertainties of the industry, its recovery with the widening of markets and the resultant prosperity up to the First World War, and the crisis afterward. What follows is not a strictly economic analysis of the industry; readers interested in such analyses may turn with profit to some of the works used and cited here. My aim is to highlight the strong element of mercantilist spirit inherent in the economic calculations of the industry. Many of the problems of jute-mill laborers followed from policies dictated by this spirit.

THE EARLY HISTORY of the Calcutta jute industry cannot be separated from that of the industry at Dundee in Scotland. The Calcutta industry started as an offshoot of the latter and some of its early problems stemmed from being a late starter. The Dundee industry was at least twenty years older.

A few words about the Scottish industry may be in order. After a checkered industrial career in the eighteenth century, when it produced coarse woolens, shoe buckles, and tanned leather, the town of Dundee on the river Tay came to develop the linen industry as its most important manufacture in the second half of the eighteenth century.[2] There were three other "linen centers" in Great Britain—Belfast, Leeds, and Inverness—but they differed from Dundee in that Dundee produced fabrics of the coarsest kind, both of flax and hemp.[3] This meant that, unlike the other three centers, Dundee operated in a market for cheap products, where survival depended on keeping prices low. Faced with a rise in flax and hemp prices early in the nineteenth century—especially in consequence of the French Revolutionary Wars (1793–1801) and the Napoleonic Wars (1804–1815)—Dundee entrepreneurs

[2] Bruce Lenman, Charlotte Lythe, and Enid Gauldie, *Dundee and Its Textile Industry* (Dundee, 1969), pp. 10–11.

[3] Dennis Chapman, "The Establishment of the Jute Industry: A Problem in Location Theory?" *Review of Economic Studies*, vol. 6, no. 1, Oct. 1938.

started looking around for a cheap "substitute for hemp in the manufacture of cotton bagging [i.e. bagging for raw cotton]" and for an
"adulterant of flax tow."[4] They tried tow and sunn before settling
upon jute in the 1830s. It was this use of jute for adulterating flax that
gave both Dundee and jute a bad name in the early nineteenth century
when some of the Dundee flax and hemp spinners felt constrained to
guarantee their products to be "free from Indian jute."[5]

In 1825–26 Thomas Neish, a Dundee merchant, persuaded the
Dundee flax spinners, Messrs. Bell and Balfour, to try spinning jute
with their machinery.[6] The experiment was unsuccessful. Circumstances, however, soon combined to place jute in a more favorable position. There was a recession in the hemp bagging trade in 1831 followed by a failure, in 1834, of the Russian flax crop on which
Dundee's dependence was total. In 1838, Dundee feared "that there
might be a war with Russia arising out of tension at the outbreak of
the first Afghan War" in the event of which the flax supply would run
out once again.[7] All this led a few more merchants and spinners of
Dundee and its neighborhood to take a more serious interest in the jute
fiber.[8] The shift is reflected in the figures on the import of jute: whereas
in 1828 the amount of raw jute imported by Dundee manufacturers
was only eighteen tons, the figure rose to three hundred tons in 1833.
By then a large part of the flax machinery had been adjusted to jute,
and 1833 saw the beginnings of the "mechanical manufacture of jute
yarns and fabrics."[9] In 1835, "pure jute yarn" was put up for sale for
the first time, and "within a few years jute appeared in the European
market as a competitor of flax and hemp."[10] Soon after this the Dutch
government placed with Dundee merchants "what were then regarded
[in 1838] as large orders for all-jute bags" for transporting coffee from
the East Indies. The experiment was considered "completely successful."[11] Linen, however, was still the more important product of Dundee and "in 1851 Dundee imported 40,000 tons of flax." But a Dundee

[4] Ibid., p. 35.
[5] Lenman, Lythe, and Gauldie, *Dundee*, p. 13. D. R. Wallace, *The Romance of Jute*
(Calcutta, 1909), "Preface."
[6] For some details see Colin Gibson, *The Story of Jute* (Dundee, 1959?), p. 12.
[7] Chapman, "The Establishment of the Jute Industry," p. 48.
[8] Rakibuddin Ahmed, *The Progress of the Jute Industry and Trade (1855–1966)*
(Dacca, 1966), p. 30, and Chapman, "The Establishment of the Jute Industry," pp. 44–
48.
[9] T. Woodhouse and A. Brand, *A Century's Progress in Jute Manufacture 1833–1933*
(Dundee, 1934), pp. 15–18.
[10] Ahmed, *The Progress of the Jute Industry*, p. 31.
[11] Ibid., Woodhouse and Brand, *A Century's Progress*, p. 18.

factory inspector reported the same year that "Dundee seemed prosperous and that an increase in the cost of flax, which was reducing the profitability of flax-spinning, was being compensated for by an increased production of a new fabric—jute."[12]

The fate of the linen trade was sealed by the Crimean War of 1854–56, which shut off the supply of flax to Dundee, and jute took its place. What placed the industry on a firm footing was the American Civil War. Lancashire's loss was Dundee's gain. Jute assumed the place of cotton, and "while the war lasted, jute packing and baggings were used very extensively in America for normal needs and to meet the insatiable demand of the war."[13] A Dundee merchant wrote later of this period that "during the American War little mills grew into big ones; big ones doubled their power, and new ones rose up everywhere. There never were such times." A Forfarshire man remarked, "The money didna only come in shoals, but in barrowfuls."[14]

The popularity of jute, soon drew competitors into the trade. The French set up their first jute mill at Ailly-s-Somme in 1843, though their industry was not a serious threat to Dundee till 1892 when the French government imposed tariff duties on imported jute products. The German jute industry was started in 1861 and was "firmly established" by 1879. It had a rapid growth through the nineteenth century and imported more than 21 percent of India's raw jute exports by 1914. Belgium and Austria started their industries in the 1860s, and Italian hemp mills began to process jute in 1885. Dundee, however, retained its lead till the first decade of the twentieth century.[15]

These developments had an important bearing on the growth of the Calcutta industry. By the time this industry came into being (in the 1850s and 1860s) there already existed a world market for jute manufacturers in which the Dundee industry predominated. The growth, behind tariff walls, of other European jute industries in the late nineteenth century would have only made the world market even harder to enter. The first few mills in Calcutta, therefore, turned to the market that India traditionally served with her handloom products of jute: the network of country ports in India and some coastal markets in Southeast Asia, mainly Burma. The first jute mill in Bengal set up in 1855 at

[12] Lehman, Lythe, and Gauldie, *Dundee*, p. 11.

[13] Dundee University Library Archives [hereafter DULA], O. Graham, "The Dundee Jute Industry, 1830–1928," MS. 15/1, p. 68.

[14] Ibid., pp. 68–69.

[15] This paragraph is based on Ahmed, *The Progress of the Jute Industry*, pp. 185–186, 191, 195, 202, 229; and [U.K.] Board of Trade, *Working Party Report on Jute* (London, 1948), p. 8.

Rishra even had a "number of hand frame looms."[16] Its location was chosen precisely because the neighboring town of Serampore was "a noted centre for hand spun jute and hemp," where "labourers possessing knowledge of hand-spinning and weaving were available in good numbers."[17] Another factory, the Gourepore Jute Mill, was started in 1862 with the express purpose of competing "with the native weavers in the Indian markets," for "at the time," as a Dundonian was to put it later, "there was no rivalry between Dundee and India."[18]

One feature of the early history of the Calcutta jute industry was the displacement of the older artisan production. From a position of near-total predominance in the 1850s,[19] the traditional industry was relegated to absolute unimportance by the 1870s (see Table 2.1) and disappeared altogether from the customs house statistics after the 1880s.[20]

For the first thirty years in the industry, that is, from 1855 to 1885, most of its products were sold in the country and coastal market that the handloom industry traditionally served. In 1850 the industry (still all handloom products) sold 70 percent of its output to these markets; by 1885 the industry was still selling 59 percent to these markets. The decline was evident in the 1880s and 1890s: in 1895 the industry was selling 29 percent to these markets, and by 1905 the figure had fallen to 11 percent. Throughout this period these markets were small and uncertain, so that profits remained a function of "exceptionally good business and high price gunnies."[21] The precarious position of the industry is indicated by the history of some of the oldest mills. The first of them, for instance, came to depend so heavily on the "fairly good profits" it made from the fortuitous boom produced in the Bombay cotton market by the American Civil War that the termination of the war caused it to collapse when no alternative marketing outlets could be found to match its scale of production.[22] "Several pioneer ship-

<hr/>

[16] Wallace, *Romance* (1928), pp. 11–13.

[17] Indian Central Jute Committee [hereafter ICJC], *Report on the Marketing of Jute and Jute Products* [hereafter *Report*] (Calcutta, 1952).

[18] *The Jute Mills of Bengal* [hereafter *JMB*] (Dundee, 1880), p. 34. This book is a collection of reports serialized in *Dundee Advertiser* in 1880.

[19] Wallace, *Romance* (1928), p. 4.

[20] Ajit Dasgupta, "Jute Textile Industry," in V. B. Singh, ed., *Economic History of India 1857–1956* (Bombay, 1965), p. 261.

[21] *JMB*, p. 4. The percentage figures in this paragraph are derived from Wallace, *Romance* (1908), pp. 10, 59, and the *Dundee Advertiser*, 17 September 1883.

[22] Ibid., p. 13. Exports to the United States fell from 7,195,409 pieces in 1863–1864 to 1,914,104 pieces in 1872–1973. See Elija Helm, "The Growth of the Factory System

TABLE 2.1.

Relative shares of power loom and handloom products in jute exports from India, 1877–82.

Year	Gunny Bags			Gunny Cloth		
	Total Export from India (in 000s)	Approx. Percentage share of		Total Export from India (in 000 yards)	Approx. Percentage share of	
		Power loom	Hand-loom		Power loom	Hand-loom
1877	32,859	89	11	6,017	—	—
1878	26,407	97	3	7,297	98	2
1879	42,354	95.6	4.4	10,427	96	4
1880	55,909	96.5	3.5	11,322	96	4
1881	52,386	97	3	10,766	97.5	2.5
1882	42,073	98	2	10,840	97	3

SOURCE: "The Cultivation of Jute" *Dundee Advertiser*, 17 September 1883, in A. C. Lamb Collection, Newspaper cutting no. 196 (23), held at the Dundee Central Library, Dundee; and "The Calcutta Jute Mills," *Dundee Year Book 1887* (Dundee, 1888), pp. 122–129.

ments having turned out disastrously," this company was "wound up" and its property put up for auction.[23]

The dependence on the "traditional" market for handloom products had another implication: there was little pressure on the mills to standardize their products. Consequently, entry into the world market for manufactured jute was even more difficult than it would have been otherwise. D. R. Wallace, a pioneer historian of the industry, wrote thus of the problem:

> We have now [c. 1870] got to five mills with about 950 looms at work. Up to this time there was very little export trade in gunnies beyond Burma. It was not found necessary to be particular about regularity in weights or counts of the two or three qualities of bags in use. . . . But now it became necessary to seek foreign outlets.

in India," *Journal of the Royal Society of Arts*, vol. 23, no. 1,172, 7 May 1875, pp. 547–555.

[23] *JMB*, p. 14.

The Borneo Co. made the first serious attempt about 1868 by shipping 400 bales of their 2⅝ lbs. twills as 2½ lbs. 3 bushel twill bags to the United Kingdom. The result was disastrous. The bags averaged on arrival anything from 2 lbs to 3 lbs. The shotting varied from 7 to 10 per inch and the result was a claim of a pound per bale.[24]

There are two points that this quotation makes. One is about the lack of standardization of the product, which came as a result of dealing in coastal markets. But it also indicates that the coastal markets were already proving a little too small for the industry. Wallace cites the year 1870 as the year "when production, by the advent of new mills, outran the local and neighboring country demand, and compelled the industry to invade foreign markets with their goods."[25] At the present moment," wrote Elija Helm in 1875,

there is reason to conclude that . . . the jute manufacturers of Bengal have been overdone. The production is large and increasing, and the difficulty of finding profitable outlets for the manufactured product is constantly becoming greater.[26]

The smallness and uncertainty of the market encouraged a spirit of speculation both in the promotion of the first few mills and their management. Floating and selling off a jute mill was often seen as a more profitable proposition than running it in the interest of the shareholders. Naturally, quite a few of the early entrepreneurs were essentially fortune hunters who had no long-term interest in the industry. George Ackland, for instance, the founder of the first mill in 1855, a one-time "middy" in the East Indian Marine Service, turned his attention to jute only to make good a loss he had suffered in Ceylon.[27] That accomplished, he was out of the scene by 1867.[28] The Baranagar Jute Mill, which was set up by the Borneo Company in 1859, was sold to the Baranagar Jute Factory, Ltd., in 1872, after the former owners had got back their capital "twice over."[29] An observer from Dundee commented that "the price which was paid by the Baranagar Company was £384 000, a figure far beyond what the mill could have been built for, and fully £125 000 more than the concern was worth." The high price was not justified by the value of the mill. It was meant "to enable

[24] Wallace, *Romance* (1928), p. 26.
[25] Ibid., p. 18.
[26] Helm, "The Growth of the Factory System," p. 551.
[27] Wallace, *Romance* (1909), p. 12, and (1928), p. 7.
[28] Ibid., (1928), p. 13.
[29] Ibid., p. 18.

the firm [Borneo & Co.] to adjust their accounts with an outgoing partner."[30]

The "quick money" mentality is also evident in the history of another of these early mills, the Asiatic Jute Mill, or the Soorah Jute Mill as it was called later. This mill was built in 1874 by Charles Smith, a small mill-owner in Dundee. Smith's attention shifted to Calcutta when he faced business difficulties in Scotland; but investing in Calcutta was only a way of repairing his financial losses. He "did not even wait to see the mill start, but took his profits from the firm of Jews who had financed him in the venture and retired."[31] This "firm of Jews," Cohen and Company, in their turn stopped all payments due to their creditors in 1878 and simply absconded from the trading scene of Calcutta; it was revealed that "they had largely helped themselves to the manufactured goods and were indebted to the Company in over Rs 20,000."[32] Yet another attempt by an Armenian trader to set up a jute mill in the late 1860s came to naught because "he lost all his capital in speculation."[33]

The person who most embodied the spirit of the times was Richard Macallister. At one time a "bus conductor in Philadelphia," he came out "to the Tudor Ice Company about 1869" and, as Wallace put it, "with Yankee instinct decided to have a hand in the golden pie."[34] In the early 1870s, when the gunny bag trade was seemingly, if briefly, prosperous, when "it was only necessary to issue a prospectus of a jute mill to have all the shares snapped in a forenoon,"[35] Macallister teamed up with "the manager of a large bank" in Calcutta and formed R. Macallister and Company.[36] This company floated a number of mills in rapid succession: the Fort Gloster Cotton Mill (1872), the Fort Gloster Jute Mill (1873), the Oriental Jute Manufacturing Company (1874), and the Rustomji Twine and Canvas Factory Company United (1875). R. Macallister & Co. were in the trade for only six years. In those six years they made enormous profits. They sold the Fort Gloster Jute Mill for Rs. 1,300,000, the Oriental Jute Manufacturing Co. for Rs. 1,800,000, and the cotton mill for about the same price (the figure

[30] *JMB*, p. 22.
[31] Wallace, *Romance* (1909), pp. 15, 32.
[32] *JMB*, p. 73.
[33] Wallace, *Romance* (1909), p. 26.
[34] Ibid., (1928), pp. 31–32.
[35] Ibid., p. 30. The "stimulation" was largely from "the demand during the famine years for bags to hold the rice supplied to the famine-stricken districts." See "The Calcutta Jute Mills" in the *Dundee Year Book* [hereafter *DYB*] 1887 (Dundee, 1888), p. 129.
[36] *JMB*, p. 28.

21

for the twine factory is unknown).[37] If the proceeds made on the cotton mill were any guide—and bearing in mind the popularity of jute-mill shares in those years—the company would have profited by at least 40 percent on each of these ventures. Besides, R. Macallister & Co. also got themselves appointed as the managing agents of these mills "for five years certain at a remuneration of 3% of the gross sales . . . and an allowance of Rs 500 a month for office establishment in Calcutta."[38]

Unsurprisingly, none of the Macallister mills was well managed. The twine and canvas factory—the idea "not proving sufficiently remunerative"—was soon converted "into a jute mill," with very little thought, it would appear, for the "spinning and preparing machinery" were reported to be "all more or less intended for flax, and [were] too light for jute." A Dundee correspondent wrote in 1880: "The concern was never worked at anything but a loss, and is now in liquidation, and when the last advices left Calcutta it was to have been exposed to public roup on the 1st March last."[39]

The directors of the Oriental Jute Manufacturing Company admitted in 1879 that the mill "cannot work to a profit, burdened as it is with debts." In 1880, the mill was stopped "with a view to liquidation and reconstruction of the Company," when it was eventually taken over by Bird and Company, and renamed the Union Jute Mill.[40] Fort Gloster Jute Mill also had a very "spasmodic" career. After a prosperous first year the mill soon tasted trouble, which only deepened with the trade crisis of 1875. On top of this, the shareholders and creditors had to bear the additional burden of their traumatic discovery, in 1878, that Richard Macallister had suddenly "disappeared" from Calcutta "on urgent private affairs" and that his firm had declared itself bankrupt. The later revelation that Macallister has also "misappropriated" Rs. 33,370 from the funds of the mill, and that "the reserve fund, Rs 40,000, [had] also disappeared and [that] in fact, it never had any existence except on paper," twisted the knife.[41]

A spirit of speculation thus reigned supreme in the flotation and

[37] Ibid., pp. 30, 62, and W.B.S.A., General Dept. Industry and Science Branch, May 1876, A Nos 28–31. The latter gives Rs. 1,800,000 as the paid-up capital for the cotton mill. Hence, going by the figures for their other factories given in *JMB*, I have assumed the selling price of the cotton mill to have been about Rs. 1,700,000.

[38] *JMB*, pp. 28–30. The profit on the cotton mill was Rs. 700,000, of which Richard Macallister got the "lion's share."

[39] Ibid., p. 66.

[40] Ibid., and Wallace, *Romance* (1909), p. 29.

[41] *JMB*, pp. 30–32, Wallace, *Romance* (1909), p. 29.

management of these early mills, often to the detriment of the interests of the shareholders. The mills in the seventies were typically set up in years of temporary boom, and shareholders were drawn in by the immediate prospects of enormous dividends. The initial dividends were sometimes attractive but their attractiveness was itself a symptom of the speculation mentality, for they were often given away in a spirit of total neglect of the financial health of the mills.

> That in the ordinary course of working the mills would require serious repairs and replacements did not occur to any one, and no allowance of any kind was ever made from time to time for depreciation, and the consequence is that many of the mills are now [1880] burdened with debenture debts, they having no funds wherewith to pay for the renewal of and replacements in the mill, when such became absolutely necessary.[42]

A typical example was Rishra Mill, which was made into the Calcutta Jute Mill in 1872. For a couple of years both profits and dividends were very good (20 percent), but with the trade depression of the mid-1870s the mill found itself in a deepening crisis.

> Large repairs and replacements were urgently required, and as all the gross profits has been paid away in dividends (the words "depreciation," "wear and tear" not then finding places in the Indian millowners' vocabulary), it became necessary to raise money on debentures mortgages, and first £30 000 and then £10 000 were borrowed on the security of mortgage debentures bearing interest at 10 per cent. This, of course, had the effect of virtually raising the capital from Rs 12,000,000 to Rs 16,000,000 without any corresponding increase in the size of the mills. Since 1874 the company had declared no dividend, and the Rs 200 shares, which at one time were selling at Rs 290, can now be picked up easily at Rs 40.[43]

The problem was of such a general magnitude that even in 1880, when the practice of having "reserve" or "depreciation" or both accounts was more common than before, six of the eleven Calcutta-owned mills had little or no such funds. "The result of this misman-agement has been a very serious decline in the value of all Jute stock, and, with exception of two concerns, the scrip of all the Calcutta-owned companies have depreciated to an enormous extent," wrote the

---

[42] *JMB*, pp. 4–5.
[43] Ibid., pp. 14–15.

correspondent from Dundee whom we have quoted before (Table 2.2).[44]

Behind this state of affairs lay the speculation spirit in which the mills were floated. Much of the initial paid-up capital raised was spent in buying the mills from their vendors, so that the mills often started with not enough working capital. The Oriental Jute Manufacturing Company, for instance, was bought from R. Macallister & Co. at Rs. 1,800,000 out of a total paid-up capital of Rs. 1,900,000.[45] And promoter-speculators like Macallister hiked up the price of a jute mill much above what could be considered an economic price for the period. The mills as a result often started with too much of their money invested in their stocks. The correspondent of the *Dundee Advertiser* estimated in 1880 that "a mill of 300 looms, with all needful accommodation, could be put up for Rs 4000 per loom, and, if this assumption is correct, no mill whatever its size, should be worth more than Rs 4000 per loom." But the eleven Calcutta-owned mills for which he could collect the information has their cost figures above this (Table 2.3). The correspondent remarked that "this would work out [to] . . . an average cost of Rs 5,673 per loom; and as two mills only are above this average, it seems to follow that the average is too high."[46]

NEW AND BIGGER markets had to be found and secured for the Calcutta industry before it could overcome the competition from Dundee and realize the benefits of its two "natural" advantages, cheap labor and proximity to the source of raw jute. But this called for determined enterprise and, above all, contacts in the already-established world market for finished products of jute. There is an element of irony in the fact that the eventual supremacy of the Calcutta mills (over their Dundee counterparts) owed a great deal, initially at least, to their Dundee connections. The Samnugger Jute Factory Company Limited (1874), which is credited with having done for the Calcutta industry "more than all the other companies put together" in their search for new markets, was floated by four businessmen in Dundee: Thomas Duff, J. J. Barrie, and "the brothers Nicol[l] of A. and J. Nicol[l]."[47] In the early 1880s, the four men held between them 60 percent of the shares of the Samnugger Jute Mill and the Titaghur Jute Mill (1883).[48]

[44] Ibid., pp. 84, 86.
[45] Ibid., p. 301.
[46] Ibid., p. 88.
[47] Wallace, *Romance* (1928), pp. 36–37.
[48] Thomas Duff and Company, Ltd., Archives [hereafter TDA]., Minutes of the Tenth

TABLE 2.2.
Financial state of Bengal jute mills, 1880.

Name of Mill	Paid-up Capital (Rs.)	Reserve, Wear and Tear (Rs.)	Debentures & Pref. Shares (Rs.)	Other Liabilities (Rs.)	1880 Market Value (Stock Exchange Quotations) (Rs.)
Calcutta	1,200,000	6,554	400,000	159,803	180,000
Gourepore	1,200,000	198,954	—	116,965	744,000
Shibpore	1,500,000	32,155	—	151,228	450,000
Howrah	1,400,000	252,072	300,000	249,164	882,000
Asiatic	399,900	3,858	—	61,397	59,985
Balliaghata	166,500	—	330,500	18,865	33,300
Kamarhatty	400,000	—	400,000	462,115	320,000
Oriental	1,900,000	—	96,500	384,242	190,000
Fort Gloster	1,400,000	—	200,000	200,615	1,386,000
Budge Budge	1,440,000	340,000	—	218,339	406,000
Baranagar	4,000,000	340,000	—	390,373	2,200,000
Total	15,006,400				6,851,285

Loss to shareholders = Rs. 8,154,755

SOURCE: *The Jute Mills of Bengal* (Dundee, 1880), p. 86.

TABLE 2.3.
Cost per loom for Bengal jute mills, 1880.

Name of Mill (1880)	No. of looms	Cost of block (Rs.)	Cost per Loom (Rs.)
Calcutta	260	1,464,909	5,632
Gourepore	224	1,112,472	4,970
Shibpore	250	1,393,072	5,572
Howrah	275	1,527,150	5,918
Asiatic	75	399,812	5,330
Balliaghata	100	469,302	4,693
Kamarhatty	202	1,020,885	5,053
Oriental	350	1,897,595	5,421
Fort Gloster	250	1,362,176	5,448
Budge Budge	320	1,424,299	4,450
Baranagar	516	3,961,970	7,619

SOURCE: *The Jute Mills of Bengal* (Dundee, 1880), p. 88.

Duff, Barrie, and the Nicolls appear to have all come from middle-ranking trading or manufacturing families of the town, and they all had, either individually or through their families, connections in the textile-trading world. Although these connections were important, it was their involvement in the Calcutta industry that made them prominent in Dundee. The Nicolls were one of "the oldest members of Dundee's textile trade," yet when Alexander Nicoll died in 1909, he was remembered, not for his doings in Dundee, but as "one of the pioneers of the great jute industry on the banks of the Hughli." Joseph J. Barrie, who rose so high as to be made president of the Dundee Chamber of Commerce in 1887, started his career in a modest way as an apprentice to a firm of flax merchants. He gradually worked his way up and became a clerk with Messrs. George Armistead and Company, a Dundee trading firm; in the 1860s he was their "market man." At this time he resigned and "began business on his own account, in which he proved very successful." In 1874 he became a partner of Thomas Duff to promote the Samnugger Company. Thomas Duff, the key man in the Samnugger story, was born into an old artisan-manufacturing family with

Annual General Meeting of Samnugger Jute Factory Company, Ltd., held in Dundee, 28 March 1883, and Minutes of Ordinary General Meeting, Dundee, 26 March 1884.

long and established connections with flax and jute. His father, Daniel Duff, "machine maker and flax spinner, South Tay street works, Dundee," was known as "the inventor of the jute teaser or devil, the softening elephant." Daniel Duff himself had some ideas about starting jute spinning in Calcutta. Thomas Duff's elder brother Robert Duff was a gunny broker who made over his business to Thomas Duff in 1855. It was as a jute merchant that Duff came to be closely associated with R. and J. Henderson and Company, in whose Liverpool and London offices he had worked before. So when the Hendersons persuaded the Borneo Company to start the Baranagar Jute Mill near Calcutta in 1859, Thomas Duff was the person selected to be in charge of the mill. "Mr. Duff's success in India was so marked," commented the *Dundee Year Book* after his death, "that after 8 years' residence in the East he returned home with ample competency, and built a large jute mill at Barking, in Essex."[49] But, as Wallace said of him, "like the old horse, he smelt the battle from afar."[50] He sold his mill and joined hands with the Nicolls and Barrie to start the Samnugger Company.

Thomas Duff's company did not go for the local and the coastal markets that other Indian mills normally served. Instead it managed to break into the Australasian market very early in its career. And once

> they got an opening into the Australian and New Zealand markets for cornsacks, woolpacks and hessian bran bags, the mill agents, without any organised combine, nursed this outlet by turning out and stocking bigger and bigger quantities of the goods in anticipation of the seasonal orders. . . . The 'Frisco central hessian wheat pocket demand was fostered in a like manner.[51]

D. R. Wallace, from whose account of the history of the industry this quotation comes, was at pains to emphasize the importance of the inherited Dundee "connections" of the company to the success of its first few raids on foreign markets:

> They were particularly fortunate in their selection of an expert to conduct their business in the agents' . . . office. This gentleman, Mr. W. Smith, had forged his way from office boy in Messrs Cox Brothers, Lochee, to a confidential position with the firm. He was endowed with indomitable assurance and when he came to Cal-

---

[49] The biographical details cited here about Barrie, Duff, and Nicoll are taken from obituaries published in *DYB 1894* (Dundee, 1895), p. 77, *DYB 1896* (Dundee, 1897), pp. 76–77, and *DYB 1909* (Dundee, 1910), p. 71, respectively.

[50] Wallace, *Romance* (1928), p. 36.

[51] Ibid., pp. 43–44.

cutta had nothing to learn in the devious ways of jute. Backed by the practical experience and *business connections of the home board in foreign markets,* this company did more than all the companies put together to invade foreign markets.[52]

The phenomenal success of the Samnugger Company in these new markets in years when many of the other mills were struggling to survive must have set an example to the latter. "In 1880," reported Sir John Leng, a Dundee M.P. who visited Calcutta in the winter of 1895, "there was a great collapse in the industry consequent upon overproduction and the Calcutta mills not having made a market for their produce, for up to this time the demand was principally local."[53] In this crisis, which had been building since 1875—when "the other mills languished or went to the wall"—the Samnugger Jute Mill with its overseas markets

> paid a steady dividend of 10 per cent per annum, besides building up a huge reserve fund, enabling them to present their shareholders with 40 per cent bonus shares in a baby mill, the Titaghur, floated in 1883, which has grown to rive its father's bonnet.[54]

If anything, Wallace probably underestimated Samnugger's prosperity in those years. The annual report of the company for 1881 described its reserve and depreciation funds as exceeding, "very considerably," "the excess expenditure of Bdgs., Plant, Boats &c.," and "over and above, the subscribed and fully paid up capital of the company" (Table 2.4).

Such an object lesson in profit making did not fail to have its effect on an industry desperate for profits and markets. Before long, other mills were also in the race for overseas outlets, and by the late 1880s "had made a fair progress" in this direction.[55] One very important development of this period was the formation in 1884 of the Indian Jute Manufacturers Association, later called the Indian Jute Mills Association, or IJMA. The association was set up with the sole object of regulating production of the industry to match demand. The idea had been mooted before. It was said in 1880 that "if all the mills were to go on the single shift or short time movement the production would no doubt be sensibly diminished, and . . . a rapid advance in the prices would naturally follow," but the problem had been a lack of unanimity

[52] Ibid., pp. 36–37. Emphasis added.

[53] John Leng, "The Indian Dundee," in his *Letters from India and Ceylon* (Dundee, 1896), p. 91.

[54] Wallace, *Romance* (1909), p. 32.

[55] Ibid. (1928), p. 48; S. B. Saul, *Studies in British Overseas Trade 1870–1914* (Liverpool, 1960), p. 192.

TABLE 2.4.
Financial figures for Samnugger Jute Mills, 1877–82.

Financial Year	Gross Profit (£-s-d)	Reserve, Wear and Tear, and Insurance funds (£-s-d)	Cumulative Reserve and other funds (£-s-d)	Dividends (%)
1877	26,623-3-11	10,767-7-4	—	15
1878	31,257-7-11	7,632-7-1	—	15
1879	22,409-13-1	7,009-13-1	259,616-7-6	15
1880	31,879-12-7	13,254-12-7	39,171-0-1	15
1881	59,841-7-6	36,216-7-6	74,387-7-7	15
1882	70,538-1-1	39,038-1-1	114,425-8-8	20

SOURCE: Archives of Thomas Duff and Company, Ltd., Minutes of the annual general meetings of Samnuggar Jute Factory Company Limited for the relevant years.

among the mills.[56] A continuing gap between demand and production, coupled with the realization that the overseas markets would yield good profits if only Bengal's supply of raw jute and cheap labor could be carefully exploited, soon made the mills wiser. On 10 November 1884 the IJMA was founded and the next year, "under an elaborate voluntary indenture, the Associated Mills agreed . . . to work short time."[57] The Calcutta agent of Thomas Duff and Company, one of the anxious architects of the short-time-working movement, assured his Home Board in December 1885 with the telegram: "Agreement completed commencing February second week," His Home Board's response—asking him "not to sell beyond about a month forward in the anticipation that the reduced production will strengthen the market"[58]—was as much an instruction as a statement of a point of view that was soon to become an article of faith with the industry and IJMA. Throughout the period under discussion, IJMA sponsored and led several short-time movements in the industry, all in the belief that "reduced production [would] strengthen the market."

These efforts soon bore fruit. By the late 1880s the Calcutta mills received "regular orders" from the United Kingdom for flour and salt bags, and had also "annexed" the "Egyptian Diara contract" and

[56] JMB, p. 12.
[57] Wallace, Romance (1928), pp. 48–49.
[58] TDA, Minute books of the Board of Directors, meeting dated 16 December 1885.

TABLE 2.5.
Indian share of the Australian jute market, 1911.

Jute bags and sacks imported into Australia in 1911		Percentage imported from India
Type	Quantity (in doz.)	
Corn and flour packs	813,123	99.9
Bran, chaff, and compressed fodder packs	259,193	100.0
Potatoes, onions, and coal packs	28,798	99.8
Ore packs	40,368	100.0
Wool packs	957,047	99.7

SOURCE: "Jute," *Agricultural Gazette of New South Wales*, vol. 24, pt. 8, 2 August 1913, p. 668.

"Levant orders for grain sacks and other twill goods."[59] By the early twentieth century, they had found new, steady and extensive markets in Australasia, the United States, South Africa, and the countries of South America. In 1913, for instance, of the total export of bags by the Calcutta mills, Australia took about 30 percent; of the cloth export, 60 percent went to the United States.[60] The importation by the United States of jute manufactures from India in that year constituted 82 percent of the country's total consumption, the rest coming from the United Kingdom. The progress that the Indian industry had made in the 1900s may be gauged from comparing those figures to the figures from 1897: in that year India had supplied only 32 percent of the total American import of manufactured jute goods, and the United Kingdom provided the balance.[61] The magnitude of the change in the Australian market, which was once a preserve of Dundee's, is reflected in the figures for 1911 (Table 2.5).

Once the Calcutta mills established themselves as a major source of cheap and coarse jute bags, these markets were to stay for a long time

[59] Wallace, *Romance* (1928), p. 48; Saul, *Studies*, p. 192.
[60] See figures given in "The Indian Jute Industry," *Agricultural Gazette of New South Wales*, vol. 25, pt. 7, 2 July 1914, pp. 578–579.
[61] Calculated from Saul, *Studies*, pp. 193–194.

with the Calcutta industry. On an average, Australia took 19 percent every year of the total export of gunny bags from India between 1920–21 and 1929–30, and America, 66 percent of the cloth exports between 1896 and 1930.[62]

The Dundee industry fell into increasing difficulties after the 1880s when rising tariff barriers in Europe and the competition from Calcutta effectively narrowed the market for Dundee products. In 1900, "no exports of jute manufactures were recorded as being sent from Britain" to Italy and France, and the amount sent to Germany was a mere 1.3 percent of that exported in 1878.[63] As one observer put it,

> in the 1880s and 1890s, the Dundee manufacturers, increasingly shut out from their established Continental markets, were simultaneously losing their extensive export outlets in Asia, Australia, and along the western sea-board of the American continent, to the Calcutta industry.[64]

The intensity of Calcutta's competition forced Dundee to specialize after the First World War in finer products like carpet backing, leaving the market for coarser goods like hessian and sacking to the Calcutta industrialists.[65] A dramatic demonstration of Calcutta's supremacy came in May 1919 "when . . . the Angus Jute Works in Dundee were sold and the whole machinery transferred to Calcutta," causing, understandably, "considerable surprise and resentment among the unemployed in Dundee."[66] That the rivalry between Dundee and Calcutta, and the consequent decline of Dundee, never quite assumed the shape or importance of the Lancashire-Bombay conflict has been put down by A. K. Sen to "three factors":

> First of all, it [the Dundee industry] was still [in the 1890s] a relatively unimportant part of the British economy, and the influence of Dundee was less than that of Manchester. Secondly, by this time the group of Scots who had been investing large amounts in Indian jute mills had become an influential force in itself. . . . [Thirdly] Indian jute goods exports were by the '90s playing a

[62] C. N. Vakil, S. C. Bose, and P. V. Deolalkar, *Growth of Industry and Trade in Modern India* (Bombay, 1931), pp. 185–186.

[63] Saul, *Studies*, pp. 159–160.

[64] I. F. Gibson, "The Revision of the Jute-Wages Structure," *Scottish Journal of Political Economy*, vol. 4, Feb. 1957, p. 47.

[65] See C. A. Oakley, *Scottish Industry* (Edinburgh, 1953), p. 9.

[66] The quotations are, respectively, from J. P. Day, "The Jute Industry in Scotland during the War," in D. T. Jones et al., eds., *Rural Scotland during the War* (London, 1926), p. 288, and Wallace, *Romance* (1928), p. 76.

crucial part in the settlement of Britain's dollar purchase . . . [i.e.] in the settlement of British balance of payments. Since this fact was considerably discussed [in Dundee and elsewhere], this too must have played its part in not allowing to develop in the case of the Indian jute mills the type of social ethos that developed against the Indian cotton industry.[67]

As the market for the products of the Calcutta industry widened and stabilized, though not without some short-lived crises in the 1880s and the early 1890s, the old spirit of recklessness in the management of funds gave place to a more confident outlook. Toward the middle of the 1890s even the companies owned in Calcutta, which had earned for the industry the notoriety of the earlier period, showed signs of financial health in their dividends and reserve fund figures. Referring to the latter, Sir John Leng remarked, "Figures like these are enough to make home manufacturers' mouths water. In the home textile trades for the same period of years such returns have been unheard of and unknown."[68] On his return to Dundee, Sir John warned the Dundee Chamber of Commerce that the "time will probably never return when the jute industry in Dundee will advance again with leaps and bounds, and when large fortunes will be realized in a few years in a very rough and easy way."[69] Indeed, by 1908, Dundee's intermittent outcries against some practices of the Calcutta mill owners and managers appeared to the latter as "nothing more serious than harmless wails from their small competitor on the Tay."[70] The tone of that statement speaks for itself; Wallace's book, from which it is quoted, is in itself a testimony to the growing sense of complacency that the Calcutta industry developed in the twentieth century.

WALLACE'S BOOK *The Romance of Jute* was published twice, once in 1909 and then again, in a revised and updated form, in 1928. The differences between the two editions are indicative of the change of mood in Calcutta jute circles. The first edition ended on an optimistic note: it envisaged a future that "would appear to be good . . . for the Calcutta mills." But its optimism was still cautious. The "scandals" of

[67] Amartya Kumar Sen, "The Commodity Pattern of British Enterprise in Early Indian Industrialization," in *Deuxième Conférence Internationale d'Historie Economique Aix-en-Provence, 1962* (Paris, 1965), pp. 799–800.

[68] Leng, "The Indian Dundee," p. 91. This also gives the relevant figures for the Indian mills.

[69] "The Indian Jute Industry," address by Sir John Leng reprinted in *DYB 1896* (Dundee, 1897), pp. 91–95.

[70] Wallace, *Romance* (1909), p. 48.

the nineteenth century were still there like unhealed scars; so the "dedication" of the book carried a reminder of the "early seventies of the last century" when "Jute Mill Management" deserved the "trenchant and businesslike criticism" they received from their friends from time to time.[71] By the time Wallace came to write the second edition he was close to retiring. The memories of the "early seventies" had faded. Wallace had seen the Calcutta industry pass through a phenomenal boom during the First World War, when, according to one observer, in spite of large increases "in the reserves and depreciation funds, the level of profits reached was incredible." "The ratio of net profits to paid up capital of the jute mill[s] . . . was 58 per cent in 1915, 75 per cent in 1916, 49 per cent for 1917 and 73 per cent for the first half of 1918."[72] The importance of trench warfare in the war created a huge demand for sandbags and the fall in India's export trade gave the industry an almost captive supply of raw jute.[73] The rates of profit for five individual jute mills in the years 1918 and 1919 remained unsurpassed for most periods in the history of the industry (Table 2.6).

Wallace wrote the second edition of his book when the industry was still gathering the fruits of the harvest it had reaped during the war. By 1925 the Calcutta mills consumed "more than five times as much jute as the Dundee industry" and "the reserve funds of the mills in almost every case" exceeded their capital.[74] The *Capital* of 3 April 1924 (the mouthpiece of the Bengal Chamber of Commerce) looked at the profit figures for the industry for 1913 to 1923 and remarked with unconcealed glee, "What a wonderful decade it has been!"

The industry now developed a new sense of its own history. The murky past of the 1870s and 1880s was forgotten, and the story of Calcutta's jute industry since 1855 was now seen as "one of uninterrupted progress."[75] The mood of the Scottish entrepreneur in Calcutta became highly self-congratulatory. The speech Sir Alexander Murray, chairman of IJMA in 1917, made that year at the annual general meeting of the association contained an unusual display of statistics and

[71] Ibid., pp. 2, 62.

[72] D. R. Gadgil, *The Industrial Evolution of India in Recent Times 1860–1939* (Delhi, 1973; 1st ed., London, 1924), p. 269; Ahmed, *The Progress of the Jute Industry*, p. 40.

[73] See C. L. Mohindra, *Die indische Jutindustrie und ihre Entwicklung* (Berlin, 1928), p. 30, for figures of "net profits" of the industry during the war. (I am grateful to Mechthild Guha for translating for me parts of this book.) See also Gadgil, *Industrial Evolution*, p. 269, Vakil, Bose, and Deolalkar, *Growth of Industry*, pp. 174–175, and C. S. Hatton, "The Situation and Prospects of the Jute Industry in India and Pakistan," Ph.D. thesis, University of California, 1952, p. 14.

[74] P. P. Pillai, *Economic Conditions in India* (London, 1925), p. 175.

[75] See, for instance, W.B.S.A., Com. Dept. Com. Br., August 1928, A 18–24.

TABLE 2.6.
Profit (in Rs.) per ton of manufactured jute for five mills, 1916–35.

Year	Samnugger North	Samnugger	Titaghur No. 1	Titaghur No. 2	Victoria
1916	170.04	144.30	137.42	146.09	136.49
1917	132.39	122.68	114.01	119.49	123.05
1918	394.40	327.49	305.73	305.35	303.16
1919	242.00	208.73	202.15	203.63	197.41
1920	195.53	184.72	183.10	184.68	181.90
1921	59.81	44.45	48.45	50.80	50.05
1922	94.90	67.57	68.60	71.09	74.62
1923	114.75	86.71	86.46	90.70	97.39
1924	90.74	76.81	69.69	69.25	82.89
1925	66.06	34.85	49.50	46.22	63.28
1926	50.43	40.65	39.14	40.37	49.16
1927	78.73	69.04	66.54	68.77	76.72
1928	104.73	90.82	86.01	91.15	97.41
1929	90.77	71.99	71.63	72.76	83.86
1930	69.28	52.82	46.80	51.20	56.92
1931	46.19	36.39	33.65	38.06	39.09
1932	45.62	32.49	30.17	35.42	36.70
1933	57.27	36.77	39.45	43.18	48.26
1934	55.41	31.43	37.67	40.44	48.11
1935	41.38	31.93	31.76	31.03	38.93

Source: Archives of Thomas Duff and Company, Ltd., computed from the confidential monthly financial statements for the individual mills for the respective years.

rhetoric. We may take note of both of these elements, for the statistics give us a good idea of the growth that the jute industry had enjoyed in its recent past and the rhetoric tells us of the spirit of complacency that this growth had generated. Both aspects are important to our story. Since 1879, Murray pointed out, the loomage capacity of the mills had increased by 500 percent while the export of raw jute had just "doubled and no more." In 1879 there were "4,946 looms . . . giving employment to 27,000 hands," whereas "the latest returns show 39,000 looms and 812,421 spindles at work in India, giving employment to 254,000 hands." Besides, the export of gunny bags had increased "over 500%," and that of gunny cloth by an unbelievable 22,000 percent. "Is not that a record to be proud of, gentlemen?" Sir Alexander asked his audience. He answered the question himself with another, rhetorical one:

> To increase the jute manufacturing industry from 10,000 looms to 40,000 in the comparatively short period of 20 years, to provide the necessary capital, to secure the required machinery, to recruit and train 175,000 new mill workers, and all the time to have the satisfaction of knowing that we are enriching Bengal, improving the standard of Indian labour and earning a fair return on our capital, what better results can be looked for by the most ardent protectionist or free trader?

"Don't those figures speak for themselves?" Sir Alexander continued. "Don't they show the sound basis of which the jute manufacturing is established, so far at least as this country's trade is concerned?"[76]

The reworked text of the second edition of Wallace's book was colored by this prevailing mood of robust confidence. "For all time" to come, it seemed to Wallace in 1927–28, the mills should be "in a position to weather . . . the fluctuating dangers of market"[77]—so long as they followed the IJMA's price-manipulation policies of restricting production to meet the demand. These policies, Wallace reckoned, were "a factor for good to the trade."[78] The revised "dedication" of the book in this late edition no longer carried any references to the uncertainties of the last century. Instead, so strong was Wallace's optimism now that he broke into poetry:

> The writer who'll be West, before
> Some future scribe takes up the score.
> Yet still, what'er the Ebb may bring
> The tang of Bengal jute shall cling.[79]

HARDLY had the ink dried on Wallace's paper when world events plunged the Calcutta industry into a period of serious depression from which it never really emerged in the years that followed. What the depression revealed was how unfortunate the industry's sense of complacency had been. Contrary to the beliefs of many jute pundits of the day, the crisis demonstrated how unstable and unsound the basis of the industry had become in the years after the First World War.

[76] *Indian Jute Mills Association* [hereafter IJMA], *Report, 1917* (Calcutta, 1918), pp. 68–69.
[77] Wallace, *Romance* (1928), p. 94.
[78] Ibid., pp. 48–49.
[79] Ibid., p. 2.

TABLE 2.7.
The jute industry in the 1930s.

Year	Index of investment (1)	Profit index (2)	Index of net profit as percentage of paid-up capital (3)	Index of consumption of raw jute by the mills (4)	Index of average rate of dividend on ordinary shares (5)
1928	100.0	100.0	100.0	100.0	100.0
1929	101.9	85.6	104.2	104.4	75.7
1930	104.7	37.9	67.2	110.9	37.3
1931	109.9	8.7	18.1	78.9	21.6
1932	110.7	12.6	4.9	73.7	18.0
1833	113.0	19.8	12.5	75.4	26.3
1934	108.6	34.4	23.0	90.2	34.9
1935	110.4	39.8	36.0	96.1	23.9
1936	110.4	39.8	36.0	96.1	23.9
1937	114.3	25.9	33.6	104.7	23.8
1938	121.1	11.1	16.4	125.4	15.5
1939	122.4	48.8	13.6	107.7	12.5

SOURCE: Cols. 1 and 2, Rajat K. Ray, *Industrialization in India* (New Delhi, 1979) p. 56; col. 3, *Report of the Bengal Jute Enquiry Committee* (Calcutta, 1939), vol. 1, p. 80, and Rakibuddin Ahmed, *The Prgress of the Jute Industry and Trade (1855–1966 Pacca, 1966)*, p. 68; col. 4, Saugata Mukherji, "*Some Aspects of Commercialization*" *of Agriculture in Eastern India 1891–1938*," in Asok Sen, Partha Chatterjee, and Saugata Mukherji, *Three Studies on the Agrarian Structure of Bengal 1858–1947* (Calcutta, 1982), Appendices; col. 5, M. H. Gopal, "Trends of Profit in India," *Sankhya*, vol. 6 pt. 3, June 1943.

The beginning of the slump in the jute industry coincided with the worldwide depression of the early thirties (Table 2.7). Jute bags were often called the brown paper of world trade, and it was natural that a fall in the volume of that trade should reduce the demand for manufactured jute. But this was not the whole story. In 1937, the volume of "world trade in materials . . . was actually higher by 8 per cent than in 1929."[80] Yet the profits of the industry had dwindled seriously, and manufactured jute fetched a much lower value on the market than be-

[80] Ajit Dasgupta, "Jute Textile Industry," p. 268.

fore. These facts point to more permanent changes occurring in the structure of the demand for jute products.

In an article published in 1934, R. W. Brock, a former editor of *Capital*, analyzed some of these changes.[81] "A more serious factor" than trade depression, according to Brock, was competition. Competition came from two sources, the first of which were the jute mills abroad, mainly in Europe. Under tariff protection, these mills prospered in the twenties. The French jute industry increased its consumption of raw jute from 357,000 bales in 1923-24 to 613,000 in 1928–29. The German jute industry became one of the largest purchasers of Indian raw jute in the 1920s; the annual average export of raw jute to Belgium shot up from 1,000 bales in 1914–18 to 174,000 bales after the war; the Italian industry also achieved "international prominence" about this time.[82] Even through the world depression of 1930–34, the effects of this competition were visible. In 1933–34, the volume of raw jute exports from India was 27 percent more than in 1931–32, "the most acute period of the depression," but "the export of jute manufactures . . . remained practically constant at the extremely depressed figure of 1931–32, which . . . marks a fall of about 30.8% as compared with 1929–30."[83]

A much graver threat came from the prospect of effective competition from substitutes for jute products. This competition, Brock reported, "has developed along two lines":

(1) the increased adoption of bulk-handling of grains is progressively eliminating jute sacks as containers for grain in transit;
(2) the substitution of jute by paper, and to a lesser extent by cotton, for the making of bags.[84]

These developments had "affected the demand for jute goods principally in the United Kingdom, South Africa, Australia, and America." Both paper and cotton interests had recently carried out extensive campaigns in favor of their products; cotton was further helped by its "low price . . . recently, its lightness and the consequent saving in freight, its greater strength and more attractive appearance, especially from the point of view of retail trade."[85] With respect to paper, "the principal

[81] R. W. Brock, "Bengal and Its Jute Industry," *Asian Review*, vol. 30, no. 103, July 1934, pp. 532–540.
[82] Ahmed, *The Progress of the Jute Industry*, pp. 186, 191, 196, 200.
[83] J. N. Sen-Gupta, *Economics of Jute* (Calcutta, 1935), p. 94.
[84] Brock, "Bengal and Its Jute Industry," p. 536.
[85] Ibid., p. 537.

CHAPTER 2

loss" had been the cement trade "of the United Kingdom, South Africa, America, Germany and Denmark."

A conservative estimate places the loss to the jute industry of Bengal involved in the change-over to paper in the United Kingdom and South Africa alone at upwards of twenty million cement bags per annum. Wide hessians have been displaced largely in the Australian dried-fruit trade by a product known as "Sisal-Kraft." . . . In the United States cotton bagging is gaining in use and popularity. . . . Agitation in favour of bulk handling of grain is active in the United States and Australia and has recently extended to . . . Argentina. . . . In Egypt, government is banning the use of jute for cotton baling, while in Australia the abandonment of jute wool-packs, in favour of some Australian alternative material . . . is under active consideration.[86]

Behind the rise of paper or cotton (and other fibers) as likely substitutes for jute lay the advances made after the First World War in the application of chemical research to textile manufacturing. "Following the war," explained S. G. Barker, a British textile scientist invited out to India by IJMA in 1934, "there came a period when . . . the modern implements of war, that is, the means of prosecution of chemical warfare, cordite, nitrocellulose and the like, together with the large factories and plants which had been constructed to produce them during the War period, had to be utilized and brought upon a peace basis."[87] Thus grew up a whole range of chemical engineering industries that in the words of E. J. Hobsbawm, were "entirely based on scientific knowledge." Their technical progress, unlike that in the case of nineteenth-century factories, was "a function of the input of scientifically qualified manpower, equipment and money into systematic research projects."[88] By the early 1930s enough of this progress had percolated into textile industries other than jute to make effective substitutes of jute possible. "Probably no other branch of textile manufacturing has made such advance as the application of chemical and other finishes to fabrics. This is more or less a direct consequence of the development of synthetic fibres on chemical lines." So S. G. Barker wrote in a paper prepared in 1938, and added that "in this regard, jute materials have, as yet, had very little attention."[89] Sir Alexander Murray, who chaired

[86] Ibid.
[87] IJMA, *Report, 1934* (Calcutta, 1935), p. 262.
[88] E. J. Hobsbawm, *Industry and Empire* (Harmondsworth, 1972), pp. 174, 254.
[89] S. G. Barker, "Scientific Research in Indian Jute Manufactures," *Journal of the Royal Society of Arts*, vol. 86, no. 4454, April 1938, p. 475.

the meeting at the Royal Society of Arts where Barker's paper was read, admitted that

> this great industry . . . has hitherto done no scientific research. It is a pity, but it is true. . . . I believe we have lost markets thereby. Take the cement industry, for example. It may be that if we had possessed a scientific research department we need not have lost that trade.[90]

Yet it was not as though the Calcutta jute circles were unaware of the possibility of substitutes. In 1917 IJMA "circulated to all [its] members . . . a series of extracts and notes regarding possible substitutes for Bengal jute." One of the conclusions it had itself drawn from the experience of the war was that paper "undoubtedly . . . provide[d] a workable substitute for jute under certain conditions."[91] Why then was the industry so unresponsive to the challenge posed by scientific and technical progress?

Speaking in 1938, Sir Alexander Murray blamed it on an "ostrich-like policy": "Manufacturers have been content to take the proceeds and not worry about the future."[92] But this criticism was prompted only by the crisis of the thirties. To someone of Wallace's generation, or even to the same Sir Alexander in 1917, the future had seemed hardly worth worrying about. Over the years the jute industry had come to recognize its strength in the cheapness of its products (deriving from the cheapness of labor and raw materials) and in the policy of curtailing outputs that IJMA followed throughout its own career. The experience of the First World War seemed to confirm this view. The fabulous profits of the times were made in the context of a very slow rise in labor wages, raw jute prices, and the number of mills in the industry.[93] These profits, the *Capital* of 3 April 1924 smugly concluded, were proof of "the advantages attaching to a semi-monopoly." As late as 1930, when the depression and competition had already struck the industry badly, the IJMA chairman still saw this aspect of the industry as a point of strength:

> But when all these adverse conditions are detailed, we must remember our unique position, we are the only textile industry in the world which can control production to meet demand. Jute is

[90] Ibid., p. 479.
[91] See IJMA, *Report, 1918* (Calcutta, 1919), p. viii.
[92] Barker, "Scientific Research," p. 479.
[93] See Gadgil, *Industrial Evolution*, p. 269, Vakil, Bose, and Deolalkar, *Growth of Industry*, pp. 174–175, and Day, "The Jute Industry in Scotland," pp. 287–288.

only grown and harvested in Bengal and 60% of it is manufactured within a radius of 30 miles of this room at much less cost than anywhere else in the world, and we should not hesitate to take advantage of our fortunate position to ensure there should be no loss in manufacture.[94]

This "semi-monopoly" was based on a small range of rather simple products. Both before and long after the war, the industry produced only four types of goods—hessian, sacking, canvas, and twine—all meant for "rough uses upon which the vagaries of fashion or the finer points of textile science has little or no influence."[95] This lack of variety in output and the coarseness of products meant a relatively stagnant technology. "Hessian, sacking or canvas has not called for any large alteration in machinery," Barker reported in 1935.[96] In the course of carrying out an investigation into the technical problems of the industry in 1934, Barker found an old outlook at work. The Scottish entrepreneur in Calcutta, like his predecessor in Dundee in the 1830s, had always regarded jute "as a cheap edition of a long fibre like flax for manipulative purposes."[97] The technology employed to manufacture jute was simply a variation of the old flax technology, which, being a rather simple proposition in mechanical engineering, did not require a highly skilled and expensive labor force.[98]

At the bottom of Wallace's or Murray's complacency, then, there was a deeply entrenched economic outlook that counterposed the cheapness of products and price-manipulation practices (like short time-working arrangements) to scientific and technological progress. This is why, as the *Indian Investors' Year Book* explained in 1911, the jute mills themselves assumed that the task of manufacturing required much less thought than the buying and selling of jute.[99] The industry acted with this merchantilist reflex when it faced the danger of substitutes: "cheap jute" became its rallying cry. "Our trade, the basis of which is after all the cheapness of the article we produce" was the ever-

---

[94] IJMA, *Report 1930* (Calcutta, 1931), p. 9.

[95] S. G. Barker, *Report on the Scientific and Technical Development of the Jute Manufacturing Industry in Bengal with an Addenda on Jute, Its Scientific Nature and Information Relevant Thereto* (Calcutta, 1935), pp. 41–42 [hereafter *Report*]; W. G. Macmillan, "Research in Jute Industry," *Jute and Gunny Review*, February-March 1950, p. 29.

[96] Barker, *Report*, p. 42.

[97] Ibid., p. 42.

[98] Ibid., p. 41. The history of adaptation of flax technology to jute manufacturing is told in detail in Woodhouse and Brand, *A Century's Progress*.

[99] See note 1, above.

recurring refrain of many speakers at the annual IJMA meetings throughout the 1910s and 1920s.[100] Jute was described as a commodity

> whose principal claim to popularity is its cheapness: raise the price still further against them [European consumers] and you may be sure that the first effect will be to stimulate the search for a substitute, and one of these days Germany will find one and your industry will be in danger of following the path of indigo.[101]

The point was repeated like a chant at later meetings of the IJMA. The industry assured itself in 1917 that "it require[d] a remarkably cheap substitute" to compete with jute.[102] What the chairman of the association said the following year on possible competition was in the same vein: "The principal factor in the success of jute has been its comparative cheapness and we should use our utmost endeavor to keep it as cheap as possible."[103] R. N. Band, the chairman in 1925, strongly recommended "cheap jute" as the weapon with which to fight substitutes and grain elevators then turning up on the market. "We know it for a fact," he said, "that suitable substitutes for jute can be grown at a price in several parts of the world, all of which have hitherto proved a commercial failure owing to high cost of labour and the difficulty of extracting the fibre." The lesson, therefore, was that the "prices of our manufactures" had to be kept low so as not to encourage the manufacture of substitutes.[104]

The implication that the survival strategy of the industry had for its labor force are examined in the following chapters. We may briefly note here that the results were not very happy for the Bengal peasantry either.[105] The industry employed several means to ensure a supply of cheap raw jute. It put constant pressure on the Bengal government for

[100] The quotation is from IJMA, *Report, 1912* (Calcutta, 1913), p. iii.

[101] IJMA, *Report, 1914* (Calcutta, 1915), pp. iii–iv.

[102] IJMA, *Report, 1917* (Calcutta, 1918), p. 81.

[103] IJMA, *Report, 1918* (Calcutta, 1919), pp. viii.

[104] IJMA, *Report, 1925* (Calcutta, 1926), p. 6.

[105] See, for example, Saugata Mukherji, "Some Aspects of Commercialization of Agriculture in Eastern India 1891–1938," in Asok Sen, Partha, Chatterjee, and Saugata Mukherji, *Three Studies on the Agrarian Structure of Bengal 1858–1947* (Calcutta, 1982); Rajat K. Ray, "The Crisis of Bengal Agriculture, 1870–1927: The Dynamics of Immobility," IESHR, vol. 8, no. 3, 1973, pp. 244–279. Wazed Ali, however, has presented some interesting details on the "positive" economic influence that the cultivation of jute had on certain sections of the rich peasantry in Eastern Bengal. See Md Wazed Ali, "Jute in the Agrarian History of Bengal, 1870–1914: A Study in Primary Production," M. Litt thesis, University of Glasgow, 1975, chap. 8.

increasing the area under jute cultivation, and often the government was only happy to oblige.[106] The industry was helped by the total absence of any organization, economic or political, among the cultivators of jute, who were distributed (according to an estimate in 1939) in nineteen different districts of Bengal and among six million individual and small plots of land.[107] Further, by following an ever-changing and arbitrary system of grading the quality of the loose jute that they purchased, the mills often got a better deal than the peasantry.[108] Finally, the mills always carried big stocks of jute in order to depress the price of the raw jute on the market. As the official history of Bird and Company, one of the biggest managing agents in the Calcutta industry, put it: "by carrying large stocks of jute they [the mills] were enabled to buy their raw materials when the price seemed most favorable."[109]

The policy of producing low-quality, low-price goods left the industry vulnerable in one important respect: its products suffered badly from a lack of standardization. Because of its neglect of the scientific aspects of its own manufacturing process, the industry had no knowledge of the chemical nature of its raw material and depended for its discrimination of bad jute from good on purely outward characteristics like, "colour, shade and lustre."[110] On the other hand, since jute was an agricultural product, its quality varied from year to year, depending on the "degree of maturity at the time of harvest, time and conditions of retting, water facilities, amount of labour available etc." The industry's classification of its own goods, therefore, allowed a "wide margin of tolerance."[111] Every year, as a result, the industry heard complaints about the unreliability of its products. We cite here only two examples that are representative. In May 1914, Ralli Brothers, leading exporters of jute and jute products, issued the following circular to the Calcutta mills:

> We have to draw your attention to the deterioration in quality, the numerous weaving faults, over-damping and under-shotting of gunnies produced by the Calcutta mills. . . . That a gradual lowering in quality has been going on during the past seven or eight years is generally admitted, but the sudden drop in quality

[106] For details, see Bagchi, *Private Investment*, pp. 267–269.
[107] P. C. Mahalanobis, "A Sample Survey of the Acreage under Jute in Bengal," *Sankhya*, vol. 4, pt. 4, March 1940, p. 512.
[108] J. N. Sen-Gupta, *Economics*, pp. 54–61.
[109] Godfrey Harrison, *Bird and Company of Calcutta* (Calcutta, 1964; privately published to mark the firm's centenary, 1864–1964), p. 143.
[110] Barker, "Scientific Research," p. 462.
[111] Barker, *Report*, p. 38.

and the innumerable weaving faults that have arisen is, to say the least, alarming.[112]

In 1925, IJMA felt it necessary to draw the attention of its members to a letter it had received from A. F. Bemis, chairman, Bemis Brothers Bag Company, a dealer in jute goods.

Let me repeat [Bemis said] the big factor for each mill to aim for in developing merchantability is uniformity of product. The big outstanding obstacles to success in this field are the uncontrollable and crude nature of jute fibre and the relatively crude nature of jute machinery. Behind these two obstacles I am sure you Scotchmen will take refuge. . . . [But] Do you know that the strength of single strands of the best 8 lb. jute warp yarn undressed from the same spindle will vary roughly 50 per cent up and down from the average, say, from 4 lbs to 12 lbs? Low grade hessian weft might vary from 2 lbs to 14 lbs. The result is that in the same piece of cloth you get strength variations in good makes of 25 per cent above and below the average and in the poorer makes 40 or even 50 per cent. The variation just cited would be increased by atmospheric and seasonal differences.[113]

"Whilst the going was good and there was little competition," as Barker put it in a note of 1934, the industry could afford to overlook these problems.[114] The industry faced a demand curve of almost unitary elasticity, and cheap jute and price manipulation guaranteed success. When "Indian mills reduced output, prices rose, and profit margins increased."[115] But with improved fiber science permitting cheaper and more reliable paper and cotton bags, and grain elevators allowing bulk handling of goods, the elasticity of demand changed in favor of substitutes. Quality now became an important issue in the market and IJMA admitted in 1934 that "jute goods have to a large extent lost their former advantage of cheapness."[116]

The Calcutta jute industry's refusal, in the twenty years between 1914 and 1934, to come to grips with the scientific problems of its manufacturing process thus displayed the mercantilist spirit of the people running it. They did not try to obtain the technology that was being developed overseas, nor were they interested in creating an indepen-

[112] Day, "The Jute Industry in Scotland," p. 271.
[113] IJMA, *Report, 1925* (Calcutta, 1926), p. 10.
[114] IJMA, *Report, 1934* (Calcutta, 1935), p. 262.
[115] Hatton, "Situation and Prospects," p. 60.
[116] See IJMA, *Report, 1934*, pp. 282–286.

dent research wing of their own. Further, the fact that "jute goods practically sold themselves" even into the 1930s may have only strengthened their complacency.[117] The industry had never had to seek orders for its products in the past, and up until 1934, IJMA had no "organized system of following up the uses to which its products are ultimately applied, and . . . it . . . made no endeavour either to keep in touch with the consumers."[118]

Immediate financial gains were considered the sign of the correctness of business policies. "Some of us have been taunted that our only desire is to make money and that we pay no attention to competition overseas," observed R. B. Laird, the IJMA chairman in 1930.

We plead guilty to the charge [he said]. The jute mills of Bengal were not built to satisfy any economic conditions, they were built to pay dividends to their owners, let us get that undeniable truth firmly fixed in our minds, and all our troubles will vanish, as mist before the Sun, as Lord Melchett once remarked. He believed in profits as the only motive force . . . which makes the wheels go round.

That is our confession of faith, we are not frightened to make money, as our friends who taunt us for our mercenary outlook seem to be, and no bogey of foreign competition will make us renounce our faith.[119]

This was no doubt a bold statement of the "faith" that guided IJMA and its members. The tragedy was that it had become obsolete by the 1930s. This became abundantly clear when S. G. Barker, the British textile scientist mentioned before, carried out his investigation into the technical aspects of Calcutta jute mills in 1934. Barker's report placed the entire technological and organizational basis of the industry in question. A thorough overhauling of the technology and diversification into finer-grade products were his recommendations. But Barker's report came twenty years too late. And probably too suddenly, given the slow, nineteenth-century reflexes of the industry. As late as 1930 the chairman of IJMA had been overly confident: "Figures are available to prove that so far as India[n] Jute Mills are concerned foreign competition is practically non-existent."[120] Huge sums of money had been spent in ways dictated by this old mode of thinking; the call for

[117] W. A. M. Walker, "Growth of the Jute Industry in India and Pakistan," *Journal of the Royal Society of Arts*, vol. 97, no. 4,794, May 1949, p. 417.
[118] Brock, "Bengal and Its Jute Industry," p. 539; Barker, *Report*, p. 42.
[119] IJMA, *Report, 1930* (Calcutta, 1931), p. 9.
[120] Ibid.

restructuring the industry in a few years' time was now bound to appear "uneconomical." IJMA started a small research department in the late 1930s but it was not important till after the Second World War.[121] None of the more thoroughgoing prescriptions of Barker was implemented. "Whatever happened in the past," reasoned two ideologues of the industry in 1936, "it is a fact that if new manufacturing methods and processed are now developed suddenly, their outcome would be nothing short of the necessity of replacing practically all the existing machinery by new ones."

> It must be realized that the changeover from old machinery to new types has taken place slowly and gradually in other industries and it can hardly be expected that it would pay to create a research organisation and change practically the entire machinery for the sake of certain improvements and some economy, the results of which could never be in proportion to the magnitude of the required capital investment.[122]

Given this mode of reasoning, the only option left to IJMA in the 1930s was to carry on with its "cheap jute," production-curtailment, and other mercantilist policies in an effort to recreate the earlier advantages it enjoyed before as a "semi-monopoly." Its first reaction, in 1929, to the news of competition was to "adopt the policy of increasing production" in order to "kill" the rivals through a glut in the market for jute goods.[123] This policy soon proving ill conceived and resulting in the first general strike in the industry, IJMA adopted other traditional means of retaining its superiority. The mills reduced their working hours to forty per week from 1931 and agreed to keep 15 percent of their looms sealed. In March 1931 they "dismissed close to 60,000 workers in carrying out this policy."[124] Thus instead of taking note of the more serious implications of Barker's diagnosis, the Calcutta industry chose to treat the problem of substitutes, in essence a scientific-technological problem, as a cost problem and hence as a price problem for the industry. In November 1935, IJMA still maintained to the government of Bengal "that the substitutes [could] only gain ground if jute products [became] relatively dearer than substitutes."[125]

---

[121] Hatton, "Situation and Prospects," p. 104.

[122] B. D. Bhatter and L. Nemenyi, *The Jute Crisis* (Calcutta, 1936), p. 68.

[123] See notes dated 7 April 1932 and 22 April 1932 by R. N. Gilchrist in W.B.S.A., Com. Dept. Com. Br., September 1932, B 87–134.

[124] Ibid.

[125] Bhatter and Nemenyi, *The Jute Crisis*, p. 18. A rise in the volume of export of jute manufactures in 1936–37 may have further encouraged IJMA in taking this view; see Saugata Mukherji, "Some Aspects."

THREE FACTORS made the traditional policies of IJMA particularly ill suited for the 1930s. First, in the depressed conditions of the period, unity among different jute mills was hard to maintain. Second, a number of new mills that were set up in the 1920s refused to collaborate with IJMA. Third, this period saw intense racial conflict between Indian businessmen (who owned most of the shares of the old mills and managed some of the new ones) and the established European (mainly Scottish) managing agency houses. To facilitate discussion we shall deal with these factors one by one and then bring them together at a later point in the chapter. Suffice it to say here that these developments combined to produce a serious crisis of trust and confidence among the jute mills that made IJMA's task of working as a "semi-monopoly" enormously difficult.

This task had never been easy. The association had of course been successful, on many occasions since 1885, in getting the industry to accept its short-time-working arrangements, but such agreements were neither easily produced nor easily implemented. Individual managing agencies looked on each other with vying, competitive eyes. Their mills were often differently placed with regard to such variables as labor supply, loomage capacity, reserve funds, and trading orders. A trade crisis, therefore, always contained a potential, and sometimes real, threat to the "unity" of IJMA.

The substantial degree of economic concentration that existed within the industry no doubt contributed to the strength of IJMA. The four biggest managing agencies in the industry—Bird & Co., Thomas Duff & Co., Andrew Yule & Co., and Jardine Skinner & Co.—controlled, between them, 41 percent of the total number of looms in 1912, 46 percent in 1925, 49 percent in 1928, and 55 percent in 1936.[126] In the fifty-two years of the existence of IJMA, up to 1938, they had supplied twenty-nine of fifty-two chairmen and in 1937 controlled about 48 percent of the votes in that body.[127] "It seems clear," wrote a partner of Bird and Company in 1935, "that if our group, Yule group, Inchcape group and Thomas Duffs are of the same mind, we can go a long way towards influencing or controlling the policy of the Association."[128] The industry was also integrated through multiple and interlocking directorships, often held by a relatively small number

[126] IJMA, *Report, 1912*, p. 28, *Report, 1925*, pp. 54–57; Bagchi, *Private Investment*, p. 195.
[127] IJMA, *Report, 1937* (Calcutta, 1938), pp. 103–106.
[128] C.S.A.S., B.P., Box 10, letter from "G.N.M." dated 23 August 1935.

of people whose interests spanned several mills and managing agencies.[129]

But in spite of these factors, agreements pushed through at IJMA meetings were often difficult to implement. The history of IJMA is marked by an intense "individualism" on the part of its members. A minimum-selling-price agreement of the association in 1890, designed "to improve the mill sale sheets" in the face of a temporary depression, ran into such trouble. "All sorts of ruses to get round the minimum scale were adopted" and "wily business dodges" became the order of the day.[130] The Calcutta agent for Thomas Duff and Company found the "scramble" among the mills for orders "very sickening." "I can give you instances," he wrote to his board, "of some Mills booking orders at Association rates, but making the broker a present of a cheque to be handed to the buyer."[131] Such "wily business dodges" were so characteristic of the managing agencies that their own commercial magazine, *Capital*, once remarked "that there were three kinds of men, good men, bad men and jute men!"[132]

In 1912–13 the problem of disunity among the managing agencies assumed such proportions that "an American organiser had to be imported in order to tell the Jute Mill Association the simple truth (which they all knew before he came) that they should organise their Association on a stronger basis."[133] Even in the prosperous 1920s and into the depressed 1930s, the competitive spirit remained a problem to be dealt with. In 1930, for example, the association noticed that the production figures of individual mills were frequently at variance with their stated loom statistics. Disturbed by this discovery, the association decided to have the looms of its member mills counted by two reputed firms of chartered accountants. "The result," in the words of R. N. Gilchrist, "was astounding."

> For several years . . . there had been an agreement that no Association mill should extend its loomage (with certain exceptions), and the enumeration by an independent authority showed a total of 58,639 looms, as against 40,898 in 1921, and 52,929, as the previously officially registered number of looms, including [the exceptions]. . . . [Thus] the Association mills had for years been

[129] See M. M. Mehta, *Structure of Indian Industries* (Bombay, 1955), pp. 291, 293.

[130] Wallace, *Romance* (1909), pp. 44–45.

[131] TDA, letters from the agent's office in Calcutta, dated 19 August 1890 and 27 October 1890.

[132] IJMA, *Report, 1925*, p. 18.

[133] W.B.S.A., Com. Dept. Com. Br., September 1932, B 87–134: R. N. Gilchrist's note of 7 April 1932.

flagrantly breaking their own agreements. . . . [They] themselves
had dishonestly and surreptitiously added about 11 per cent. to
their productive capacity against their own agreements. . . . [But
this] was not the only type of dishonesty practised. Time stealing
was as common as loom piracy. . . . The appointment of two firms
of Chartered Accountants to check the number of looms in itself
was an unpalatable confession of weak morality.[134]

Undoubtedly, the "weak morality" of its members left IJMA weak
as an organization. As the chairman of the association admitted in
1925, "the Association had no power to control its members." The
association could draw up an agreement, but "it must be left to the
members to see that the agreement was observed."[135] Without the dramatic prosperity that the First World War gave the industry, interne-
cine quarrels between mills would have paralyzed IJMA quite early in
its career, as it almost did in 1912–13 when the association had to
bring in an overseas consultant to cure its own internal problems. A
year later, however, before any of the recommended organizational reforms could be seriously considered, came the First World War, with
its "unheard and undreamt of" profits. Here again, as in so many other
respects, the war proved only a mixed blessing for the industry and its
organization. For even though it helped the IJMA on to its feet, it was
no cure for its inherent weaknesses. The former spirit of mistrust and
competition remained; the superprofits of wartime and the 1920s only
made them more bearable. As Gilchrist explained, "the old intense individualism of the mills did not matter now." "Money poured in so
fast that almost literally the owners did not know what to do with it,"
apart from distributing "enormous dividends" and building up "huge
reserves." Even "loom piracy" (i.e. surreptitious additions to loomage
capacity), a well-known practice in the industry, did not cause as much
worry as before: "indeed," said Gilchrist, "it was regarded as something of a joke. No action was taken as long as trade was favorable;
exposure had to wait for bad times."[136] As conditions worsened from
the late twenties onward, the fissures within IJMA surfaced once again
and the association found it more and more difficult to maintain discipline among its members.

These old problems of internal unity of IJMA were compounded by
the establishment, after the First World War, of a number of jute mills
under Indian management. These mills came to be known as the non-

[134] Ibid., Gilchrist's note of 22 April 1932.
[135] IJMA, *Report, 1925*, p. 18.
[136] See note 134, above.

association mills because they refused to become (or stay) members of IJMA and abide by its rules of short-time working. When the IJMA mills agreed to work only forty hours a week in 1931, these mills worked for 81 hours, upsetting the calculations of IJMA.

The nonassociation mills had good "economic" reasons for the policies they adopted. R. N. Gilchrist thus explained their behavior:

They are attempting to do their best, within the law, to earn a return on their capital. Their investment was made in the knowledge that there was an Association of manufacturers which prescribed the commercial policy of its members. They knew they need not join the Association or if they did they could resign from it. Soon after their investment was made, trade conditions deteriorated. They could not make money under the Association rules; they therefore had to resign and make their own policy. They had no reserves, no special standing for the purposes of credit [unlike the IJMA mills]. They simply had to make money or go to the wall.[137]

Gilchrist's point that these mills had "no special standing for the purposes of credit" should be carefully noted, because it is of importance to our story. For there were other mills established in the postwar period—Meghna, Craig, Waverley, Nuddea—whose reserves and dividends were much smaller than those of the prewar mills.[138] But they were set up and managed by old and established European managing agencies already belonging to IJMA. "On general grounds," Gilchrist remarked, "one might have expected a division of interests into pre-war and post-war [mills], but the truth is that the bigger brothers have carried the younger children on their backs. . . . Thus the pre-war Gourepore sponsored the post-war Nuddea, the pre-war India the post-war Megna, the pre-war Alliance the post-war Craig and Waverly, the pre-war Ganges the post-war Bansberia."[139] These mills, therefore, did not pose any threat to IJMA; they remained tied to the latter through their European managing agencies. The problem of the nonassociation mills was precisely that they were all owned and managed by newly set-up Indian managing agency houses (most of them by Marwaris), except for the American Ludlow Jute Mill, which declined to join the association ostensibly on antitrust grounds.[140]

The fact that the nonassociation mills were mostly Indian managed

137 W.B.S.A., Com. Dept. Com. Br., September 1932, B 87–134.
138 Ibid., gives the relevant figures.
139 Ibid.
140 The Benthall papers are a most useful source for the history of this conflict.

may give their conflict with the European-dominated IJMA the appearance of yet another confrontation between imperialism and nationalism.[141] There are problems, as we shall see, with this characterization. Yet the racial element in this conflict is important for the purpose of understanding the problems of the industry in this period. The confusion and distrust created by racism certainly contributed to IJMA's inability in the thirties to impose any discipline on its members.

THE RACIAL CONFLICT between Indian (mainly Marwari) and Scottish businessmen in the jute industry was aggravated by a particular historical feature of the situation. Even though Scotsmen managed most of the mills and had an almost exclusive control over managerial positions, the capital they managed was for the most part Indian and became increasingly so after the First World War. "Out of a total capital of £10 000 000 sunk in jute mills in India" in 1912, "only about one-eighth [was] from Dundee and District."[142] The capital was largely raised in India, initially, as A. K. Bagchi has shown, mainly from European civilians and military residing in India, and later from Indians as well.[143] The Marwari Association of Calcutta claimed in 1922 that "Indians held not less than 60% of the shares in jute mills."[144] By 1937 the figure was somewhere close to 67 percent.[145] This is also seen in the place of registration of the companies.[146] Of twenty jute mills running in Calcutta in 1880, only four were registered in the United Kingdom.[147] In 1921, the number was seven out of sixty-five.[148]

The reasons for the unwillingness that established Scottish capital historically displayed toward the question of direct investment in the Calcutta industry are difficult to determine. But the "last period of heavy investment" in the Dundee jute mills was the year 1873, and the rise of the Calcutta mills "coincided with a return of prosperity in the United States," when Dundee financial circles transferred their invest-

[141] For example, see the "Editorial" in the *Modern Review*, vol. 72, August 1942. For a recent analysis on different lines, see Omkar Goswani, "Collaboration and Conflict: European and Indian Capitalists and the Jute Economy of Bengal, 1919–1939," *Indian Economic and Social History Review*, vol. 29, no. 2, April–June 1982, pp. 141–179.

[142] British Association, Dundee, *Handbook and Guide to Dundee and District* (Dundee, 1912), p. 120.

[143] Bagchi, *Private Investment*, pp. 159, 263.

[144] Ibid., p. 278, n. 47.

[145] Ibid., p. 192.

[146] Ibid., p. 161.

[147] Figure taken from *JMB*.

[148] H. Venkatasubbish, *The Structural Basis of the Indian Economy: A Study in Interpretation* (London, 1940), p. 134.

ment interest . . . across the Atlantic." In 1873 Sir William Reid, then vice-consul for the United States in Dundee, promoted the Oregon and Washington Trust Investment Company Limited, which was financed by twenty-five of the major Dundee financiers. The original board of the company had such men on it as "Thomas Bell and William Lowson, merchants; James Neish, solicitor; Thomas Couper, shipowner; Thomas H. Cox, manufacturer; and John Leng, newspaper publisher."[149]

It also seems quite possible that the early "scandals" of the Calcutta jute industry left the important Dundee financiers and industrialists unenthusiastic about investment in that direction. Thomas Cox, who was a senior partner of Cox Brothers, Dundee, specializing in finance and investments, is a case in point.[150] In 1872, a year before he decided to invest in the American company mentioned above, he turned down a proposal to invest in a jute mill in Calcutta that he thought would only be a "very heavy financial burden on the business." This is what Thomas Cox wrote to his brother Henry about the proposal in 1872:

> We note what you say about engaging in a spinning and manufacturing company at Chandernagore. After giving this matter due consideration, we concluded to advise you to get out of it in the best way you can. We see no great objection to your managing the mercantile part of it if you think you can accomplish it, but we would decidedly advise you against investing money in it. In such a climate, the deterioration and difficulty of keeping up a jute mill must be very great. No doubt the Borneo Co. saw it was time to get part of their immense place realised. Our Mr Williams was told by Mr Fergusson, one of the partners of George Henderson and Co., that the Barnagore [mill] at that time—10 years ago— had never remitted any dividends home and we see Duff got out of it in as easy a way as he could.[151]

Thomas Cox's views were apparently shared by other Dundee investors. The special correspondent of the *Dundee Advertiser*, who reported in detail on the financial state of individual jute mills in Calcutta in his book *The Jute Mills of Bengal* (1880), ended his series of reports by saying: "Our advice just now to people desirous of investing capital

---

[149] W. Turrentine Jackson, *The Enterprising Scott: Investors in the American West after 1873* (Edinburgh, 1968), pp. 22–24.

[150] Lenham, Lythe, and Gauldie, *Dundee*, pp. 10–11.

[151] Dundee University, History Department Archives, card collection on Cox Brothers, card titled, "Spinning in India?"

in the jute manufacturing trade at Calcutta is similar to that of *Punch* to those about to marry —'DON'T'."[152]

Even though Scottish capital did not flow out to Calcutta in any large measure, Scottish enterprise did. The British Association of Dundee found in 1912 that the "overseers, managers and mechanics in the Indian jute mills [were] almost wholly recruited from Dundee."[153] By the time of the First World War, the composition of the Dundee middle class had been perceptibly affected by fortunes made in Calcutta. An economic study of the town as it was in this period observed: "Undoubtedly some of the new middle-class mill owners had emerged from the artisan class by means of a period of employment in Calcutta."[154]

This domination of jute-mill management by Scotsmen was not based on the proverbial Scottish enterprise alone. It was also based on a degree of clannishness. The Scottish managers and supervisors of the Calcutta jute mills did not owe their position to any special skills or qualifications, as Bagchi has duly noted, but to their "connections."[155] One William Ure, who was interviewed by Sir Edward Benthall of Bird and Company for employment with them in Calcutta, had no special qualifications "apart from a course in Book-keeping" that he had taken "through the International Correspondence people." Benthall even noted that "he [did] not read, except in the winter, when he [read] chiefly thrillers." But what made him eligible was that he knew "Anderson in Hooghly Mill and the two Golds in Birds" and his father was "Cashier in the Victoria Mill." Besides, he had always "wanted to go to India as does every young man in Dundee." He was, Benthall said, "just the normal type we take on in Calcutta."[156]

This clannishness could easily give rise to racism. The Marwari Association of Calcutta complained to the Indian Fiscal Commission of 1922 that "the European [mill] managers did not buy jute through Indian traders."[157] The complaint was voiced also to the Bengal Provincial Banking Enquiry Committee of 1930, which was told of the considerable "difficulty" that Indian traders of jute in Calcutta had to face "in disposing of their stocks to the mills." The mills did not recognize their marks and names and compelled them "to sell through European firms of brokers."[158] The practice was old and established.

[152] *JMB*, p. 87.
[153] British Association, *Handbook and Guide*, pp. 118–119.
[154] Lenham, Lythe, and Gauldie, *Dundee*, pp. 10–11.
[155] Bagchi, *Private Investment*, pp. 205–206, 289.
[156] C.S.A.S., B.P., Box 10, Note from Benthall to G. B. Morton, 7 September 1935.
[157] Bagchi, *Private Investment*, p. 278, n. 47.
[158] *Report of the Bengal Provincial Banking Enquiry Committee 1920–30* (Calcutta, 1930), vol. 1, p. 107, quoted in Ray, "The Crisis of Bengal Agriculture," p. 263.

A Dundee gentleman visiting Calcutta in 1894 noticed "a grave defect in the management of the Indian mills," which arose "from the presence in the jute trade of Dundee men as sellers and brokers." "These men have friends or relations among the jute mill agents, who naturally place confidence in them and employ them in preference to others." The Indian jute brokers had to "obtain a Dundee partner in order to qualify to enter the magic ring."[159]

The story of the rise of the Marwaris in the European-dominated business world of Calcutta deserves a much richer and fuller account than can be provided here. According to Thomas Timberg, "more than one-half" of the jute balers in 1900 were Marwaris. By 1907 they had started direct shipping of jute overseas and in 1909 formed their Baled Jute Association. Before the First World War some Marwari merchants "acquired a large number of 'pucca' or export-oriented jute presses," which were "formerly a European preserve." In 1917, the most important Marwari firm, Birla Brothers, opened a branch office in London; by 1920 they were "one of the top three exporters of raw jute" from Calcutta. During and after the war the Marwaris also entered the export trade in hessian and gunnies, and started speculation in jute-mill shares, the value of which increased by "three times" between 1915 and 1926.[160]

The 1920s also saw a very large increase in future trading in raw jute—and later in hessian as well—by Marwari merchants. Known as the operations of the *fatka* (lit. bubble) market or the *bhitar bazar* (lit. inside or secret market), such speculative trading in jute was started in Calcutta about 1911–12 by one Jewanmal Bengani, a Marwari dealer in raw jute.[161]

> As the number of . . . speculators increased, an "exchange" was formed at 68 Cotton Street in the year 1912, where dealings in 25 bales or its multiples used to be carried on. There was no question of delivery [of jute] and only difference used to be paid. When the great war broke out and the jute trade was temporarily disorganised . . . this "exchange" had to stop its operations. With the return of confidence by 1916, a limited company, styled the Cal-

---

[159] "The Calcutta Jute Mills," *DYB 1894* (Dundee, 1895), p. 117.

[160] This paragraph is based on Thomas Timberg, *The Marwaris: From Traders to Industrialists* (New Delhi, 1978), pp. 53, 54, 62, 166–167, 171. See also Bagchi, *Private Investment*, p. 279, n. 51.

[161] H. Sinha, "Jute Futures in Calcutta," *Economica*, no. 27, Nov. 1929, pp. 330–337, and Timberg, *Marwaris*, p. 193. Sinha explains the word *fatka* thus: "Literally, a bubble; a speculative market is so described because it swells up and bursts like a bubble."

cutta Pat Association Limited, was started for those speculative deals.[162]

A temporary short supply of raw jute in 1925–26 helped the Calcutta Pat Association to do brisk business till the government closed it down in 1926 under the gambling act "on the complaint of a few parties who had suffered loss on this market."[163] Significantly, ten of the eleven men convicted in this connection were Marwaris.[164] Soon after the suppression of the Pat Association, a new organization called the East India Jute Association was formed with a view to running a futures market in jute. All its leading members were Marwari balers and shippers of jute, the Birlas heading the list. There were also two other, less formal, exchanges—called Gudri and Katni—where the units of transaction were kept small in order to accommodate small-time speculators, whose ranks swelled as the trade depression of the late twenties deepened, adding to the profits of the balers who sold in these markets. "It cannot be substantiated," wrote M. N. Roy in his 1934 pamphlet we have referred to before, "but the report goes that the drivers of motor cars . . . and the numerous Biri[wallas] and panwallas, and Darwans occasionally buy and sell 5 bales in the Katni."[165]

While enriching themselves in the *fatka* market, the Marwari balers, following the lead of the Birlas, also reached out for the foreign market in jute, where their performance impressed even their competitors. "The enterprise and efficiency of the modern Marwari Baler," wrote Benthall in a long note in 1935, "cannot be appreciated abroad and this applies particularly in the case of large operators of the type of Cotton Agents (Birla Brothers) and Surajmal Nagarmall."

> I understand that [a] number of [Marwari] Balers are frequently in communication now a days with their direct connections abroad by phone. They do not confine their operations to the London market but are directly represented in such markets as Dundee and New York, and there is a distinct tendency to encourage Continental business directly through Hamburg. In this connection the activities of Khubchand Sethia here on the London Market are a special feature particularly as regards Russian business which seems to have gone completely past us sometimes.[166]

[162] M. N. Roy, "Jute Futures in Calcutta," in W.B.S.A., Com. Dept. Com. Br., July 1934, A 33–43.
[163] Ibid.
[164] W.B.S.A., Com. Dept. Com. Br., August 1927, A 18–24.
[165] W.B.S.A., Com. Dept. Com. Br., July 1934, A 33–43.
[166] C.S.A.S., B.P., Box 10, note dated 25 June 1935.

Marwari incursion into the jute industry was thus only an aspect of their overall success in the world of Bengal jute. Here again the Birlas were among the leaders. In 1918–19 they set up their Birla Jute Mill, which was followed soon by the Hukumchand Jute Mill, belonging to the Sarupchand Hukumchand family.[167] By 1926–27 several other Indian traders made their way into manufacturing, the more prominent among the new mills being Premchand Jute Mill owned by Janakinath Roy, Gagalbhai Jute Mill belonging to the Mafatlalls, Hanuman Jute Mills set up by Surajmall Nagarmall, Agarpara Jute Mill owned by B. N. Elias and Company, and Haji Adamji Dawood Jute Mill owned and run by Haji Adamji Dawood and Company. By 1932 these were joined by some other smaller mills, such as the Calcutta Jute Manufacturing Company, Ltd., Kedarnath Jute Mills, Shree Ganesh Jute Mill, Kathiar Jute Mill (owned by Hardutroy Chamaria and Sons), and the Swadeshi Jute Mill.[168]

The appearance of the Indian "intruder" on the scene naturally did not please the entrenched European businessman. "The Indians are determined to get into the industry" was Benthall's grim comment on the margin of a letter he received in December 1928 from a Marwari firm of "Stock and Share Brokers and Dealers."[169] A month earlier his partner M. P. Thomas had described the Indian mills as "our new and undesired competitors."[170] Benthall himself wrote in 1929: "These people . . . are hopeless gamblers, it will be to the good of India if they retire from the scene."[171]

A special target of European hostility was G. D. Birla, the most up-and-coming of the Marwari entrepreneurs. Thomas reported to Benthall in December 1928 that Birla "has had more to do with encouraging New Mills than any one [else]." "If he can't get us by kicking us out he will try to get us out by unfair competition."[172] Even when he was away in England Benthall worried about competition from Birla. "In Calcutta," reads the entry for 10 February 1929 in his diary,

the Birla party continued their efforts to control the jute trade and at the moment have paralysed the export business by [selling at] Rs 6 below the Calcutta packing cost and bearing the phatka

[167] Timberg, *Marwaris*, pp. 64, 171.
[168] See W.B.S.A., Com. Dept. Com. Br., September 1932, B 87–134, for details on some of these mills.
[169] C.S.A.S., B.P., Box 1, letter from Mokandlall dated 13 December 1928.
[170] C.S.A.S., B.P., Box 1, letter from M. P. Thomas dated 15 November 1928.
[171] C.S.A.S., B.P., Box 7, diary 1929–33, entry for 7 March 1929.
[172] C.S.A.S., B.P., Box 1, letter dated 12 December 1928.

while the forward position here commands a ruppee premium for each month.

In the privacy of his personal diary Benthall's hostility was frank and unconcealed:

It is his [Birla's] policy (on a 5 year basis) to establish himself as the leading figure in the trade and it may be necessary to form a combine against him. A plan is being hatched. Both in jute and gunnies his advance has been tremendous. . . . It is a sign of the times: we must dig in our toes and fight for our position.[173]

Indeed, the signs of the times were too obvious to be overlooked. By the middle of the twenties, the Marwaris were being openly assertive about protecting their business interests. This can be seen in the letters written by Marwari shareholders to the editor of the *Capital* complaining of arrogance on the part of some European managing agents of jute mills and in the references in Benthall's diaries to "Bajoria's attacks" on Europeans at shareholders' meetings.[174] In 1926 the Marwari businessmen formed the Indian Chamber of Commerce at Calcutta with G. D. Birla as its president and took a leading role in the founding of the all-India organization of Indian employers, the Federation of Indian Chambers of Commerce and Industry (FICCI).[175] The following year they founded the East India Jute Association, which soon evoked opposition from European businessmen in Calcutta and elsewhere.[176] About this time Birla also managed to become "the only Indian member" of the London Jute Association.[177] It was in these years that reports of Marwari traders like "Choudri Chhajuram" buying "considerable number of jute shares" led Benthall to make the unfriendly remark, "the Indians are determined to get into the industry." In February 1929 Benthall was still "considering means of giving the Birla party a slap in the jute market" and was not pleased to discover the next month that Birla was still "up and by registering more share in Titaghur is showing signs of intensified hatred towards us."[178]

The years 1926–30 appear to have been the period when relations

[173] C.S.A.S., B.P., Box 7, diary 1929–33, entry for 10 February 1929.

[174] See letter of Mugneeram Bangur, Mokandlal, and others in *Capital*, 12 November 1925, and C.S.A.S., B.P., Box 7, diary 1929–33, entry for 6 May 1929.

[175] Rajat K. Ray, *Industrialization in India: Growth and Conflict in the Private Corporate Sector 1914–1947* (New Delhi, 1979), pp. 306–309.

[176] For details, see W.B.S.A., Com. Dept. Com. Br., July 1934, A 33–43.

[177] Ray, *Industrialization*, pp. 306–309.

[178] C.S.A.S., B.P., Box 7, diary 1929–33, entries for 19 February 1929 and 7 March 1929.

between Indian and Scottish businessmen in Calcutta reached a low point. The peculiarly marginal position of the Scotsman in the world of Bengal jute—his domination being based more on enterprise and clannishness than on capital investment—perhaps contributed to the intensity of the conflict. Once when asked by Benthall in 1929 if "he hadn't been insulted" by "Scotchmen" while negotiating the sale of jute to a Calcutta mill, G. D. Birla gave the rather sarcastic reply, "not more than usual."[179] The hostile exchanges were by no means confined to the verbal. In March of the same year, while Birla tried to reach the viceroy's ear with complaints about "racial discrimination" by the Europeans in the jute trade,[180] Benthall made the following note about Birla's jute mill near Calcutta:

> He [Birla] has had five fires in four months at his mill—due to his Indianisation policy and refusal to employ Scotsman. Jute gone to dust and burnt: more burnt to cover up the delinquencies and then finally a fire in the finishing house (affecting also 150 looms) which [even] if he recovers from the Ins-Coys. will about square the rest.

It is a small monument to the racism of the day that Benthall held the Marwaris squarely responsible for these jute-mill fires. "These people [the Marwaris] carry racial hatred to [an] extreme" was his only gesture at apportioning blame.[181]

Racism could easily be stretched into "imperialistic" and "patriotic" feelings on the two sides. G. D. Birla later recalled that he had always "smarted" under the "insults" he suffered in dealing with "Englishmen who were my patrons and clients": "I was not allowed to use the lift to their offices, nor their benches while waiting to see them. . . and this created within me a political interest."[182] Yet the Scottish-Indian conflict in the jute industry never quite became an all-out war dividing the industry into two clearly defined, mutually opposed, ethnic interest-groups. The problem of unity that IJMA faced in this period would have been much less complicated had this been the case. In reality, the lines of unity and division in the industry ran in bewilderingly different directions, often across and within the warring races. The Scots and the Marwaris were, after all, interested in the same industry, often in

---

[179] Ibid., entry for 6 May 1929.

[180] India Office Library [hereafter IOL], MSS. Eur. C. 152/5, Irwin Papers, letter from viceroy to the secretary of state for India, dated 6 March 1929.

[181] C.S.A.S., B.P., Box 7, diary 1929–33, entry for 7 March 1929.

[182] G. D. Birla, *In the Shadow of the Mahatma: Personal Memoirs* (Calcutta, 1953), p. xv.

the same mill, with the Marwaris as substantial shareholders in the twenties and the Scots providing the crucial managerial element. Each group stood to profit from the other's activities. To a managing agency firm like Bird and Company even the rival, nonassociation mills were potential fields for their business activities. For all his anger at "vilification of us by Narayandas Bajoria to sundry Assembly members," Benthall was too good a businessman to lose sight of this. "Adamji will not be friends," he noted with genuine regret on 7 March 1929. "There is now no chance of obtaining his mill agency if hard times come." Hence, "we must not make the same mistake . . . and I must continue friendly relations with other new mill owners e.g., Magneeram Bangur, Mafatlall, Surajmull Nagarmull etc."[183] He even took care to write to his archenemy Birla in December 1928, emphasizing his "trust" in "friendly relations."[184] The tie-up of economic interests between a colonial capitalist like Benthall and a "nationalist" businessman like Birla comes out clearly in another extract from Benthall's diaries. It was written on 26 September 1930, when relations between the two races were far from cordial.

> The most significant feature of the last few months has been the crash in Jute and Gunnies which has taken Birla far down with it. There is no doubt whether he will survive: he owes us money at the end of October but if he fails after that we will be delighted. . . . Even if he does not go, he should not be the danger that he has been, but without the support of B[irla] we may not get the tariff on paper. So I hope he survives, that he doesn't sell his shares or if he does, that they go into other Indian hands.[185]

The opposition between Scottish and Marwari interests was weakened also by serious divisions among the Marwaris themselves. Some of these divisions were caused by religious and cultural questions that had arisen in the community as a result of its contact with Western ideas and institutions. The inevitable conflict between the "orthodox" and the so-called westernizers, a familiar theme in the history of British India, seriously occupied the Calcutta Marwaris in this period, and such was the irony of the situation that G. D. Birla, the thorn among the European businessmen in the city, was seen by the "orthodox" Marwari as the leading "westernizer" of the community.[186] These ideological issues, along with individual trade rivalries, often divided the

[183] C.S.A.S., B.P., Box 7, diary 1929–33, entries for 7 March 1929 and 18 April 1929.
[184] C.S.A.S., B.P., Box 1, Benthall's letter to G. D. Birla, 4 December 1928.
[185] C.S.A.S., B.P., Box 7, diary 1929–33, entry for 26 September 1930.
[186] An account of this conflict is available in Timberg, *Marwaris*.

Marwaris against themselves, creating strange alliances in a "race war" that otherwise might have been total. Thus it was not only the Scotsmen who would have been "delighted" to see Birla go down but "so will [be] most of his own community!!!" wrote Benthall.[187] The "Swarajist" connections of a Bajoria or Birla could be countered by what Benthall thought was "inestimably more valuable, the support of the orthodox Marwaris." It is interesting to note that in the "open war" that Benthall privately and unilaterally declared on Bajoria in the pages of his diary, the combatants mentioned on his side were all Marwaris: "three of the principal loose jute balers i.e., Hari Singh, Lohia and Surajmull Nagarmull," the last named being also the owner of one of the rebel mills. Indeed, Benthall received much of his "secret" news about the business moves or the social situation of the Birlas from rivals within their own community—a "Sheokissen at Goenka's garden party tonight" or a "Swedayal Ramjeedas" of the firm of "Tarachand Ganshyamdas" would often volunteer the information. As if to add to the confusion of this picture of "war of all against all," Birla and Benthall had their own private parleys where it would now be Birla's turn to speak ill of the Marwaris "by whom I was surrounded . . . particularly . . . Bunga and Chokhany."[188]

Thus what the European-Marwari competition produced in the end was an atmosphere of suspicion and mistrust in the jute circles of Calcutta, where men now saw each other as playing ambiguous games. Benthall's private correspondence gives indications of how people felt in such circumstances. Mungneeram Bangur, an important Marwari shareholder of jute mills, for example, left some of the senior officials of Bird and Company extremely unsure of his motives. M. P. Thomas wrote to Benthall in December 1928 that he suspected Bangur of being "up to some dirty work": "I think he is keen on putting up a mill himself. He denies it and laughs, but I feel there is something in it." Benthall himself was utterly confounded and angry that Bajoria should play such games with him. To all appearance, Bajoria behaved like a sworn enemy of Benthall's. He "vilified" the Europeans in the Bengal Legislative Assembly. He also fought Benthall at shareholders' meetings of the Titaghur Mills with the help of men like "Mookerjee or Banerjee," who, Benthall wrote, "was briefed for Rs 16/- to speak on their behalf and who offered for Rs 32/- to speak on our side." But what left Benthall breathless was that Bajoria should also "at the same

[187] C.S.A.S., B.P., Box 7, diary 1929–33, entry for 26 September 1930.
[188] C.S.A.S., B.P., Box 7, diary 1929–33, entries for 19 February, 6 May, 17 June, and 9 August 1929.

time . . . protest his friendship to me by the gift of a Banares cloth!" "Such a man is he!" exclaimed a disgusted Benthall.[189]

WE CAN now pick up the main thread of our story and see how the problem of racism and Indian competition affected IJMA. The magnitude of the competition offered by the nonassociation mills was not very large. They controlled about 2,000 looms, compared to IJMA's 57,387 in 1932.[190] But even so, the situation posed a serious problem of "discipline" to IJMA at a time when this was badly needed. IJMA's plan of retrieving the earlier monopolistic supremacy of the Calcutta industry through production and price agreements called for a certain degree of cohesion among different mills and their owners. This was where Indian competition hurt most. By producing an atmosphere of mistrust and suspicion, it added to the complexity of IJMA's task, already made difficult by the depression.

"I will be glad when the matter is finished," M. P. Thomas of Bird and Company wrote to Benthall in November 1928 regarding a move for a fresh working-time agreement that he had been spearheading within IJMA. "The position this morning is that with the exception of Birla, Angus, Barry and Gillanders, all have signed . . . it's been a dickens of a worry, and the market has been mad, reacting hysterically to every fresh rumour."[191] The confusion created by the Indian competition and the feelings it aroused in different quarters compounded the problem. Four Indian mills that had joined the association briefly "during the first half of 1930" left while the IJMA mills worked only forty hours a week with 15 percent of their looms sealed under an association agreement. So feeble was the solidarity within IJMA now that even the prospect of the small competition that these four mills offered threw the association into complete disarray. The association now swallowed its much-vaunted principle of "non-interference of Government in industry" and involved the governor of Bengal, Sir John Anderson, in coercing the nonassociation mills into a temporary truce.[192]

The association admitted its organizational weakness in the petition in which it requested government intervention. It said:

[189] C.S.A.S., B.P., Box 1, M. P. Thomas to Benthall, 12 December 1928; Box 7, diary 1929–33, entries for 18 April and 6 May 1929.

[190] W.B.S.A., Com. Dept. Com. Br., September 1932, B 87–134; Note by J. A. Woodhead dated 15 April 1932.

[191] C.S.A.S., B.P., Box 7, letter from M. P. Thomas, 28 November 1928.

[192] W.B.S.A., Com. Dept. Com. Br., September 1932, B 87–134, gives details of the negotiations.

The attraction of trebling production and thereby reducing overhead costs by 30 per cent is likely to prove irresistible to a few of the associated mills, and to all non-associated mills, and it is altogether certain that resignations from the association will be handed in very soon. The situation at the present moment is that, if measures are not taken by Government . . . the ability of the association [IJMA] to regulate [production] must disappear within a few months.[193]

The internal problems of IJMA in the thirties were also evident in a proliferation of rules and bylaws designed to "tighten up" its organization.[194] In the past the association had always depended to some extent on the informal social control that a small group of expatriate Scotsmen could exercise on itself. A "word of honour," though often somewhat indifferently kept, served IJMA well enough in its better days; no policing of the members had been necessary.[195] With Indians breaking into the industry at a time when the trade took a turn for the worse, such informal control soon proved inadequate. Working-time agreements had to be backed up throughout the thirties by an elaborate set of rules and, on occasion, governmental authority. To someone like Sir Alexander Murray, the change from the earlier days of "informality" was too marked for it to go unnoticed. "They [the mills] have all signed agreements for five years," he said in 1949, "which have been renewed for another five years, with rigorous rules and by-laws. I was the chairman of the Mills Association in Calcutta in 1913 . . . and at that time there were no rigorous rules and by-laws by which to get people to work four days, or five days, or to get down hessian and sacking looms."

I remember once having to persuade members that the time had arrived for a short-term agreement. I got on fairly well until I came to an old Scotsman who had a grievance of some description. In the course of earlier discussions he had said: "I will not sign any more short-time agreements." Eventually he agreeed . . . [but] said: "No, we will not sign this agreement, but have you ever found me letting you down in any way? I can assure you my word is as good as my bond." I said "Thank you very much" and got up and walked out before he could qualify that in any way.[196]

[193] IJMA's letter dated 26 February 1932 in ibid.
[194] See IJMA, *Report, 1930*, pp. 3, 19–20.
[195] IJMA, *Report, 1925*, p. 18.
[196] See Alexander Murray's "discussion" appended to Walker, "Growth of the Jute Industry," p. 418.

In the middle of the trade crisis, suspicions, bitterness, and race conflicts of the 1930s, such informal arrangements were no longer possible.

The more desperately the association pursued its elusive goal of monopoly in the 1930s, the more deeply the Calcutta industry became embroiled in its own contradictions. IJMA's policy of restricting output ran up against the opposition of the mills that refused to join the association, which in turn endangered IJMA's own fragile unity. IJMA hoped, on the one hand, to undercut "substitutes" and foreign competition through the cheapness of its products; on the other hand it wanted to deal with the competition from the nonassociated mills by forcing them to buy their jute dear. This meant a price war over raw jute and frequent fluctuations in jute prices as a result of interested manipulation. Such fluctuations, on the other hand, encouraged "substitutes," which enjoyed a comparative price stability.[197]

> The market [wrote G. B. Morton of Bird and Company to Benthall in August 1935] undoubtedly fears the results of conflict between outside and Association Mills and this is undoubtedly part of the reason for uncertainty and may be the root of the trouble. Association Mills hold large stocks of cheap Jute and therein lies their strength in a conflict. To reduce the price of jute is to reduce this advantage, so it is [in] the interest of the outside Mills to get Jute prices down and keep them down. It will suit them also to have small margins now between cost and selling prices whilst restriction of hours still places Association Mills at a disadvantage.[198]

Unsuccessful in its attempt to eliminate competition through either restriction of output or manipulating jute prices, IJMA decided in 1937 to "crush" the nonassociated mills "out of existence" by glutting the market: "their object was to spoil the market so that every mill would be incurring losses." The strategy boomeranged. The "outside" mills were generally smaller in size and their cost structure saved them from heavy losses, but the price of jute manufactures plunged "to [a] very low figure" and the association mills suffered.[199]

IJMA had not taken into account a growing volume of "excess capacity" that had been accumulating in its afflicted mills over the years, adding to their costs. High profits during and after the First World War

[197] IJMA, *Report, 1933* (Calcutta, 1934), p. 51.
[198] C.S.A.S., B.P., Box X, letter from G. B. Morton, 23 August 1935.
[199] Sibnath Banerjee's note in *Report of the Bengal Jute Enquiry Committee* (Calcutta, 1939), vol. 1, p. 119.

had drawn more and more capital into the industry. Even after the depression the trend continued as the industry continued to offer dividends from its large reserve funds. In 1935, the Government of India, when approached by the industry for the grant of protection, pointed out that compared to the years "immediately preceding the war," the capacity had been "increased by an addition of about 60% to the number of jute mills and of about 90% to the number of looms and of about 60% to the number of spindles."[200] The Jute Enquiry Committee of 1939 reported that although the "total loomage of the jute mills in 1932 registered an increase of 11.3 per cent over the quinquennial annual average of the years 1927–31 . . . the average consumption of raw jute by Associated mills had increased by only 1.8 per cent during this period."

> The productive capacity continued to increase uninterruptedly till, at the end of 1938, the total loomage had increased by 9.4 per cent over the figures for 1932. The consumption of raw jute during this period had fallen by 15 per cent.[201]

Such excess capacity was bound to affect profitability, especially since the price obtainable for jute manufactures fell and the price could not be raised for the fear of substitutes, revealing once again the dilemma of the industry.

THE STORY of entrepreneurship in the Calcutta jute industry is thus one of an old trading outlook persisting in the face of several changes in the political and economic environment of the industry. The outlook was an anachronism in a post-First World War era of close alliance between scientific research and industrial success. Barker's investigations into jute-mill technology gave the industry a moment of introspection but that moment was brief. In the perception of the people who mattered, the report came too late in the day. Nor do all of its implications seem to have been comprehended. Instead, the industry sought to face its new problems with its old strategies. These did not work very well in the changed circumstances. It is true that the crisis of the thirties shook the industry out of its earlier mood of complacency, but the old habits of thinking died hard. In 1932 the IJMA chairman John Sime evinced a different mood for poetry from that displayed by Wallace in 1928. "Let us not deceive ourselves," said

---

[200] C.S.A.S., B.P., Box X, "[GOI] Memorandum relating to the question of controlling the output of Manufactured Jute in Bengal" (1935).

[201] *Jute Enquiry Committee Report*, vol. 1, p. 22.

Sime, "conditions are changed and changing rapidly," and he went on to quote Shakespeare:

> Not poppy nor mandragora nor all the drowsy syrups of this world can ever lull us back to that sweet sleep that we had yesterday.[202]

Sime's love of Shakespeare was not matched by the accuracy of his quotation, but his choice of metaphor was apt. The Calcutta jute industry had chosen to sleep through scientific and technological changes in its rival industries for twenty years. Even when it woke up in the thirties, it still behaved like a Rip Van Winkle of the industrial world and spent more than a decade looking for its old position in a trading structure that no longer existed. This anachronistic nature of the industry—the trading mentality that guided its economic policies and technological choices—was to have a profound influence on the history of the labor force it created, especially in matters of discipline, authority, and, consequently, workers' protest as well. Even though this was by no means the only influence shaping that history, it was an important one and is considered in more detail in the chapters that follow.

[202] IJMA, *Report, 1932* (Calcutta, 1933), p. 111.

· 3 ·

OF CONDITIONS AND CULTURE

When the Government of India appointed a committee in 1946 to enquire into the conditions of the jute-mill workers of Calcutta, the committee found that there was "very little literature available" in regard to the subject.[1] These conditions, in other words, had not been investigated before with any degree of thoroughness. Today, this creates a special problem for the historian, for any projected history of the conditions of this working class is soon bedeviled by the paucity of sources. True, this scarcity of documents can be explained in part by the characteristics of the Bengali intelligentsia, who seldom, if ever, produced social investigators like Henry Mayhew. Some of it may also be explained by the nonliterate nature of the working class. A problem, however, still remains.

This is the relative poverty of the information in the documents of the state—especially documents that needed the cooperation of employers, such as the factory inspectors' reports—which compare rather badly, say, with the apparent richness of similar, English documents that Marx, for one, put to such effective use in the first volume of *Capital*.

To discuss this question, we shall treat the problem of "paucity of sources" as constituting in itself an important problem in the history we are trying to understand. We will therefore read the available documents on jute workers' conditions for both what they say and their "silences." We will look at the conditions of production of these documents and in this way try to make sense of their gaps and omissions. For, as we argue below on the basis of our reading of Marx, an attempt to analyze these silences invariably takes us into questions of culture and demonstrates a point central to our overall argument: that a theoretical understanding of the working class needs to go beyond the "political-economic" and incorporate the "cultural."

The discussion in the first volume of Marx's *Capital* raises the possibility of a relationship between the day-to-day running of capitalism and the production of a body of knowledge about working-class con-

---

[1] S. R. Deshpande, *Report on an Enquiry into Conditions of Labour in the Jute Mill Industry in India* (Delhi, 1946), p. vi.

ditions. Marx in fact presents us with the elements of a possible theoretical approach to the problem. Even at the risk of appearing to digress, it may be worthwhile to go over that theoretical ground once again, since the rest of this chapter will use that discussion as its own framework. Perhaps it should also be emphasized that what we are borrowing here from Marx is essentially an *argument*. Marx used the English case to illustrate his ideas, but the specifics of English history do not concern us here. We are not reading Marx as a historian of England and this is not an exercise in comparative history.

As is well known, Marx used the documents of the English state for the wealth of detail they usually offered on the living and working conditions of the English proletariat. But Marx also noted in the process that the English state's interest in closely monitoring the conditions of labor had an extremely useful role to play in the development of English capitalism. "This industrial revolution which takes place spontaneously," wrote Marx, "is artifically helped on by the extension of the Factory Acts to all industries in which women, young persons and children are employed."[2] This the acts achieved in two important ways. First, they sought to make "the conditions of competition" between different factories uniform: Marx referred in his discussion of the factory acts to the "cry of the capitalists for equality in the conditions of competition, i.e. for equal restraint on all exploitation of labour." Second, by regulating "the working day as regards its length, pauses, beginning and end"—that is, by making "the saving of time a necessity"—they "forced into existence" more developed and complex machinery and hence, by implication, a more efficient working class.[3]

For the factory acts to secure these aims, however, the state needed to ensure that the knowledge generated by the administration of the acts was not influenced by the narrower considerations of any particular industrialist. Individual masters, it is true, were often in "fanatical opposition" to the acts. But the very fact that Marx derived a lot of his details of the "cruelties" of early capitalism directly from factory inspectors' reports speaks of the "political will" that the English state was capable of mustering, the will that allowed it to distance itself from particular capitalists and yet serve English capitalism in general.[4]

Marx's discussion clarifies some of the conditions for this success. The "political will" of the English state did not fall from the skies. Even though Marx saw the factory acts as "that first and meagre concession wrung from capital" by the government and the working

[2] Karl Marx, *Capital*, vol. 1 (Moscow, n.d.), p. 474.
[3] Ibid., pp. 474, 476–479, 490.
[4] Ibid., pp. 480, 482–484.

people, he also noted that important sections of English industrialists were in fact themselves in favor of the factory acts, their humanistic impulses often spurred on by the forces of competition. Competition was the key to the demand for "equal restraint on all exploitation of labour." "Messrs. Cooksley of Bristol, nail and chain, &c., manufacturers," Marx noted, "*spontaneously* introduced the regulations of the Factory Act into their business" (emphasis added). The Children's Employment Commission of the 1860s explained why: " 'As the old irregular system prevails in neighbouring works, the Messrs. Cooksley are subject to the disadvantage of having their boys enticed to continue their labour elsewhere after 6 p.m.' " Marx also gave the instance of one "Mr. J. Simpson (paper box and bag maker, London)," who told the commission that "he would sign any petition for it [legislative interference]." Summarizing such cases, the commission said:

> It would be unjust to the larger employers that their factories should be placed under regulation, while the hours of labour in the smaller places in their own branch of business were under no legislative restriction. . . . Further, a stimulus would be given to the multiplication of the smaller places of work, which are almost invariably the least favourable to the health, comfort, education, and general improvement of people.[5]

Even if competition in the economy is regarded as instrumental to the autonomy of the English state, one still has to explain why the factories, in the first place, produced the necessary documents without the state having to do much policing. Marx's answer lies in his discussion of the industrial discipline that the capitalist system of manufacture involved. In the process of "disciplining" the labor force, the interests of individual capitalists and those of the state meshed, since, in England, the pressure toward discipline arose both from within and from without the factory. If one effect of the factory legislation was to produce "uniformity, regularity, order and economy," within "each individual workshop,"[6] these were also produced internally, according to Marx, by the capitalist division of labor: "continuity, uniformity, regularity, order," are also the words that Marx used to describe discipline.[7]

Discipline, in Marx's discussion, had two components. It entailed a "technical subordination of the workman to the uniform motion of the instruments of labour," hence the need for training, education, and so

5 Ibid., pp. 488–491.
6 Ibid., p. 503.
7 Ibid., p. 345.

forth. Second, it made supervision—the labour of overlooking—an integral part of capitalist relations of production. The supervisor or the foreman was the executor of the "private legislation" of capital, the "factory code in which capital formulates . . . his autocracy over his workpeople." The supervisor thus embodied the authority of capital, and documents representing factory rules and legislation, such as attendance registers, fine books, and time sheets, became both symbols and instruments of his authority. Supervision, so crucial to the working of capitalist authority, was thus based on documents and produced documents in turn. In Marx's words:

> The place of the slave-driver's lash is taken by the overlooker's book of penalties. All punishments [in capitalist production relations] *naturally* resolve themselves into fines and deductions from wages.[8]

The everyday functioning of the capitalist factory, therefore, produced documents, hence knowledge, about working-class conditions. This was so because capitalist relations of production employed a system of supervision—another name for surveillance—that, in the language of Michel Foucault, "insidiously objectifies those on whom it is applied."[9] It was thus in the nature of capitalist authority that it operated by forming "a body of knowledge" about its subjects. In this it was different from, say, precapitalist domination, which worked more by deploying "the ostentatious signs of sovereignty" and could do without a detailed knowledge of the dominated.[10]

In pursuing Marx's ideas on the relationship between industrial discipline and the documentation of the conditions of workers, we thus end up with the notion of "authority." Marx was quite clear that the supervisor represented the disciplinary authority of capital over labor; but "authority," in Marx's hands, was never a one-sided affair. Quite early in his discussion on capital, Marx wrote: "A . . . cannot be 'your majesty' to B, unless at the same time majesty in B's eyes assumes the bodily form of A."[11] Or a few pages later:

> Such expressions of relations in general, called by Hegel reflex-categories, form a very curious class. For instance, one man is king only because other men stand in the relation of subjects to him.

[8] Ibid., pp. 423–424. Emphasis added.
[9] Michel Foucault, *Discipline and Punish: The Birth of the Prison*, trans. Alan Sheridan (Harmondsworth, 1979), p. 200.
[10] Ibid.
[11] Marx, *Capital*, vol. 1, p. 51.

They, on the contrary, imagine that they are subjects because he is a king.[12]

A particular form of authority or a system of power then implies a particular cultural formation producing and supporting it. As discussed in chapter 1, the laborer of Marx's assumption belonged to a culture characterized by the "formal equality" and the "formal freedom" of the "contract," in this case the contract of the wage. The disciplinary power of capital embodied these very notions. If our exposition of Marx's ideas is correct, then it would mean that such power was rooted as much in the factory codes that capital legislated out of its own needs as in the culture of the working man over whom the authority was exercised. The point seems important in a further respect. By assuming a particular kind of culture on the part of the worker, Marx assigns the working class a place, an active presence, in the whole process of disciplining by supervision and record keeping. And this he does, not just for moments of protest when the working class is obviously active and shows its will, but even when it does not protest and is seemingly a passive object of documentation and knowledge.

Marx's argument can thus be used in two ways. It can be used as a measure of how different capitalism in colonial Bengal was from the paradigm developed by him. There is another question he helps us raise. The Calcutta jute-mill workers, being mostly migrant peasants from Bihar and U.P., did not have a culture characterized by any ingrained notion of "human equality" and were thus very unlike the workers of Marx's assumption. Theirs was largely a precapitalist, inegalitarian culture marked by strong primordial loyalties of community, language, religion, caste, and kinship.[13] Since, in Marx's argument, the question of documentation of conditions of work within a factory was linked to the problem of "disciplinary authority," and that in turn was linked to the question of working-class culture, the cultural specificities of the Calcutta working class raise a whole series of problems. Were relations of production within a Calcutta jute mill still characterized (in spite of differences in working-class culture) by the disciplinary authority that Marx described? The answer would appear to be no. What then was the nature of "supervision" in a Calcutta jute mill? Did it behave like a huge apparatus documenting the conditions

[12] Ibid., p. 57, n. 1.

[13] This is discussed in more detail later in this chapter and in the ones that follow. See also my "Communal Riots and Labour: Bengal's Jute Mill-Hands in the 1890s," *Past and Present*, May 1981, pp. 140–169.

of labor? Did it have a bearing on the problem that a historian of the Indian working class faces today: paucity of "sources"?

In the following sections I will pursue these questions. These discussions have two objectives. They aspire to draw a picture, however incomplete, of the conditions of the jute-mill workers of Calcutta in the period mentioned. At the same time, they seek to account for the gaps in our knowledge and argue that the gaps are as revealing of working-class conditions as any direct reference to them. They provide, therefore, a history both of our knowledge and of our ignorance. Since knowledge of labor conditions ultimately relates to the problem of discipline and authority within the factory, the culture of the workers must occupy a special place in the history of such knowledge.

GOVERNMENT interest in working-class conditions in India is of relatively recent origin. It was only after the end of the First World War that the conditions of Indian workers became an object of knowledge for the Government of India. A Labour Bureau was set up in May 1920 "to collect all available information on labour conditions in India, and classify and tabulate it."[14] One important factor contributing to this development was the establishment of the International Labour Office (ILO) immediately after the war. The Indian government had been an "active participant" in the process of the formation of the ILO and was pledged to its goals.[15] A second important factor was one internal to the Indian political scene. The conclusion of the war and the subsequent period of nationalist agitation had seen trade unions mushroom all over the country on a scale previously unknown. This was accompanied by a countrywide outburst of labor unrest. With the Russian revolution still fresh in its memory, the Government of India's reaction to these developments was colored by its fear of Bolshevism.[16] "Labour is growing more conscious of its own wants and power," the government warned its provincial heads in 1919, "[and] it is showing signs of a capacity for organization."[17] By its militancy, therefore, labor was drawing upon itself the gaze of the government.

What distinguished this new outlook on labor from the traditional law-and-order view of the state was a desire to reform the conditions of labor and thus change the nature of the work force. In an impressive range of labor legislation considered (and partly enacted) in the twen-

[14] *Report of the Royal Commission on Labour in India* [hereafter RCLT] (London, 1931), vol. 5, pt. 1, p. 327.
[15] Ibid., and W.B.S.A., Com. Dept. Com. Br., April 1922, A5–9.
[16] See for example W.B.S.A., Home Poll. Confdl., 405(1–3)/1919.
[17] W.B.S.A., Com. Dept. Com. Br., November 1919, All–25.

ties and afterward, the Government of India sought to take a direct role in structuring the situation of working classes. The amended Factories Act (1922), the Workmen's Compensation Act (1923), the Trade Unions Act (1926), the Trade Disputes Act (1928), the Maternity Benefits Bill (1929), the Payment of Wages Act (1933), and others were all aimed at creating a working class different from the traditionally held image of the industrial labor force in India. The worker was henceforth to receive a new "legal" personality, more welfare, and even some official help in organizing into trade unions (naturally, of a noncommunist kind). Introducing a bill for the "registration and protection of trade unions," the Government of India wrote to the local governments in September 1921 that "in so far as the [trade union] movement makes for the organization of labour, and for the steady betterment of the conditions of labour . . . every facility should be offered for its development along healthy lines."[18]

The government's concern for a "steady betterment of the conditions of labor" was sustained and animated by a recently acquired vision of burgeoning industrial growth in India. The war had left the government in a "developmentalist" mood, from which sprang the arguments regarding working-class conditions.[19]

> There are indications of a considerable expansion in the near future in the number and size of industrial establishments. Moreover machinery and power are being employed in factories to a much larger extent than . . . before. Mines are being worked at greater depths. . . . The transport industries are developing.

With these words the government pleaded in August 1921 the case for creating a system of rules for compensations to be awarded to workmen injured in accidents in the course of work.[20] The argument was elaborated during the discussion that followed. The Government of India explained that the "growing complexity of industry . . . with the increasing use of machinery" required a more efficient labor force than had hitherto been available. It was therefore "advisable that they [the workers] should be protected . . . from hardship arising from accidents," because this would not only increase "the available supply of

[18] W.B.S.A., Com. Dept. Com. Br., August 1922, A32–51.

[19] For details, see Clive Dewey, "The Government of India's 'New Industrial Policy,' 1900–1925: Formation and Failure," in K. N. Chaudhuri and C. J. Dewey, eds., *Economy and Society: Essays in Indian Economic and Social History* (Delhi, 1979), pp. 215–257.

[20] W.B.S.A., Com. Dept. Com. Br., July 1922, A34–72.

labour" but also produce "a corresponding increase in the *efficiency* of the average workman."[21]

"Efficiency," in this logic, was a function of working-class conditions. The government noted in 1919 that although there was "a keen and increasing demand for factory labour" in India, there was "little apparent desire on the part of the labourers to increase their efficiency," and—more to the point—"little prospect of their being able to do so under present *conditions*."[22] Improving efficiency meant improving these "conditions," and they included not only "education, housing and social welfare" but also such aspects as the "comfort" and "spare time" of the worker.

> The efficiency of workers is closely connected with their education, and their standard of comfort; the shortening of hours may not prove an unmixed good, if the workers are not put in a position to make a proper use of their spare time.[23]

The argument was broader than it might appear at first sight. For it was not only a question of giving the workers "spare time" but of structuring that "spare time" as well, of ensuring that the workers made "proper use" of it.[24] It was thus that the government's eyes fell— for the first time in Indian history—on several aspects of the worker's life that had so far been held to be beyond the ken of capital. Issues of indebtedness, the "monetary reserve" of the worker, his wages, food, health, home life—all came under the scrutiny of the government.[25] "Efficiency" produced its own code of ethics, which opposed the image of the vigorous and healthy worker to that of the overworked and fatigued:

> They [the Government of India] believed that the longer interval [of rest] is desirable in order to enable the worker to maintain his *vigour*, and that its enforcement should ultimately prove beneficial to the employer. There are grounds for believing that the absence of sustained work, characteristic of many factory employees in this country, has been due . . . to the fact that the hours fixed did not in the past allow sufficient opportunity for the *rest* necessary to prevent fatigue.[26]

[21] W.B.S.A., Com. Dept. Com. Br., January 1923, A65–107. Emphasis added.
[22] W.B.S.A., Com. Br., November 1919, A11–25. Emphasis added.
[23] Ibid.
[24] See also W.B.S.A., Com. Dept. Com. Br., May 1927, A1–6.
[25] See for instance W.B.S.A., Com. Dept. Com. Br., February 1927, A1–8, and May 1929, B196–9.
[26] W.B.S.A., Com. Dept. Com. Br., March 1924, A45–61. Emphasis added.

It was only in the context of this search for an "efficient" working class that working-class conditions became an object of knowledge in India. How did the Government of India propose to produce and gather this knowledge? Provincial governments were equipped with new departments that were meant to perform this task. For instance, under pressure from Government of India, the Bengal government established in July 1920 the office of the industrial intelligence officer, later named the labour intelligence officer, whose duty it was to "maintain a proper watch over the industrial situation," and "in particular to investigate and report on labour conditions and the facts and causes of labour disturbances."[27] The Government of India also realized that much of this knowledge would have to be generated within the factories and that the provincial staff of factory inspectors might need to be employed on collecting and monitoring the information. Since "leisure," "rest," "fatigue," and "spare time" were some of the key concepts supporting the government's notion of "efficiency," control over the laborer's working hours naturally emerged as a problem of the highest importance. The attendance registers maintained by individual factories and the factory inspectors' reports now came to be regarded as crucial documents from the Government of India's point of view. With this end in view, the Factories Act was amended in 1922 with a new section 35, which required the manager of a factory "to maintain . . . [an attendance] register of all persons employed and of their hours of work."[28]

THE CONDITIONS of jute-mill labor in Bengal were never as fully documented as the Government of India wished. The inaccuracies in the attendance registers of the jute mills were witness to this failure; the chief inspector of factories admitted to the Royal Commission on Labour in 1929 that "the records given in such registers [did] not represent the true conditions . . . of . . . labour."[29] The Labour Office of Bengal, moreover, suffered from a peculiar bureaucratic malaise, the history of which only indicates that the Bengal government never shared the Government of India's enthusiasm for knowledge of labor conditions. For one thing (as the labor commissioner of Bengal recalled in 1939) the office was set up with "no immediate purpose of having a large investigating office, with cost of living indices and other standard concomitants of an organized labour office."[30] Besides, so low was the

[27] W.B.S.A., Com. Dept. Com. Br., April 1922, A5–9.
[28] W.B.S.A., Com. Dept. Com. Br., February 1926, A1-46.
[29] RCLI, vol. 5, pt. 1, p. 92.
[30] W.B.S.A., Home Poll. Confdl., no. 392 (1–3)/1935.

priority of his office in the eyes of the Bengal government that when "the first Retrenchment Committee" reported in 1921, "the Labour Office seemed bound to go"; but "instead of abolishing it, the [Bengal] government changed its character." To economize, the labor intelligence officer was saddled with various other responsibilities and his investigative functions suffered badly in consequence. He was placed "in charge of the Commerce Department, and later of the Marine Department." He was made responsible for the administration of all the labor laws that were to come in the twenties, as well as for other legislative measures only "partly concerned with the welfare of labour, e.g., the Boilers Act and the Electricity Act." The labour intelligence officer thus became, in his own words, "an ordinary secretariat officer" who had little time to investigate the conditions of labor.

> With the growing volume of office work and the addition of one duty after another, the Labour Intelligence Officer found it impossible to continue his personal investigations regarding every strike, and also to some extent, his visits to factories . . . , although, as far as possible, he continued these visits up to 1929 when the enormous increase of work due to the advent of Whitley Commission tied him completely to his desk.[31]

The atrophy of the Labour Office was not a matter of simple bureaucratic mindlessness. What calls for analysis is precisely the "mind" of this bureaucracy. To this "mind," any interest in labor conditions beyond that called for by the immediate needs of capital, or of law and order, was suspect. "For some peculair reason," wrote a rather frustrated labor commissioner in 1935, "in Bengal, interest in labour matters or desire for knowledge of labour developments is read as sympathy for the labour point of view."[32]

The "reason" for this suspicion is not difficult to see. The Government of India's "desire for knowledge of labour developments" assumed that the investigating authority would be capable of maintaining a degree of independence from the point of view of particular capitalists. The government wished to stand above the "unevenness" of such particular views. For example, in insisting on "uniform rules" for fines or accident compensations, the Government of India argued that the question of the "welfare of the working classes" could not "any longer be left to the uneven generosity of employers."[33] Such

[31] Ibid.
[32] Ibid.
[33] W.B.S.A., Com. Dept. Com. Br., July 1922, A34–72.

"neutrality" by the state threatened to rupture the almost "natural" unity that had existed in Bengal for years between the provincial government and owners of capital (especially those represented by such powerful organizations as the Bengal Chamber of Commerce and IJMA).

This "natural unity" had received its fullest expression in the nineteenth century when the moral order of the day had been unashamedly procapitalist and when the government of Bengal plainly considered it its duty "to do all it can to afford moral support to the [jute] millowners" in the face of labor unrest.[34] In the 1890s even the meager provisions of the first two factory acts of India were seen by senior officers of the government of Bengal as "needlessly harassing to the [mill] managers."[35] A factory inspector who once insisted on age verification for all jute-mill child workers in his jurisdiction was sharply pulled up by the chief secretary of the government of Bengal. "Inspectors," he was told, "by making the [medical] examination of every child compulsory, would give to owners or managers of factories the maximum of trouble, and to the government the maximum of expenses without conferring any compensating benefit on the majority of the children employed."[36]

It would not be very profitable to see this merely as an instance of ruling-class hypocrisy. The evidence yields more value when treated as an expression of ruling-class outlook on conditions of labor. The Bengal officials were not just displaying their lack of respect for the factory laws; underlying their statements was also the conviction that the labor conditions themselves did not leave much to be desired. To most of the factory inspectors, therefore, contrary to the aims of the factory legislation, the conditions always seemed satisfactory. A typical example of their attitude is to be found in the report of the working of the Factories Act in Bengal for the year 1893. The "general conditions of the [mill] operatives" were found "very satisfactory," they said; the coolie lines were "well laid out," their work was "not arduous," the water supply was "good," the latrines were "well kept," the children were "thoroughly healthy," their work "in no way detrimental to them," and the arrangements for medical care of the workers were "satisfactory." Even the "fact" that "five or ten per cent" of the children were "weak, feeble in growth and stunted for their age" could not be attributed, it was said, "to the work they perform in the mills,

[34] W.B.S.A., Judicial Dept. Police Br., January 1896 A6–11.
[35] W.B.S.A., General (hereafter Genl.) Dept. Miscellaneous (hereafter Misc.) Br., July 1882, A73–81.
[36] Ibid.

as about the same proportion of undersized and weakly children may be observed among the outside population."[37]

To such an official "mind," labor conditions deserved investigation only when they posed law-and-order problems. A government of Bengal file discussing a sudden outburst of working-class unrest in the jute mills in 1894–95 gave some attention to the question of housing of labor. But the concern here was merely with issues of public control and no more. The lieutenant governor of Bengal invited IJMA to "cooperate with the [Bengal] Government in improving both direct control [i.e. policing] over the mill-hands in case they should break into violence, and also indirect control which will make acts of violence less likely by *bettering* the *conditions* of the employees":

> His Honor therefore confidently invites the co-operation of the mill-owners to provide comfortable and well-ordered homes for mill-hands, and thus avoid such conditions as those at Samnagar and Titagar, which offer temptations to the disorderly and make control difficult.

But the amount of improvement desired in the "conditions" was severely limited. Too much "bettering" of conditions might make the task of control harder. "Rice is very cheap, and this makes them [the laborers] independent," was the diagnosis of a police officer in the same file, who quoted jute-mill managers' views in support of his own: "Experienced mill managers seem to think that . . . when the labour market becomes once more over-stocked, as they said it will be, mill hands will grow less independent, and matters will quiet down to their normal state."[38] In taking a law-and-order view of labor conditions, then, the state incorporated within its own outlook the point of view of capital.

Much of this nineteenth-century spirit can be read in twentieth-century documents as well, especially those coming from the years before the First World War. There was, for instance, the civil surgeon of Serampore who thought (in 1909) that "the mills in Hooghly need no legislation for the well-being of the operatives"; or the factory inspector who felt (in 1910) that he was "legitimately entitled to place the telescope to his blind eye" if he came across "a child of seven or eight years sewing or hemming a gunny bag in the vicinity of the mother," even though the law demanded "the Manager . . . be prosecuted for employing a child under nine"; or the even more striking case of C. A.

[37] W.B.S.A., Genl. Dept. Misc. Br., August 1893, A1–36.
[38] W.B.S.A., Judicial Dept. Police Br., January 1896, A6–11.

Walsh, the chief inspector of factories, boldly declaring in 1912: "I see no poverty in the quarters surrounding the great [jute] mills at Khardah, Titagarh, Shamnagore, Kankinara, Naihati, Budge-Budge or Fort Gloster."[39]

The tone of the official pronouncements changed somewhat after 1920, thanks to the efforts of the Government of India and of nationalist and radical politicians who espoused the cause of labor. "The increasing solidarity of labour" entered the calculations of the government of Bengal and the realization dawned upon it that "industrial disputes will in future form an integral part of the industrial life of this province."[40] Yet this did not mean any "epistemological shift" in the status of the "conditions of labour" question. It never acquired any priority over the question of control. The Industrial Unrest Committee of 1921 recommended that the Bengal government set up machinery for investigating strikes but made it clear that the machinery proposed "must be designed for the purpose of alleviating unrest . . . rather than for a detailed investigation of current labour conditions."[41] It was the same "disease" that had warped the career of the Labour Office in Bengal. The periodic reports the labor intelligence officer sent to the Government of India were, it was admitted, "nearly always" the view of the local police—"merely thana officers' views," as Donald Gladding, a senior official of the Bengal government, once described them. "Neither superior police officers nor Magistrates go about seriously to find out the truth by questioning the workmen on the one hand and the employers on the other—and this," Gladding insisted, was "polite and correct."[42]

The factory inspectors' reports bore ample testimony to this absence of a spirit of investigation. A good example is the treatment they gave to the question of the "health" of the workers. This was an important question from the Government of India's point of view, carrying obvious implications for the dietary conditions, the standard of living, the wages situation, and the efficiency of the worker.[43] None of these latter considerations, however, ever influenced the Bengal factory in-

[39] W.B.S.A., Genl. Dept. Misc. Br., August 1910, A33–86; August 1911, A18–63; and Medical Dept. Medical Br., January 1914, B287–95.

[40] W.B.S.A., Com. Dept. Com. Br., December 1923, A8.

[41] W.B.S.A., Com. Dept. Com. Br., July 1921, A43–5.

[42] W.B.S.A., Com. Dept. Com. Br., August 1925, A7–8.

[43] For evidence of the Government of India's interest in these questions see W.B.S.A., Com. Dept. Com. Br., February 1927, A1–8; November 1933, A1–27; June 1935, A35–48. For the government of Bengal's reluctance to carry out a wage census see W.B.S.A., Com. Dept. Com. Br., November 1921, B200–1.

spectors. For years, their reports carried a section called General Health of the Operatives, where the workers' health was always described as "good" if there had been no epidemics. "The general health of operatives has been good," said the Factories Act report for 1928, "no outbreak of disease in epidemic form having been reported during the year."[44] Why was health a question of epidemics, and not one of diet, nutrition, or standard of living? The following quotation from the factory inspection report for 1921 suggests the answer:

> The Naihati Jute Mills at Naihati, Baranagar Jute Mills at Baranagar, [etc.] . . . reported a shortage of labour in the month of August last owing to outbreaks of malaria and influenza. The shortage . . . was not serious and the general health of the operatives . . . has on the whole been satisfactory.[45]

Or, to put the argument in an even more precise form, as did the report for 1923:

> The general health of operatives during the year . . . has been comparatively good, no shortage of labour on account of epidemic diseases or sickness having been reported by the mills.[46]

At heart, this was the employer's argument. In the jute mills, health care for workers was essentially aimed at prevention of epidemics. Information regarding diseases treated free by the doctors of twenty-three jute mills in 1928 was collected by the government of Bengal for submission to the Royal Commission on Labour. It is interesting to observe that none of the diseases treated was of nutritional origin; chief among them were cholera, smallpox, malaria, typhoid fever, relapsing fever, kala azar, dysentery, diarrhea, pneumonia, tuberculosis of the lungs, and respiratory diseases "other than infectious."[47] Clearly, most of them were infectious diseases or water or food borne diseases, capable of affecting a number of people at the same time, especially under conditions of overcrowding. In other words, attention was confined to diseases that were potentially epidemic. It was epidemics that caused large-scale absenteeism and thus affected production; besides, they respected no class barriers. Speaking to IJMA in 1918, Alexander Murray, then chairman of the association, referred to a proposal put up by mills "in four different municipalities up the river . . . to spend anything up to Rs 100 per loom" in improving workers'

44 W.B.S.A., Com. Dept. Com. Br., September 1929, A12–15.
45 W.B.S.A., Com. Dept. Com. Br., June 1921, A29–30.
46 W.B.S.A., Com. Dept. Com. Br., August 1924, A34–7.
47 W.B.S.A., Com. Dept. Com. Br., April 1930, A7–12.

housing, and remarked that he could "imagine no more profitable investment from a mill labour point of view." Supporting this view, he said:

> In proof of this I might refer to the experience during the influenza epidemic last year of the mills with which I am most closely associated. Our mill doctors' reports show that the hands living in the bazar suffered far more severely than those living in the mills' own coolie lines. At most of our mills the production for the week ending 20th July, which witnessed the epidemic at its worst, was anything from 15 to 30 per cent below normal. But in the case of one of our mills which houses nearly all its labour in its own lines, the drop was only 5 per cent.[48]

Clearly, to Murray, as to the jute industry, the measure of the severity of epidemics was the drop in production. Epidemics therefore became the most important issue whenever the employers turned their minds to the question of the health of the workers.

One implication of such an outlook was that large areas of working-class life remained out of view. Once again, the health question illustrates the problem. As a result of the recommendations of the Royal Commission on Labour, an investigation was carried out into the condition of women workers in jute mills in 1931–32. The investigating doctor discovered several diseases that had never found their way into the records of the mill dispensaries. She noted that many of the working-class children had "a tendency to rickets, shown by slight bending of the legs and bossing of the forehead." This was "probably due to deficiency of vitamin D in the food." Although many children looked "fine" "in the first year of life," a "healthy appearance was less common" after that age. Venereal diseases were "said to be wide-spread," yet there was "no evidence on the subject." In the lines of one mill, she came across a young girl "obviously dying of a pernicious type of anaemia," but "she was having no treatment." "In the lines of another mill," she found "a woman suffering from a severe degree of ostcomalacia, unable to walk. This is a very great danger in childbirth and with careful treatment can be cured or greatly relieved." She noticed "several cases of children reduced to almost extremity." Another time she saw "a woman obliged to stop her work for blindness and suffering great pain in her eyes [which] . . . would have been susceptible to treatment." But a certain kind of "blindness," in these cases, was what characterized the employer's outlook. The investigating doctor re-

[48] W.B.S.A., Com. Dept. Com. Br., July 1919, A1–2.

marked: "None of these cases were known to the mill doctors, who always accompanied me when I visited the lines."[49]

Thus, in claiming as their own a view of labor conditions that really belonged to the owners of capital, the documents of the Bengal government reproduced something else as well: the "optical errors" of that vision. Significant aspects of working-class conditions remained hidden from it. This was what in the end undermined the Government of India's project for "knowledge" of these conditions. The government of Bengal lacked the political will necessary to distance itself from the employers in the jute industry. This was well known even to the Government of India, which, however, never felt powerful enough to force anyone's hand. On 13 September 1928 Lord Irwin, the viceroy, wrote to the secretary of state:

> We had a discussion in Council this week on the contemplated enquiry into labour matters . . . no Local Government except Bengal had any objection to our announcing now that such an enquiry would be held; but the Bengal Government entered a strong protest. . . . Bengal have on other occasions lately shown a disposition to act as a brake in questions of this kind; for example they stood alone in adopting an uncompromising attitude in respect of maximum wages, and they were nearly alone in pressing for the circulation of the Trade Dispute Bill when we asked if Local Governments would agree to our pushing on with it.

Irwin's conclusion was significant: "The influence of the employers—and particularly the European employers—is strong there [in Bengal], and they were not likely to receive the news of an enquiry with joy."[50]

It would once again be wrong to see this "influence" as a conspiracy of state and capital against labor. Its expressions were too aboveboard and direct for it to be treated as such. It is better seen as part of the existing political culture. In deciding, for instance, if commercial bodies like IJMA should be approached directly with the recommendations of the Industrial Unrest Committee (1921), Sir J. H. Kerr, a member of the Governor's Council, wavered:

> We must walk warily [he wrote]. . . . Sir Alexander Murray warned me specially that the Jute Mills Association would have to be led, not driven, and I think we should be safer in leaving the matter in his hands.[51]

[49] W.B.S.A., Com. Dept. Com. Br., July 1932, A2–6.
[50] IOL, MSS. Eur. C152/4, Irwin Papers, letter to Birkenhead, 13 September 1928.
[51] W.B.S.A., Com. Dept. Com. Br., July 1921, A43–5 K.W.

Kerr felt frightened even to start an office like a Labour Bureau with some pretension toward investigation of labor conditions. "The term bureau frightens people," he wrote; "I would not start anything in the nature of a Bureau even on paper without consultation with employers."[52]

So keen was the government of Bengal in its desire to avoid any confrontation with the owners of jute mills that factory inspectors were actually encouraged to leave all "controversial" matters out of their reports. Further, the capitalists themselves sometimes had a direct role in weeding out statements unfavorable to their interests. The report for 1923 had to be redrafted because of objections from industrialists like Alexander Murray. As the labor intelligence officer explained:

> Normally the Chief Inspector of Factories sends in his report to Government without previous sanction, but last year owing to a number of controversial paragraphs being inserted, the report was first unofficially examined. The report had ultimately to be reprinted as strong objection was taken by Sir A. Murray and others to the remarks of the Chief Inspector. There is nothing objectionable in the report [now being] put up, but I have toned down some of the remarks.[53]

Even the attendance register that the 1922 Factories Act required the factories to maintain was modified in Bengal to suit the convenience of the jute-mill managers. It was made into a less detailed document than it could have been and as a result, admitted the chief inspector of factories in 1930, it became "a type of register satisfying the view of the employers [in the jute industry] but futile and inadequate for ensuring establishment of the provisions of Chapter IV [relating to working hours] of the [Factories] Act."[54]

Thus if working-class conditions in the jute mills never quite became an object of knowledge in the way envisaged by the Government of India, the "failure" occurred at two levels. The industry never produced the necessary documents; and the government lacked the political will to carry out its own investigations.

THE QUESTION of the lack of a "political will" on the part of the government of Bengal, its inability to force any issue on IJMA or the jute industry, can be partly comprehended as a negative illustration of

[52] Ibid.
[53] W.B.S.A., Com. Dept. Com. Br., August 1924, A34–7.
[54] RCLI, vol. 5, pt. 1, p. 328.

Marx's argument. I say "partly" because some of the spirit of cooperation prevailing between the state and capital must have derived from the tight racial bonds that existed between European employers and the British bureaucracy in colonial Bengal.[55] But one also has to note that the industry (or any sections of employers) never put any pressure on the government to equalize "the conditions of competition" between different mills. "Conditions are different in different [mill] centres," said IJMA to the Royal Commission on Labour. "One mill provides housing accommodation for all their workers whereas another mill provides none whatever. One mill provides good water, another provides no water.[56] An official of the government of Bengal was to use much stronger words in 1929:

> Perhaps in no industry in the world, situated in such a circumscribed area, is the wage position more inchoate. The mill groups under different managing agents work under wage systems which have developed many local idiosyncrasies during the long and short years of their existence. Even in mills under the same managing agents there are differences which to persons not acquainted with the position would seem incredible. . . . In . . . groups of mills situated close to each other and under different managing agents, the wage-rates in individual mills are kept, or are supposed to be kept, strictly secret.[57]

Yet the jute industry was always content to let all this be; there never arose any significant demand for the standardization of wage rates. At the instance of the Royal Commission, IJMA decided in 1931 to set up a subcommittee to look into the latter problem. The committee admitted in its report the following year that "nothing can be done in the direction of general standardisation [of wages] for all the mills," since there were "circumstances which preclude any immediate steps being taken."[58] The report ended with extremely cautious recommendations for slow and gradual standardization of rates for mills "in the same districts," but very little came of this. A confidential report, "Jute Mill Labour Conditions" written in October 1945 by J. Lee, the senior labor officer of IJMA, referred to the lack of standardization of wage rates as a continuing problem:

> Over the last year I have collected statistics of wage-rates paid in the mills and these have all been transferred into a rate paid as

[55] A. K. Bagchi, *Private Investment in India 1900–1939* (Cambridge, 1972), chap. 6.
[56] *RCLI*, vol. 5, pt. 2, p. 163.
[57] Ibid., pt. 1, p. 141.
[58] IJMA, *Report*, 1932 (Calcutta, 1933), pp. 314–315.

"pies per hour." . . . I prepared a list of all occupations, and then gave the maximum rate paid as well as the minimum. The differences in many occupations was very great, and in itself, was . . . a good case for wage-standardization.[59]

The lack of standardization of wages remained a problem even in the 1950s.[60]

Why was it that the jute industry, notorious for the feelings of rivalry that mills often harbored against one another, was happy to carry on with an "inchoate" wage position? Several answers suggest themselves. To consider outside competition first, the relationship between the Calcutta and the Dundee industries was never one of straightforward competition, like that between Bombay and Manchester. With Dundee branching off into fine products for survival and Calcutta providing a big employment market for Dundee technicians and managers, the pressures of that potential competition eased off a great deal after 1914–19. The kind of uproar that Dundee industrialists often caused in the 1890s over labor conditions in Calcutta became a matter of the past in the twentieth century.[61] At the same time, the state of organization of the Calcutta jute-mill workers was too weak for them to exert any effective pressure on the wage question. Third, the "individualism" of individual (or group of) mills was something that IJMA accepted as the price of its organizational unity, which the industry saw as crucial to its overall prosperity. And fourth, one must take into account the concentration of economic power within the industry; this must have gone some way toward mitigating any spirit of competition between mills.

There were, however, two other factors that were perhaps more important than those mentioned above. Paradoxical though it may sound, the expenditure incurred by the mills per capita of their respective labor force might have varied in fact far less than the discussion on wage-rate differences suggests. In other words, it is possible that the "conditions of competition" between mills remained more or less at a par and thus made state intervention superfluous. It will be interesting, in this respect, to depart from the practice of calculating bonuses and wages by themselves and try instead to study these along with other expenditures on labor, such as housing, sanitation, water supply, and health clinics. Since the amounts spent under these heads also varied

[59] IJMA, Labour Office, "Circular and Notes of the Committee," 1945-46.

[60] See Raghuraj Singh, *Movement of Industrial Wages in India* (Bombay, 1955), pp. 223–225.

[61] See, for instance, the *Dundee Advertiser*, 28 January 1893, and IJMA, *Report, 1893* (Calcutta, 1894), pp. 22–24.

from mill to mill according to differences in the volume of labor supply, employers who paid lower wages might well have ended up by spending more on housing, for example, and vice versa. It then seems quite possible that the average amount spent per unit of labor worked out to be roughly the same for different mills, so that the disparities in the "conditions of competition" did not matter very much.

The point cannot be statistically verified here, detailed information on wage rates and other matters being extremely hard to come by. But there is some evidence to suggest that the industry had developed certain informal means for equalizing "labor conditions" between the mills (especially those close to one another) or at least for keeping the "inequalities" well within "tolerable" limits. For one thing, it was hard to keep the information about wages a secret however much the managing agents might desire this. "The total earnings [for different occupations] are not necessarily kept secret," the government of Bengal told the Royal Commission on Labour, and the piece rates or bonus rates could easily be "ascertained by spy-work in the bazar."[62] Further, the worker's idea of a "fair wage" often involved a principle of parity with those paid by mills in the neighborhood. Localized strikes, therefore, often tended to bring local wage rates in line with one another.

Even more important perhaps was the fact that managers could effectively create an informal climate (and pressure) of opinion that also had a homogenizing influence on labor conditions. When an American firm, the American Manufacturing Company, started a jute mill in Calcutta in the early 1920s, it was said that "the Directors in the States . . . sanctioned large amounts to be spent on sanitation and welfare of workers, as they were accustomed to such outlay in connection with their jute mills in the United States." Yet the eventual amount spent turned out to be much less than that sanctioned, for the managers of the other jute mills had objected.

> In many cases they [the Directors] would have been willing to go much further than they had actually gone e.g. to give electric light in the workers' houses, as well as a plentiful installation outside in the lines, but had been told that this had never been done here. So at present electric light is limited to the durwans' houses.

It is significant that this mill ultimately settled for the "district rate" of wages and followed "the custom in jute mills in the district" in respect of accident compensation. It also "modelled" its leave rules (or their absence) on those at the "neighboring jute mills." And even though the

[62] *RCLI*, vol. 5, pt. 1, p. 141.

"agents had been willing to put in as good a drainage system as possible," the actual "type copied was that used by the other Calcutta Jute Mills."[63]

A lack of standardization in wage rates, therefore, did not necessarily reflect a competitive situation among the mills regarding their labor conditions. Any effective pressure from international competitors was also conspicuously absent. The Bengal government's views on labor conditions were therefore governed solely by its relationship with capitalists in the jute industry, and in this relationship, the latter always predominated. What the state reproduced in its documents therefore, was the blinkered vision of capital.

THIS LEAVES us with the more crucial question: Why was the "vision" of capital "blinkered"? Why did the jute mills fail to produce the daily records that the Government of India had asked for? Or to put the question differently: Why were the attendance registers kept in such a state that they did not "reflect the true conditions of labour"? Once again, Marx's argument is useful. To understand the lack of documentation at the level of the factory we have to turn to the problem of "discipline." A discussion of "discipline" has to begin by considering the nature of work and technology in a jute mill, for discipline is, in the first place, a question of training and skills, the "technical subordination of the worker" to the motion and requirements of the machine. Discipline of course also involves supervision, but we shall take that up later.

Work inside a Calcutta jute mill involved mechanical processes broadly similar to those in a nineteenth-century cotton mill, except that jute was a rougher material than cotton and the humidification necessary for cotton was not needed for jute.[64] After the raw jute had been sorted and batched as it came into the mill, it went through a process of softening and preparing for the eventual spinning and weaving of jute. Softening included passing the jute "through a softening machine consisting of fluted rollers under heavy pressure when simultaneously an emulsion of oil and water . . . [was] applied," the oil being necessary "to facilitate the succeeding process of manufacture as jute fibre contains no natural lubrication." After softening came the preparing stage, which included three distinct operations: carding, drawing, and roving. The object of carding was "to break down long stalks

[63] W.B.S.A., Com. Dept. Com. Br., April 1923, B77.

[64] This description is based on the following sources: C.S.A.S., B.P., Box 18, note entitled "Indian Jute Industry" (n.d., 1940s?), and N. C. Saha, "Inside a Jute Mill," *Jute and Gunny Review*, February-March 1950, pp. 139–143.

or strips of fibre into a continuous broad ribbon of fine fibres" and to lay the fibers parallel to one another. The carding process involved the use of two machines, the breaker card and the finisher card. The former "breaks and hackles the stalks of [the] fibre" to make it into a broad ribbon "termed sliver in the trade." About twelve such slivers were then fed manually into the finisher card, "where the carding operation is continued on finer scale."[65] The carded slivers were still not uniform or straight and were therefore subjected to processes called drawing and doubling, where the aim was to obtain "a greater length of [uniform] fibre for the same unit of weight." The operations of drawing and doubling were "combined into one machine called [the] drawing frame." Drawing thinned out the sliver, doubling counteracted it by combining "two or more such drawn out slivers into one at the delivery end of the machine." The last of the preparatory processes was roving, the object of which was to draw out the slivers even further, according to the spinning requirements, while strengthening them by giving them a partial twist. The twisted sliver was called "rove." The next step was spinning, when yarns were made by spinning frames that drew out further the rover, spun it, and finally wound it on spinning bobbins. Warp yarns were twisted harder than weft yarns. Winding followed next and "the yarn forming the warp of the cloth . . . [was] wound round . . . bobbins into the form of comparatively large rolls, thereby obtaining a greater continuity in length." The yarn for the weft in the cloth was wound into " 'cops' fitting exactly into the shuttles employed in weaving." Warp yarn, saturated with a starchy material to prevent breakage in weaving, was then "drawn on to large beams" (the "beaming" process) and placed at the back of the loom for weaving. The final stages in the manufacture constituted the finishing process, whereby the woven cloth was passed through the heavy rollers of a calendering machine for ironing and eventually cut and sown into bags. The bags again were "made into bundles of 25 or 30" and packed by a hydraulic press.

The technology accompanying these processes had been "perfected" in the nineteenth century. S. G. Barker, who investigated the technical side of Calcutta jute mills in the 1930s and whose findings we have discussed in the previous chapter, found the technology so stagnant that he likened the industry to a gramophone needle: "It runs in a groove and plays a nice tune. If either needle or record gets worn, new

[65] "The principle of these [carding] machines is a rapidly revolving cylinder armoured with pins whilst smaller pinned rollers revolving at a slower speed are placed parallel to this cylinder and retard the fibre, thus promoting the combing action": C.S.A.S., B.P., Box 18, note entitled "Indian Jute Industry," p. 2.

ones are demanded."[66] The "groove" in Barker's description referred to the lack of diversification of products in the history of the industry and to the crude and rough nature of what was produced. This, as we know, he saw as a fundamental factor in the technological stagnation of the industry. In Barker's words:

> Jute being a cheap material producing fabrics for rough usage . . . the machinery and technique in India became standardised upon an elementary mechanical basis. Simplicity of operation without the necessity for textile science, since changes [in output] were practically non-existent . . . soon led to the mass production of the limited range of Indian jute products becoming almost automatic. The conversion of Jute fibres into fabrics therefore became a mechanical engineering proposition, a position largely maintained to this day. The mechanical influence was greatly enhanced by conditions in India, since spare machine parts and renewals were difficult to get from home. Thus each mill or group was equipped with an efficient mechanics' workshop, which not only maintained the machinery in excellent order but even extended to the construction of duplicates of existing looms, etc. Again the simplicity of the machine principles facilitated this. . . . Machinery in the mills in general, therefore, has had a long working life, perhaps too long.[67]

The industry considered this technology so adequate for its purpose that it placed very little premium on the scientific and technological training of its workers and its superior technical staff. Barker was surprised to discover many large and crucial gaps in the technical knowledge of the Scottish managers and assistants, gaps that they usually filled up with that rather undefined human quality called "experience." The softening process contained a number of "unknowns" like "temperature, moisture content and distribution in the [jute] pile" as well as the optimum pressure between the rollers, "the actual value for which seemingly . . . [had] no criterion but *experience*." He was also struck by "the lack of finality in technical knowledge of the carding process." The same went for drawing and doubling, where "the ideal roller pressure" and "the size of flutings for Jute . . . [had] been determined by *experience*." For the process of roving, the list of things unknown was formidable. "Roller covering and pressure, surface speeds,

---

[66] S. G. Barker, *Report on the Scientific and Technical Development of the Jute Manufacturing Industry in Bengal with an Addenda on Jute, Its Scientific Nature and Information Relevant Thereto* (Calcutta, 1935), p. 42.

[67] Ibid., pp. 41–42.

spindle speeds, the flyer mechanism, the distribution of fibre length in the rove, the degree of levelness along its length, fibre control and, in addition, the factors concerning twist and the form of bobbins" were all yet "to be studied."

Barker's correspondence with some of the mill managers on technical problems dramatically revealed the low priority that the industry gave to technical education. Technical issues were often treated merely as matters of the *"experience,"* "opinion," or personal judgment of the people concerned:

> From my experience [wrote one manager to Barker] I have found that certain makers' machines are suitable for one class of fibre, while others are suitable for a different class. . . . A number of people favour pinning with light pins whilst [others] prefer a coarser pinning with a corresponding heavier pin, again only a matter of opinion.
>
> Another point which allows a certain latitude to be taken is roller speeds and ratios, but to my mind this item is not nearly as important as pinning and setting.[68]

If the manager's knowledge of the machinery had such a glaring "lack of finality" about it, one can imagine the want of understanding that separated the worker from the machine. This is not to say that the machine did not in any way affect the worker's life in the factory. The mechanical processes in a jute mill were continuous with one process feeding another, and the work was heavier and noisier than in a typical cotton mill.[69] The continuous motion and speed of the machinery was something that the worker had to adjust to. "Continuous and even flow" of the jute sliver was the responsibility of the laborers working on the softening, carding, drawing, and roving machines.[70] "The work of feeding the breaker cards," for instance, was "heavy" and needed "constant attention." The finisher card required the cooperation of three women at a speed matching that of the machine: "one arranges the slivers side by side at the feed end, one takes delivery at the other, and one carries."[71] In the spinning department, the shifting of bobbins "must be done quickly for with bulky material such as jute, the bob-

[68] The quotations in this paragraph are from ibid., pp. 26–27, 30–31, 33, 36. Emphasis added throughout.

[69] See B. Foley, *Report on Labour in Bengal* (Calcultta, 1906), note (dated 19 September 1905) on Bengal Cotton Mill.

[70] See *Report of the Central Wage Board for Jute Industry* (Delhi, 1963), Appendix 17.

[71] J. H. Kelman, *Labour in India* (London, 1923), p. 82.

bins fill fast and require frequent changing, which necessitates stopping the machine."[72] But since the payment of the managing agents and managers often depended on the output, such stoppages were seen as time lost and therefore had to be as brief as possible. Pace also characterized the work in piece-rated departments like weaving or sack sewing where the worker's earnings depended on how much, and hence how rapidly, he could produce.

The "subordination" to the machine that the worker suffered in the jute mill, however, was not very "technical." The worker did not come to terms with the machine on the basis of even an elementary understanding of its working principles. The story here is poignantly told in the nature of the accidents that occurred in the jute mills. Many of the fatal ones resulted from the workers' attempting to clean the machinery while it was still in motion or from their (especially the women's) loose-fitting clothes being caught up in its moving parts.[73] Accidents of this kind revealed the emphasis that the mill managements placed on continuous running of the machinery, the laxity of factory rules (e.g., about dress), and the little value attached to a worker's life, but also the worker's incomprehension of the running principles of the machinery. In fact, the worker's relationship to the machine, instead of being mediated through a technical knowledge, was mediated through the North Indian peasant's conception of his tools, whereby the tools often took on magical and godly qualities. A religious outlook rather than "science" determined this relationship, with the difference that in a jute mill, the laborer's tools were far more powerful and malign than the peasant's implements and were capable of taking lives at the shortest notice. The vivid details of a report from the 1930s bear witness to this religious consciousness:

> In some of the jute mills near Calcutta the mechanics often sacrifice goats at this time [autumn: the time of the Diwali festival]. A separate altar is erected by the mechanics of each of the four or five departments in the mill. Various tools and other emblems of their work are placed upon it, together with heaps of sweetmeats and decorations. Incense is burned during an entire day and . . . the buildings are effectively filled with smoke. Towards evening a male goat is thoroughly washed, decorated with proper colors and flowers and prepared for a parade and final sacrifice. The little

---

[72] D. H. Buchanan, *The Development of Capitalistic Enterprise in India* (New York, 1934), p. 247.

[73] The factory inspection reports for different years have material supporting this observation.

procession, made up principally of the goat and a band, then marches through the grounds and up and down the aisles of the department to the altar. The animal is fed as many sweets as he will accept, and is then decapitated at one stroke by a long knife and sword. With proper ceremony the head is deposited in the river, in this case . . . the sacred Ganges, while the meat is retained for a feast in the evening. . . . The factory and the power-machine have been readily adopted and given due place in religious ceremony.[74]

It is of course not being claimed here that this religious outlook of the workers would have vanished only if they were given a scientific knowledge of the machinery. That modern Indian "holy men" have always counted a good number of Ph.D.'s in physics among their camp followers should act as a sufficient deterrent against any such view. The point is that the man-machine relationship inside a factory always involves culture and a techno-economic argument overlooks this. Relevant here is also the point that the Calcutta jute worker's subordination to the pace and requirements of the machinery was not effected through training and education. It was not, in that sense, a case of the "*technical* subordination" of Marx's description. The mills in fact were largely averse to the idea of giving their workers or their children any education at all. In 1929, the IJMA said to the Royal Commission that it did not think that to provide education was a "duty" of the employers.[75] But their deeper attitudes were revealed in 1914–15 when the government of Bengal, acting under pressure from Delhi, made some money available for the education of working-class children in the jute-mill areas and was forced by IJMA to confine such education only to those children who were not yet old enough to work in jute mills. And the lessons, insisted the mill owners, had to be confined to the teaching of "the three 'R's" and nothing beyond.[76]

---

[74] Buchanan, *Capitalistic Enterprise*, p. 409. The practice of worshiping machine tools seems to have been widespread among factory workers in eastern India. The author of this study remembers being present, as a child, at some of these ceremonies at a small engineering factory in Calcutta. The Jamshedpur steel-industry workers had their annual day of Hathyar Puja (tool worship) when "tools and implements attained the status of deity." "Bedecked with flowers, the giant cranes and traveling derricks clanked to their appointed tasks; caparisoned with blossoms, the locomotives snorted about on the sidings; streaming garlands, the wheelbarrows squeaked from coalpit to furnace." Lillian Luker Ashby (with Roger Whatley), *My India* (London, 1938), pp. 287–288.

[75] *RCLI*, vol. 5, pt. 2, p. 160.

[76] W.B.S.A., Genl. Dept. Education Branch [hereafter Ed. Br.], March 1913, A69–85; January 1914, A31–36; April 1915, A172–75.

The argument that IJMA put forward to the government (and one that was accepted by the latter) explained the "reason" for their lack of interest in workers' education:

> The character of the education must not be such as to draw the children away from the profession which they would adopt if they were allowed to continue illiterate . . . it must not render them unfit for *cooly* work.[77]

Literacy, in other words, was irrelevant to work in jute mills. The reason for this, according to the employers, was that the work was easily learned and required no rigorous training. Indeed, the bulk of the labor force was made up of totally unskilled laborers (called coolies) employed without exception on manual work. The census of 1921 found that of a total of 280,854 workers in the Calcutta jute mills, no less that 156,633 (i.e. over 55 percent) were engaged in work involving no machinery at all.[78] Even of the work that involved the use of machinery it was said in 1937 by jute-mill owners themselves that "up to spinning . . . most of the work is mechanical or routine and can be easily learnt, and labour for these departments is plentiful; winding, weaving and [machine] sewing required skilled labour."[79] How "easily learnt" was explained in 1906 by the chairman of IJMA, who spelled out the different amounts of time that were needed to train in the different occupations in a jute mill:

Coolie['s] [work]	[one] week
Women['s][work: mainly preparing and hand-sewing]	[one] week
Shifter['s] [work]	[one] week
Spinner['s] [work]	Graduate from shifters; may be a year or more on shifting
Weaver['s] [work]	A year to be first-class workman.[80]

This "learning," again, was purely experiential. It was pointed out by several witnesses to the Royal Commission that there was no ap-

[77] W.B.S.A., Genl. Dept. Ed. Br., April 1915, A172–75. Emphasis added.

[78] *Census of India 1921* (Calcutta, 1923), vol. 5, pt. 2, table 22, pts. 4 and 5. This census report defined all work involving machinery as "skilled work."

[79] C.S.A.S., B.P., Box 12: Mimeographed note dated 27 April 1937, captioned "Jute Strike Situation," by J. R. Walker, M.L.A., circulated for the information of the European Group, Bengal Legislature.

[80] Foley, *Report*, Appendix.

prenticeship system in the jute mills.[81] IJMA said in its evidence that "the bulk of the work in the mill is unskilled, and where training is necessary, as for instance in the spinning department, this is obtained in the course of actual employment, by the efforts of the worker himself."[82] On the preparing side, "a few weeks at any of the machines . . . [was] long enough to make the worker proficient." Weaving needed "skilled" work "but, generally speaking, weavers become proficient very quickly." Even mechanics, joiners, blacksmiths, had no system of formal training: "[they] . . . start as boys, and are paid a nominal wage until they become of use."[83]

The informality of the jute-mill system of recruitment and training—two important features of industrial discipline—was the subject of comment in 1945 in a note entittled "Apprenticeship to Jute Mill Weaving Departments," prepared by the newly formed Labour Office of the IJMA. "Notwithstanding that the Jute Industry has prospered and expanded upon the output of its many looms," the note said, "there has never been established any common method of selecting recruits or of teaching young workers the business of weaving." Worse still, such informal training as the worker could receive by watching or helping others was often a matter of breaking factory rules or legislation: "[the] knowledge of power loom weaving could only be gained by the efforts of the novice himself in time spent, *usually surreptitiously*, beside a friendly weaver already employed in a mill factory." What permitted such a state of affairs to continue was the stagnation in technology, which reflected, as we have seen, a lack of diversity in the products of the mills and their rather crude nature. This, again, was commented on in the note:

> Of recruits who had any specialised tuition in weaving there were none, and there are very few today. . . . No lasting improvement of quality or quantity of outturn could possibly result from this system, and it is probably true that the operative himself is no better equipped technically to turn out good fabric today than was his grandfather fifty years ago. Pride of craftsmanship has not been fostered, nor have any efforts been made to improve or widen the outlook of the operative who frequently never attains greater proficiency than is needed for operating a loom weaving [only] one type of fabric.[84]

[81] *RCLI*, vol. 5, pt. 1, p. 262; pt. 2, pp. 129, 157.
[82] Ibid., vol. 5, pt. 1, p. 280.
[83] Ibid., p. 298.
[84] This and other quotations in this paragraph come from IJMA, Labour Office, "Cir-

This discussion helps explain why the owners in the jute industry took a rather selective view of working-class conditions. Given the easily learned nature of jute-mill work, individual workers remained highly replaceable so long as the supply of labor was adequate. The task of structuring a labor force was therefore largely a supply proposition to the mills and not a question of skill formation, training, or efficiency. An "ample supply of [cheap] male labour," and not efficiency, was what was always seen as an important key to the prosperity of the mills.[85] It was in fact a concern with the supply of labor that often produced a certain atmosphere of laxity of rules within a jute mill. As the factory inspector explained in his report for 1893:

> A number of men, women and children can at most times of the day be seen in the grounds of the large [jute] mills, either asleep under the trees or shady parts of the building, taking their meals, bathing or smoking in a special shed . . . built for the purpose. The question might suggest itself to some . . . as to why so many are able to leave their work at all times of the day when in the Home Mills everyone is kept under lock and key. The answer is simple but a very striking one. There are 100 per cent more hands employed in every Jute Mill in Bengal than is required to work a similar sized mill in Dundee.[86]

The mills obviously found it cheaper to carry with them an amount of excess labor (to meet contingencies like epidemics and high absenteeism) than to invest in a healthy, vigorous, efficient working class. As late as 1929, the Indian jute-mill worker was half as efficient as a worker in Dundee. IJMA explained that this was not because "the work [in India] is unduly hard." Nor was it caused by the "climatic conditions," but "simply because this has been the custom so far as the Calcutta jute mills are concerned."[87]

In the eyes of the employers, then, certain aspects of working-class conditions gained priority over others and received more attention. And the knowledge produced as a result of this attention bore an unmistakable stamp of the employers' concern about the supply of labor. The "areas of origin" of the workers, for instance, became an object of investigation, especially at moments of inadequate supply of labor.

---

cular and Notes of the Committee," 1945–46: Note entitled "IJMA Apprenticeship Scheme." Emphasis added.

[85] W.B.S.A., Com. Dept. Com. Br. November 1919, A11–25: Alexander Murray's note on the jute industry.

[86] W.B.S.A., Genl. Dept. Misc. Br., August 1893, A1–36.

[87] *RCLI*, vol. 5, pt. 1, p. 304.

Hence the availability of such information. Foley's report of 1905, it-self a document on labor supply, gave evidence of this. J. Nicoll of IJMA told Foley that "he had experienced some difficulty [in procuring labor] in his three Jute Mills in 1902, and had *therefore* caused a cen-sus to be made that year, showing the districts from which the hands came," and it was these data that Foley reproduced in his report.[88] But Foley also noted that such information was not collected except in times of labor scarcity. The average jute-mill manager, who was "usu-ally a kindly Scot from Dundee," was "generally . . . unable to say from where his hands come, and if told the information would convey no meaning to him."[89] Foley's impressions are confirmed by a 1921 report entitled "The Conditions of Employment of Women before and after Child-Birth in Bengal Industries," by Dr. D. F. Curjel of the In-dian Medical Service.[90] Of the twenty-five jute mills Curjel visited, none was able to offer any information about the number of children born to their female workers. Curjel was struck by the managers' lack of interest in working-class conditions. The manager of the Soorah Jute Mill "did not concern himself with conditions affecting lives of his workers." She found the manager of the Lawrence Jute Mill "rather vague as to [the] class of labour employed," and he "seemed to take little interest" in their conditions. The manager of the Union Jute Mill, who "had been in charge 6 months," told Curjel that "he had been too busy to think about the health of the workers." This lack of interest was once again reflective of capital's view of labor conditions: they mattered only if and when they affected labor supply. "It is interesting to find," Curjel noted after talking to the manager of the Howrah Jute Mills, "how little managers know of the origins of the labour em-ployed in their mills. As long as the sirdars produced the required num-ber of workers, it does not concern them from what district it is drawn." Even more telling was the reception that Curjel had from the manager of the Ballighata Jute Mill. The manager "would scarcely dis-cuss" the subject of labor conditions with Curjel. He said "he did not concern himself with the workers' lives." "He took no interest in mod-ern labour questions [and] 'thought it all useless.' " Curjel notes why this was so:

> The manager who had been in this mill for many years, did not appear to be the very least interested in conditions affecting his workers, so long as he got the labour.[91]

[88] Foley, *Report*, Appendix. Emphasis added.
[89] Ibid., par. 23.
[90] W.B.S.A., Com. Dept. Com. Br., April 1923, B77.
[91] Ibid.

Thus it was that in the jute mills of Calcutta the employers' vision of labor conditions developed its particular blind spots: the worker's health became a question of epidemics and not one of nutrition; in this connection sanitation became a matter of interest but not the worker's general standard of living.[92] And although areas of "origin" of laborers became on occasion a subject of documentation and research, the individual worker remained largely undocumented almost throughout the period under consideration.[93] The political encomy of the jute industry thus goes a long way toward explaining why the mill managers were not particularly careful about the proper maintenance of records relating to conditions of labor.

THE SELECTIVENESS with which the industry treated the question of labor conditions meant that the factory documents covered a narrow range of issues, touching upon only a few aspects of the workers' lives. But apart from the narrowness of their scope, there was yet another problem that the authorities faced in handling these documents: their unreliability. This is why the attendance registers of jute mills were described in 1930 as not reflecting "the true conditions" of labor. Factory inspectors, courts of justice trying cases involving jute-mill workers, the managers of the mills—all complained of this. "You will admit," J. A. Murray of IJMA was asked by Sir Victor Sassoon of the Royal Commission on Labour, "that it must be very difficult for the management to be sure that the attendance books that come before them are accurate?" "It is difficult," Murray agreed.[94] The extent of the "difficulty" was underscored in the factory inspector's report for 1927, where he quoted a letter "from a Subdivision Officer" as only "an example of the value" of such documents. The letter read:

> In connection with a bad-livelihood case one * * * said to be the clerk in charge of the attendance register of the * * * Jute Mills, was summoned on behalf of the defence as witness. He gave sworn testimony that the undertrial prisoner * * * had attended the

[92] For examples of jute mills' interest in sanitation see W.B.S.A., Local Self-Government Dept. Public Health Br., October 1928, A7–42; December 1931, A15–21; December 1931, B24–26; June 1932, A70–81. For evidence relating to the extreme scarcity of information about the workers' indebtedness, see *RCLI*, vol. 5, pt. 2, p. 172, and W.B.S.A., Com Dept. Com. Br., January 1933, B242–74.

[93] For example, up to 1924 the jute mills did not keep any records of the home addresses of individual workers. The Workmen's Compensation Act made such records necessary. See *RCLI*, vol. 5, pt. 2, p. 21. Up to 1937 the mills did not keep any employment cards bearing the service histories of individual workers. These were to be introduced in 1937 at the instance of the Bengal government but not properly till 1948. See IJMA, *Report, 1937* (Calcutta, 1938).

[94] *RCLI*, vol. 5, pt. 2, p. 144.

mill from the 10th to 13th January 1927 and had drawn Rs 4–11 as wages. He stated that he had noted the attendance personally. It transpired, however, that the said * * * was arrested by the Police on 30th December 1926 in connection with a dacoity case and since that day he was continuously in the Jail lock-up to the end of February 1927. The entries in the attendance register must be false entries. . . . The attendance register has been kept in a very slovenly manner and there are many unattested corrections and many entries are in pencil.[95]

Similar remarks were made by the subdivisional officer of Serampore who tried the "Time Babu" of the Champdany Jute Mill in 1913 for employing a child on the basis of a canceled medical certificate.

I would point out [he said] that the provisional certificate shown to me does not bear any doctor's signature, and appears to be merely a blank form filled up by an unknown person. This suggests a lack of supervision, specially as I was told [that] this was the customary practice.[96]

The problem of unreliability of documents, then, takes us back to a question already highlighted in our discussion of Marx's argument: the nature and quality of supervision inside the mills. The "subordinate supervising staff" in the jute mills contained two classes. "In the first class there would be the more or less educated babu who has never been a mill operative himself." Initially appointed as an apprentice, the *babu* was soon promoted to supervisory work under a Scottish assistant. The duties of the *babu* were to "check attendances, to keep attendance registers," to prepare wage books, and to "generally assist in the supervision and work of the department."[97] Below the *babu* was the *sardar*, who was both a supplier and supervisor of labor and often of the same social origins as the ordinary worker himself. The government of Bengal pictured the *sardar* thus:

The immediate employer of a worker is his sirdar. The sirdar gives him his job and it is by his will that the worker retains it. . . . The sirdars are the real masters of men. They employ them and dismiss them, and, in many cases, they house them and can unhouse them. They may own or control the shops which supply the men with food. The operative, too, pays his lump or recurring sum to the

[95] W.B.S.A., Com. Dept. Com. Br., September 1928, A21–25.
[96] W.B.S.A., Finance Dept. Com. Br., March 1915, A58–59.
[97] *RCLI*, vol. 5, pt. 1, pp. 280–281.

sirdar to retain his job. His life, indeed, at every turn is coloured by sirdarism.[98]

The IJMA described the *sardars* and the under-*sardars* as constituting "the lower subordinate supervising staff of the mills."[99]

The *sardar* assisted the *babu* in the latter's task of maintaining factory documents. The process was explained in the conversation that took place between Victor Sassoon and J. A. Murray during the proceedings of the Royal Commission on Labour;

> *Sassoon [S]*: Is the only check as to attendance after men are at their machines?
> *Murray [M]*: That is right.
> S: Tokens [designating shifts] are not taken at the gate and put on their machines?
> M: No. The check is taken after the workman is at the machine.
> S: The *baboo* walks round the machinery and puts down the number of people he happens to see working at the machines or probably the *sardar* tells him are present?
> M: He is supposed to check up each worker individually.
> S: But I take it the *sardar* tells him who is there and he takes the word of the *sardar* to a great extent?
> M: That may happen.[100]

As the government of Bengal's description of the *sardar* will have made clear, *sardari* was primarily about supervisory workers making money at the expense of the ordinary worker through such means as moneylending and bribery. *Sardars* "dismissed labour and engaged fresh hands just at their pleasure," the IJMA complained to the Royal Commission, and "each man who signed on had to pay for the job."[101] In this the *sardar* often acted in league with the *babu*.

It is easy to see that the "corruption" of the *sardar* and the *babu* would have necessarily imparted a perverse character to the mill documents relating to working-class conditions: wage books, attendance registers, fine books, shift tokens, medical certificates, and others. This at any rate was the burden of the official complaints. One example that the authorities often gave to support their contention was the way the medical certificates of child workers were treated in the mills. In point of law, these certificates were meant to protect the health of the work-

[98] Ibid., p. 153.
[99] Ibid., pp. 280–281.
[100] Ibid., pt 2, pp. 144–45.
[101] Ibid., p. 142.

ing class by preventing the employment of underage children. But the practice of each child recruit having to bribe the *sardars* and the *babus* made this impossible of attainment. As the chief inspector of factories explained to the Royal Commission:

> The sirdar produces the children and, in many cases, allows them to be employed whether they are fit, certified or not, and he being illiterate cannot satisfy himself as to the correctness of the entries in the register. He must, however, keep the spindles going, if not directly to maintain continuity of production, to maintain his receipts on a child capitation basis.[102]

This apparently led to a fairly rapid turnover of children from individual mills, a process that contributed to the "unreliability" of documents. Captain O'Connor, the senior certifying surgeon of factories, Barrackpore District, wrote: "The principal reason why children migrate from mill to mill is that they are forcibly turned out by sirdars for pecuniary gain." The result was that it became "quite normal . . . for a child to have a certificate in each of a number of mills in a district," and a child "whose certificate is cancelled for not being produced" could "easily be re-certified under another name."[103] Colonel Nott, the civil surgeon of Howrah, reported a case in 1913 in which the same child applied to him on the same day for certificates in two different names, one Muslim and the other Hindu: Pir Mohamed and Banojowah. Enquiries revealed that he had done it at the *sardar*'s instruction.[104]

A similar phenomenon could be observed in the case of adult labor as well. "When checking registers," wrote the factory inspector in 1930, "a woman under examination may give two or three names with a certain amount of persistence."[105] The manipulation of the attendance registers (and other documents) by *sardars* and *babus* invariably led to an inflation of the wage bill. "You may have 10 per cent of the names on your books," the Royal Commission suggested to the manager of the Caledonian Jute Mill, "who actually do not exist as far as working is concerned and that money goes somewhere?" "Yes," replied the manager, "it is divided between the baboos and the sardars and the man who is doing the two men's jobs."[106] Another manager admitted in his evidence that about 7.5 percent of his labor force were

[102] Ibid., vol. 5, pt. 1, p. 92.
[103] Ibid., pp. 333–334.
[104] W.B.S.A., Finance Dept. Com. Br., March 1915, A58–9.
[105] W.B.S.A., Com. Dept. Com. Br., August 1931, A33–6.
[106] *RCLI*, vol. 5, pt. 2, pp. 142, 144–145.

probably such ghost workers.[107] The chief inspector of factories, however, thought these figures to be underestimates. Even though "theoretically" and "according to the register" the multiple-shift mills carried 22 or 25 percent more labor than in single-shift mills, the inspector knew that in reality it was "considerably less than 10 per cent."[108]

A study of the process of "supervision" within a jute mill—a problem that Marx saw as central to the question of documentation of the conditions of work—turns on the problem of "corruption" of the supervisory staff. Why was "the labour of overlooking" in a Calcutta jute mill riddled with "corruption"? How does one account for the widespread practices of falsifying documents?

ONE COULD obviously and easily develop a "needs of capital" argument in response to these questions. It could be argued, for instance, that the *sardar* existed only because he served the "needs of capital" in the jute industry and that his so-called corrupt practices—recruiting workers for bribes, housing them, lending them money at high rates of interest—constituted a kind of service to capital in a labor market that the industry had done very little to structure.

There is a body of evidence that supports this view. The mills, it would appear, were prepared to tolerate the "corrupt" practices of the *sardar* because he was considered indispensable. Even though the IJMA bitterly complained to the Royal Commission about *sardari* "corruption," they nevertheless insisted that "you [could] not do without sardars."[109] The financial outlays made by the mills on wages to be paid to the laborers clearly allowed for a certain amount of leakage through *sardari* corruption. Admittedly, this was not true of the (relatively) high-wage, piece-paid department of weaving; here "a check [was] made by calculating the total production of each section of the department, so that the total amount actually earned by production must equal the amount to be paid out."[110] In weaving, therefore, *sardari* extortion of ordinary workers took the form of bribery, money-lending, and the like.[111] But in every other department the wage policy followed the simple aim of keeping the "corrupt" practices of the *sardar* and the *babu* (e.g., inflating the wage bill by employing "ghost workers") under control rather than attempting to abolish them altogether.

[107] Ibid., p. 143.
[108] Ibid., p. 195.
[109] Ibid., p. 150.
[110] ibid., pt. 1, p. 281.
[111] Ibid., pt. 2, p. 120.

In each department throughout the works . . . a complement is drawn up, showing the number of hands it requires to run satisfactorily; and against this number is shown the amount in wages that such departments are bound down to.[112]

There is also evidence suggesting a direct complicity, in some cases, of the Scottish overseers and managers of the mills in the "corrupt" acts of the *sardar* and the *babu*. The Kankinarrah Labour Union (formed in 1922) "once exposed a case of bribery when Rs 3000 had been paid for the position of a Head Sardar." The president of the union, K. C. Roy Chowdhury, noted in his diary that "the money had been received by a friend of the manager of the [jute] mill concerned."[113] His diary also had the following entry, which is even more revealing:

Sen, the Head Babu of the Union [Jute] Mill, informed me today that numerous false tickets [tokens] are distributed every day at their mill. This means that tokens are distributed in the names of people who have not actually done any work. The money is then divided between the sardars, the Head Babu and the European overseer sahib. Bima sardar reportedly even supplies the weekly groceries for the overseer sahibs free of any cost.[114]

How did all this suit the "needs of capital"? Why were the owners of capital in the jute industry prepared to overlook, and at best contain, this "corruption" rather than stamp it out? Obviously, the *sardar* in his role of labor supplier was important to the industry's view of its own interests. The chief inspector of factories explained this in 1913:

All mills have to rely on the Sirdars and Time-Babus of their various departments for the supply of labour, [and therefore] the Manager has either to overlook irregularities practised by these men or to deal strictly with them and face a shortage [of labour] which results in a reduced weekly outturn in tonnage of gunnies, and seriously affects his position with the Managing Agents.[115]

But as we shall see, finding inexpensive ways of controlling labor was a problem of even greater concern to the industry than simply the problem of labor supply. This is why the *sardar* remained important even when the supply of labor was adequate. To understand why this

---

[112] Ibid., pt. 1, p. 281.
[113] K.C.R.P., Bengali diary no. 3, entries for 25 August 1929 to 28 November 1929.
[114] KCRP, Bengali diary no. 3, entry for 6 October 1929.
[115] W.B.S.A., Finance Dept. Com. Br., March 1915, A58–59.

was so, we have to look at the nature of the demand for labor that the industry created and the way it proceeded to meet that demand.

A plentiful supply of labor was considered necessary for the progress of the industry. Between the years 1895 and 1926, when the industry enjoyed an almost uninterrupted period of prosperity and expansion of output, the number of workers employed in the mills grew from 73,725 to 338,497. The supply of labor had to be adjusted to the IJMA-devised strategy of short-time working, which frequently imposed weekly "idle days" on the mills as a way of reducing output (to match temporary fluctuations in demand) and wage bills.[116] From 1913 onward, the mills kept changing "from four to five days a week or from five days to six days a week and so on at different intervals," sometimes changing "twice or three times a year."[117] But since the mills offered no incentives for long-term service, a temporary closure of a mill often meant a temporary loss of labor. The problem was an old one.[118] It assumed critical importance in the prosperous years of 1895–1926 when individual mills always wanted to conserve labor for days when they might be called upon to expand output. The means devised to meet this end was the multiple-shift system, whereby the labor force was worked in three or four shifts during the day and into the night.[119] Between 1913 and 1926 more than 90 percent of the jute mills worked on this system.[120] The main advantage of the system was not economy. An "abundance of labour or surfeit of it . . . [was] a necessary concomitant of multiple-shift employment," since that was the only way it could be ensured, at least on paper, that the workers did not work beyond the legally allowed hours.[121] There was, for instance, an elaborate relief system for weavers that necessitated employing extra "daily-weavers."[122] It was generally agreed in 1929 that a multiple-shift mill carried 25 to 30 percent more labor (at least on its

[116] Cf. IJMA, *Report for the Half-Year Ending 30 June 1886* (Calcutta, 1886), p. 14.

[117] *RCLI*, vol. 5, pt. 2, pp. 168-169.

[118] *The Jute Mills of Bengal* (Dundee, 1880), p. 48, mentions the case of Seebpore Jute Manufacturing Co., Ltd, whose directors decided to continue working "rather than temporarily close the mill and lose the workpeople," even when they were faced with a depressed "bag market."

[119] For a good description of the multiple-shift system, see W.B.S.A., Com. Dept. Com. Br., January 1929, B261–8.

[120] See *RCLI*, vol. 5, pt. 2, pp. 168-169, 195. Between 1926 and 1929 half of the mills transferred to the single-shift system as a result of the worsening of the trade position. After 1930, all the mills were working in a single shift. Ibid., vol. 5, pt. 1, pp. 81–82.

[121] W.B.S.A., Com. Dept. Com. Br., May 1929, B196–99, and January 1929, B261–68.

[122] *RCLI*, vol. 5, pt. 2, p. 167.

books) than a single-shift mill.[123] But therein lay its advantage, a reduction in the risk of a bottleneck developing in labor supply should the trade ever demand an increase in output.

By an accident of history, the industry's search for an ample supply of labor took place at a time that saw enormous increases in emigration of labor from Bihar and U.P. and other regions into Bengal. "Twenty years ago," Foley wrote in 1905, "all the hands [in jute mills] were Bengalis. These have been gradually replaced by Hindust[h]anis from the United Provinces and Bihar . . . so that at present in most of the mills two-thirds of the hands are composed of up-countrymen."[124] Once the flow started "from upcountry," it flowed—as the Royal Commission on Labour was told—"very strongly."[125] The situation was considered so satisfactory by 1895 that an official enquiry committee formed to investigate the question of labor supply to the Bengal coal mines felt that "there was no necessity" to conduct any "exhaustive enquiry into the subject of labour supply for jute mills." Nor did the mills particularly press for one.[126] Foley was "somewhat astonished" in 1905 to find that large increases in demand for jute-mill labor between 1895–96 and 1903–4 had been easily met in spite of "no recruitment on any systematic method . . . at all" and without any "material" rise in wages.[127] Even the problem of seasonal shortage of labor, during harvesting months, for example, that Foley and other early observers of the industry often commented on seems to have lost its importance in the later years. In their memorandum dealing with "methods of recruitment," IJMA said to the Royal Commission in 1929 that "labour is in good supply all the year round." When asked about the seasonal shortage of the "olden days," the IJMA representatives remarked that even those conditions had changed after 1914: "the fact remains that since 1914 labour has never been scarce."[128]

Evidence of the industry's sense of satisfaction regarding supply of labor may also be seen in certain significant changes in the geographical location of the mills. In the early days, when the mill hands were local, that is, "mostly Bengalis," an "isolated site" for a mill was "recognized as an advantage, the hands . . . living in the neighbour-

[123] Ibid., pt. 1, p. 15.
[124] Foley, *Report*, par. 28.
[125] RCLI, vol. 5, pt. 2, p. 237.
[126] *Report of the Labour Enquiry Committee of 1895* (Calcutta, 1896), pp. 49–51. See also Bagchi, *Private Investment*, p. 135.
[127] Foley, *Report*, pars. 18, 21–24.
[128] RCLI, vol. 5, pt. 2, p. 162.

hood."[129] In those years "it was considered by the mills a matter of life and death to prevent a rival company settling down in proximity to their labour supply."[130] The first two years of the Victoria Jute Mill, built in 1885 on the river bank opposite the Samnugger Jute Mill, were marked by what Wallace called "the celebrated land dispute" between the two mills.[131] "We are a little short of hands this week," ran a typically complaining letter from the Samnugger Mill to its directors in 1887, "and this may affect us. The Victoria [Mill] has taken up all our spare hands . . . [and] we do not have so many to fall back on and that injures us a bit."[132] In 1894 the Hastings Mill made a rather "unremunerative" decision to work day and night by electric light.[133] This decision was "said to have been suggested by a rumour that another . . . firm contemplated putting up a large Mill near Hastings, whereupon the proprietors of the latter thought they might as well find employment for all the hands in the neighbourhood . . . by running 22 hours, instead of from daylight to dark."[134] As labor became "chiefly immigrant" and came of its own in abundant numbers, the situation soon reversed itself. Mills were no longer located in isolation from one another. Instead, noted Foley, "it is considered now [1905] . . . an advantage to have a site in a centre, such . . . as Kankinara, where immigrant labour congregates."[135] This explains why the number of mills on the 24 Parganas side of the river Hooghly—where Kankinara, Jagaddal, and other centers of immigrant labor were located in close proximity to one another—eventually grew much faster than the numbers in other districts. In Hooghly District, there were four jute mills in 1880 and nine in 1921; in Howrah District there were five mills in 1880 and twelve in 1921; in Calcutta there were three mills in 1880 and five in 1921; but in the 24 Parganas side there were six mills in 1880, fifteen in 1896, thirty-one in 1911, and thirty-eight in 1921.[136]

A significant aspect of this migration of labor from U.P., Bihar, and

[129] Foley, *Report*, par. 26. The early mills like Fort Gloster, Gourepore, Budge Budge, and Kamarhati all followed this policy. See *JMB*, pp. 27, 35–36, 43, 45, 68, 81.

[130] D. R. Wallace, *The Romance of Jute* (Calcutta, 1909), p. 38.

[131] Ibid.

[132] Archives of Thomas Duff and Co. Ltd., Dundee (hereafter TDA), letter from the Calcutta agent dated 10 May 1887.

[133] Wallace, *Romance* (1909), p. 47.

[134] John Leng, "The Indian Dundee," in his *Letters from India and Ceylon* (Dundee, 1896), p. 79.

[135] Foley, *Report*, par. 26.

[136] For 1880, *JMB*; for 1896, John Leng, "The Indian Dundee," in his *Letters from India and Ceylon* (Dundee, 1896); for 1911 and 1921, *Census of India 1921*, vol. 5, pt. 1, p. 403.

other places into Bengal was that it enabled the industry to replace Bengali workers by their "cheaper," upcountry substitutes and this at a time when the industry was looking for ways of saving expenses. The IJMA's move in 1886 to reduce wage expenditure by short-time working was in fact preceded by "most of the Mills . . . taking action to effect a reduction of wages," for "the tone of the market . . . [was] still very unfavourable."[137] Just how large these reductions were is suggested by a letter that the Dundee directors of the Titaghur Jute Mill received from their Calcutta manager toward the end of 1885. The letter reported, to the directors' delight, "that the wages at the works have now been reduced by Rs 1000 per week below what used to be paid, which the Directors considered very satisfactory and creditable to the Manager."[138] Working hours were prolonged with the introduction of electricity into the mills about 1895,[139] and this also seems to have caused a decline in the Bengali component of the labor force.[140] Whatever the specific factors aiding these changes in the social composition of the jute-mill working class, the result was that by the 1920s the labor force was of a predominantly migrant character (see Table 3.1).

It is important to emphasize that the industry provided little service in helping these migrant workers settle down in the city and in thus developing a permanently stable labor force. The reason for this inaction lay in the very mercantilist spirit in which the jute mills handled their economic affairs. In the minds of the entrepreneurs in the industry, as we have seen in the last chapter, profit was firmly linked to the idea of "cheap products." It was thought that their cheapness gave these products—sacking and hessian of a very crude quality—a competitive edge over any natural or synthetic substitutes. Hence the insistence within the industry on keeping products crude and cheap, a policy that resulted in a stagnant technology and an unskilled labor force. A cheap product has to be produced at a low cost, and the availability of cheap labor in eastern India was therefore considered a definite advantage. Thus developed the labor-intensive nature of the industry, where labor alone accounted for about 50 percent of the cost of converting raw jute into the finished material. In 1880 the authors of *JMB* estimated the labor cost of two mills to be 40 to 45 percent of the cost of conversion; the figure for a hypothetical Calcutta mill in

[137] T.D.A, Minute books of the Titaghur Jute Factory Co., letters from the Calcutta agent dated 25 June 1884 and 20 May 1885.
[138] Ibid., minutes for 21 October 1885.
[139] Wallace, *Romance* (1909), pp. 49–50.
[140] See the *Report of the Indian Factory Labour Commission* (London, 1909), vol. 2, p. 271.

TABLE 3.1.
Areas of origin of jute-mill workers, 1921–41.
(figures in percentages)

Year	Bengal	Bihar	Orissa	United Provinces	Madras	Central Provinces	Others
1921	24.1	33.4	11.4	23.1	4.6	—	3.2
1928	24.8	37.1	(inc. Orissa)	15.7	11.2	9.1	1.9
1929	17.0	60.0	(inc. Orissa)	5.0	14.0	4.0	—
1941	11.6	43.1	3.4	36.4	1.6	—	0.8

(Figures have been rounded off to the first decimal place.)

SOURCES: Ranajit Das Gupta, "Factory Labour in Eastern India: Sources of Supply, 1855–1946: Some Preliminary Findings," *Indian Economic and Social History Review*, vol. 8, no. 3, 1976, p. 297, Table 6; W.B.S.A., Com. Dept. Com. Br., April 1930, A7–12. The 1921 figures apply to the whole labor force and the 1928 figures relate to twenty-five jute mills. The 1929 figures are approximate; the 1941 figures are drawn from a sample survey of mill workers in the Jagaddal area and hence are not representative of the whole working class.

1900 was estimated by Cox Brothers, Dundee, to be in the region of 50 percent. Buchanan gives 50 percent as the actual figure for one mill in 1927, and figures derived from information available in the Benthall papers range from 49 to 55.[141]

The bulk of this "labour cost" was constituted by wages. Given their concern for keeping down the prices of their products while using labor-intensive methods of production, we should not be surprised that the owners of the jute mills were reluctant to spend on any individual laborer anything beyond the minimum necessity of a wage. And even the wages paid were single-worker wages; they were not enough to support a worker's family. According to an estimate of 1929, the "average income" of a jute-mill worker was Rs. 5 per week, but it would cost him at least Rs. 7 to maintain a family of himself, his wife, and,

[141] See *JMB*, pp. 20, 47; Archives of the Modern History Department, Dundee University, Card Collection on Cox Brothers, card entitled "Cost of Mill, and Factory" (c. 1900); D. H. Buchanan, *The Development of Capitalistic Enterprise in India* (New York, 1934), p. 250; C.S.A.S., B.P., Box 13, "Paul" to Edward Benthall, 20 September 1937, enclosures.

say, three children.[142] The increase over the years in investment in workers' housing was extremely tardy. An 1897 survey of about 73,000 of the Bengal jute-mill workers showed only 13.5 percent of them living in company-built coolie lines. The rest had to make their own arrangements.[143] Thirty years later, in 1929, when the mill labor force had increased to 339,665, only 30 percent of the jute-mill labor were housed by the mills, according to the Bengal Chamber of Commerce and IJMA.[144] Stability of labor was obviously not in itself a crucial concern to the industry—semiskilled or unskilled workers being highly replaceable—so long as the supply of labor remained abundant.

One can also see this in the extremely underdeveloped nature of the factory rules that were in operation in the jute mills. The service rules, for instance, had been left largely uncodified. Graded wage systems (with provisions for regular increments), pensions, provident funds, sickness insurance, leave rules—all the usual inducements for long-term service and stability—were conspicuous by their absence. Leave as a rule was without pay and the amount of pay due to a worker during his or her sickness remained "a matter for the manager's discretion."[145] Sickness insurance was considered "impossible."[146] So too were provident funds and pensions. When the workers of the Fort William, the Howrah, and the Ganges jute mills went out on strike in February 1937, the secretary to the government of Bengal concluded that they could not have had any "serious grievances" because their leaders asked for "such obviously impossible terms as provision of provident funds and pension."[147]

For this uncared-for and poverty-ridden working class, the *sardar* performed functions that ideally should have been performed by the employers, such as supplying work, credit, and housing. R. N. Gilchrist, the labor intelligence officer of Bengal, thus pictured the average migrant worker in 1930 "as he sets out from his village to find work":

> The sirdar may oblige him with his fare and a little money to buy food on the way. . . . The sirdar may advance him a little more money, for a job may not be immediately available, and he may also direct him to live in certain quarters and to buy his rice at a certain shop. The day when there is a vacancy comes, and the sir-

[142] *RCLI*, vol. 5, pt. 2, p. 132.
[143] W.B.S.A., Judicial Dept. Police Br., September 1897, A95–99.
[144] *RCLI*, vol. 5, pt. 1, p. 282; pt. 2, p. 284.
[145] Ibid., pt. 2, p. 155.
[146] Ibid., pt. 1, pp. 283–285.
[147] W.B.S.A., Home Poll. Confdl., no. 60/1937.

dar may say: "Your pay on the books of the mill is twelve rupees a month, but I have incurred some expense for you. Usually when I give a job, I require thirty rupees down and one rupee a month for two years. You have no money to give me as a lump sum, so you will pay me two rupees a month for as long as I secure you a job. If you do not, I cannot be certain your job will last." The grateful youth . . . gratefully accepts. . . . As he grows older and wiser, he gradually finds out that the sirdar owns the house in which he shares a room with six others and for which they all pay rent, and that he also owns the shop were he buys his rice.[148]

This of course was part of the "corruption" that the industry and the government complained of. The *sardari* practices undoubtedly constituted a kind of secondary exploitation of ordinary workers by their supervisory or superior colleagues.[149] But it could be legitimately argued that the employers allowed such "corruption" to exist because it saved them the expense of investing in institutions otherwise typical of capitalist control of labor. *Sardari* control was cheaper than housing, health care, or an articulated body of rules guiding the conditions of work.

A "NEEDS OF CAPITAL" argument then tells us that the *sardar* existed along with his invariably "corrupt" practices mainly because they were allowed to exist. They suited the strategy of capital. This is an important consideration, but it does not go far enough for the purpose at hand. More important, it does not answer the question that Marx helps us to raise: What was the relationship between the *sardar*'s authority and his "corruption"? As we have seen, it was *sardari* "corruption" that ultimately distorted the documents the supervisors in a jute mill were required to produce and keep. The nature of supervisory authority in the Calcutta jute mills was thus significantly different from the one discussed in Marx's argument. For Marx, the supervisor's authority in capitalist relations of production manifested itself in the keeping of time sheets, fine books, attendance registers, wage rolls, and the like. Such maintenance of documents implied a keeping of the wage

---

[148] R. N. Gilchrist, *Indian Labour and the Land* (Calcutta, 1932), pp. 6–7.

[149] The expression "sardari practices" is used here in a general sense to designate activities not only of the head *sardars* but of the under-*sardars* and some other workers as well. In an industry devoid of any structuring by skills or promotions, exploitation of the fellow worker was one important way of material advancement. The more ambitious and the luckier worker often followed the *sardar*'s example of being a moneylender or a landlord to the less fortunate. *Sardari* is thus best treated both as a real institution and as a working-class ideal of success. See *RCLI*, vol. 11, pt. 2, pp. 358, 365.

contract between capital and labor. And the notion of the contract took us back to Marx's specific assumptions regarding working-class culture, assumptions that informed his category of "capital," Our jute mills, however, presented a very different picture. The supervisory authority of the *sardar* (or of his accomplice *babu*) produced unreliable, falsified documents. One could in fact go further and argue that falsifying documents was integral to the operation of the power and authority that the *sardar* wielded over the ordinary coolie. What appeared to the state as "corruption," "abuse," or breaking the rules was precisely the form in which the *sardar*'s authority was manifested. Or to put it in another way, it was an authority that was incompatible with any bourgeois notions of legality, factory codes, and service rules.

We would be mistaken, for example, to see the bribe that the ordinary coolie gave the *sardar* simply as an economic transaction. The bribe was also a sign, a representation, of the *sardar*'s authority and its acceptance by the worker, which is why an act of refusal to pay the bribe was seen as a gesture of defiance and exposed the worker to a degree of anger, vendetta, and violence from the *sardar* that was often out of proportion to the amount of money involved. K. C. Roy Chowdhury's diaries mentioned the not untypical case of one Abdul, a worker of the Hukumchand Jute Mill, who was stabbed by the followers of a certain *sardar* called Sujat for having refused to pay the latter his *dastoori*, or customary commission.[150] The nature of the *sardar*'s authority and power is visible in the details of the letter that twenty-eight workers of the Budge Budge Jute Mill wrote to a Bengali barrister in December 1906:

> We have to get permission for leaves from the Sahib. But we have to pay bribes to the babu and the sardar at the time of the leave; further, they take bribes from us every month and also when the Durga Puja season approaches. If we refuse to pay them they get the sahib to fine or dismiss us on false charges of bad workmanship. Till recently we felt compelled to meet their unjust demands. But as prices ran very high last year at the time of Durga Puja, we expressed our intention to pay them a little less than in earlier years. At this the Head Sardar Haricharan Khanra has been going around instigating the Assistant Babu Atul Chandra Chattopadhyay to collect even more *parbani* [gifts customarily due at times of religious festivals; *parban* means religious festival] than usual. The two of them have even advised the in-charge Panchanan Ghose, a nice gentleman otherwise, to force us to pay a much

[150] K.C.R.P., Bengali diary no. 2, entry for 12 April 1928.

larger *parbani* this year. When [in protest] we stopped paying any *parbani* whatsoever, they got the sahib to fine us on cooked up charges. . . . But, in truth, we are not guilty.[151]

A large part of the *sardar*'s authority was then based on fear: "we felt *compelled* to meet their unjust demands." So great was the fear of the *sardar*'s vengeance that several of the workers interviewed by the Royal Commission strenuously denied having paid any bribes for their employment. But their denial lacked the force of conviction. Sorju, an under-*sardar* of the Anglo-Indian Jute Mill, admitted that there was bribery "in every department" of the mill but claimed that there was none in his own. Kalil, a weaver in the same mill, said that he had heard "that *sardars* take Rs 5 or Rs 10 but so far as I am concerned I did not pay anything."[152] Harilal, a spinner in the Titaghur Jute Mill, insisted that he "did not pay any *bakshish* for getting my job," although he thought it possible that "other people might be paying *bakshish* to the *sardar*."[153] A Madrasi female worker of the Howrah Jute Mill told her interviewers that she got her employment only after promising the *sardar* two rupees from her "first wages." On the statement being read out to her, however, she retracted it. "It is probably true," remarked the interviewers.[154]

It is undeniable that much of this fear of the *sardar* derived from the employers' allowing him to "dismiss and engage fresh hands just at [his] pleasure" (to repeat the words of IJMA). Babuniya, a Bihari female worker of the Titaghur Jute Mill, expressed her fear to the Royal Commission:

> When I was first entertained I had to pay Rs 4 *bakshish* to the *sardar* who appointed me. Each time I return back from the village I have to pay the same amount as *bakshish* to the *sardar*. I also pay him 2 as. every week. My husband paid Rs 6 when he was first appointed. He pays 4 annas a week to the *sardar*. If we refuse to pay the *sardars* we will not get work. Every worker pays a similar amount to the *sardar*.[155]

Another important element in the *sardar*'s domination was the use of naked physical force. For the ordinary worker, as we have noted, there was always "the fear of being beaten." The child workers, it was said,

[151] The letter is quoted in Sumit Sarkar, "Swadeshi Yuger Sramik Andolan: Kayekti Aprakashita Dalil," *Itihas*, vol. 4, no. 2, Bhadra-Agrahayan 1376 (1969), pp. 113–115.
[152] *RCLI*, vol. 5, pt. 2, p. 26.
[153] Ibid., p. 78.
[154] Ibid., vol. 11, pt. 2, p. 360.
[155] Ibid., vol. 5, pt. 2, p. 77.

would not normally speak up against the *sardar* for this very reason.[156] Narsama Kurmi, a female of the Howrah Jute Mill, was "obliged to leave" Howrah because "she had trouble with a sirdar." She returned only after "she found [that] the sirdar who annoyed her [had] gone."[157]

Like all domination, however, the *sardar*'s domination was not based on fear alone. There was always an undercurrent of tension between the *sardar* and the ordinary worker, and pushed beyond a certain point, the worker could become openly hostile. To be effective, therefore, the *sardar*'s authority also needed legitimacy and acceptance. Fear had to be balanced by respect. According to R. N. Gilchrist, the typical jute-mill *sardar* was more respected than feared. "The sirdar [is] a man of considerable importance," Gilchrist wrote. "He is . . . respected, perhaps even feared."[158]

We should note that even physical violence, which remained an important element of the *sardar*'s authority, could itself provoke both fear and a sense of awe that sometimes bordered on admiration. The ambivalence with which the workers looked on physical prowess is sharply illustrated by the life histories of working-class *goondas* (neighborhood bullies), whose oppressive activities often resembled those of the mill *sardars*.[159] The *goonda*, like the *sardar*, dominated life in working-class *bustis* (slums) and bazaars.[160] Again like the *sardar*, he presented to the ordinary worker a "spectacle of excess." Of humble origin himself, he enjoyed, for however short a period, a lavish style of life that contrasted strongly with the poverty of the average mill hand. The police described the typical *goonda* as "extravagant," someone who "always lived beyond his means." An "inveterate" drinker and gambler, to use the words of the police again, he terrorized shopkeepers, fellow workers, and the neighborhood women with his

[156] Ibid., pt. 1, p. 333.

[157] Ibid., vol. 11, pt. 2, p. 360.

[158] Gilchrist, *Indian Labour*, p. 6.

[159] During my trips to the jute-mill municipalities, *burra* (head) *sardars* were often described to me as well-known *goondas*. See also the fictionalized account of jute-mill *sardars* in Mohanlal Gangopadhyay's Bengali novel *Asamapta Chatabda* (Calcutta, 1963), pp. 98–99. Having said this, however, one must make an important distinction between a *goonda* and a *sardar*. The *goonda*, from the point of view of law and order, had the status of a criminal, whereas the *sardar* was a functionary of capital and his illegal oppressions, such as they were, formed an important part of the relations of production in jute mills.

[160] Thanks to the operations of the Goonda Act of 1923, some information regarding the life histories of individual working-class *goondas* is available in the police files of the Bengal government. My brief statement here is based on, among others, the following sources: W.B.S.A., Home Poll. Confdl. 18(1–6)/1925; 219/1925; 74(1–5)/1925; 376(1–8)1925; 93(1–10)/1925; 94(1–2)/1925; 554/1931.

immoderate, if not immoral, demands, which were always backed up with the threat of physical violence. Police files give ample evidence to show that the mill workers lived in fear of such *goondas* and, when offered a chance, complained bitterly of their extortions, just as they did with their *sardars*. Yet the often conspicuous presence of so-called *goondas* (or for that matter, *sardars*) in strikes and in other forms of group actions by mill workers (including riots) suggests a certain position of leadership and prestige that the former may have enjoyed in the eyes of the latter. For example, four out of the six "leaders" of a strike and riot at a mill in Barrackpore in June 1926 were, according to the police, "known *gundas* of Kankinara [who] ... [did] not work."[161] Similarly, reporting on a clash between striking and "loyal" workers of the Kesoram Cotton Mill in May 1937, the police said that although some of the "assailants" of the "loyal" workers were "strikers," "others were *goondas* who [had] nothing to do with the mill."[162] There are other instances like this.[163]

Physical prowess, on the part of the *goonda* or the *sardar*, may also have been validated by the prestige that was attached to it in the peasant society of Bihar and U.P., where physical culture had been elevated to an art form in the shape of preindustrial sports such as traditional wrestling. It was said of male upcountry laborers in Calcutta in the late nineteenth century that their one common aspiration was to earn a name for themselves as wrestlers in the *akharas* (gymnasiums; societies for physical culture) set up in north Calcutta by their fellow immigrants.[164]

[161] W.B.S.A., Home Poll. Confdl. 286(5–7)/1926.

[162] W.B.S.A., Home Poll. Confdl. 128/1937.

[163] See, for instance, W.B.S.A., Home Poll. Confdl. 484/1937; 283(1–11)1926. It might be objected that police reports could not be taken at face value, since it would have been characteristic of the police to see striking workers as *goondas*, or simple criminals. Although this is true, one should also remember that it is not uncommon in the history of oppressed classes for a "criminal"—whose normal presence is a challenge to the legally constituted order—to become a "hero" when that order comes under scrutiny and is challenged by the oppressed. The *goonda* or the oppressive *sardar* exemplifies in this regard what Guha has recently described as the ambiguous relationship between "crime" and "rebellion." See Ranajit Guha, *Elementary Aspects of Peasant Insurgency in Colonial India* (Delhi, 1983), chap. 3.

[164] See Sankariprasad Bosu, *Sahasya Vivekananda* (Calcutta, 1974), p. 296. The connection between such *akharas* and the subculture of the Calcutta *goonda* is suggested in a police file on a carter called Sheikh Rahim Bux, who was arrested under the Goonda Act in 1925. The police described him as "a member of the gang of Bara Karim, a noted wrestler who had an akhara in Rajabazar where a large number of roughs and bad characters used to assemble." W.B.S.A. Home Poll. Confdl. 74(1–5)/1925. See also Dilip K. Basu, ed., *Malla-Bir: The Autobiography of a Calcutta Killer* (forthcoming). For a

Nevertheless, as I have said before, the *sardar* cannot be equated to the *goonda*, and to be effective, the former's authority needed a more enduring acceptance and legitimacy than a simple "criminal" existence could provide. The respect that the *sardar* commanded had roots in certain other aspects of the culture to which both the *sardar* and the worker belonged. It derived from a precapitalist culture with a strong emphasis on religion, community, kinship, language, and other, similar loyalties. It seems significant, for instance, that all the words used by the workers (and others) to describe *sardari* extortions—payments summed up in the legalistic expression "corruption" or "abuses"— were words of precapitalist, pre-British origin: *dastoori, bakshish, batta, parbani, salami*, and so on. *Dastoori*, the most widely used of these words, came from the word *dastoor*, which meant "custom" or "tradition." Even the word *sardar* in its meaning of "labor supplier" (literally it meant "a headman") was in vogue in the late eighteenth century and perhaps even earlier.[165] Besides, the *sardar*'s mode of operation had certain crucial precapitalist elements. He usually recruited on the basis of the often overlapping networks of community, village, and kin. The government of Bengal wrote:

> Sirdars in the jute mills, engineering works, and other concerns recruit in their own native villages and surrounding areas; hence there is a tendency for people from the same village or the immediate neighbourhood to congregate in the same industrial area in Bengal.[166]

Much of the basis of the *sardar*'s social control of the work force lay in the relationships of community, kinship, religion, and so on, and in the ideas and norms associated with them. For example, it was usual for important upcountry *sardars* to build temples or mosques for the workers under them. On this depended a lot of the *sardar*'s prestige

---

discussion of the culture and history of wrestling in the Banaras region, see Nita Kumar, "Popular Culture in Urban India: The Artisans of Banaras, c. 1884–1984," Ph.D. thesis, University of Chicago, 1984, chap. 4.

[165] See, for example, the use of this word by Krisnakanta Nandy in his account books of 1787–88, in S. C. Nandy, "Krisnakanta Nandy's Book of Monthly Accounts of 1195 B.S. (1787–88)," *Bengal Past and Present*, January-June 1980, p. 10. Bishop Heber's *Narrative of a Journey through the Upper Provinces of India from Calcutta to Bombay 1824–1825* (1828) had references to such laborers as "Sirdar bearers and bearers." Heber is quoted in Brajendrath Bandyopadhyay's "Introduction" to Bhabanicharan Bandyopadhyay's *Kalikata Kamalalaya* (Calcutta, 1951), p. 21. See also Jadunath Sarkar, *Mughal Administration* (Calcutta, 1972), pp. 55–56, for an instance from 1662 illustrating the custom of *dastoori*.

[166] *RCLI*, vol. 5, pt. 1, p. 11.

and authority. Mosques in jute-mill areas are even today named after important *sardars* and stand as monuments to their once enormous presence. Manbodh Sardar ki Musjid, Birbal Sardar ki Musjid, and Ishaque Sardar ki Musjid are, to give a few instances, the names of three working-class mosques that exist today in the Kankinara area.[167] *Sardari* thus seems to have been an instance of a precolonial, precapitalist institution being adapted to the needs of industrialization in a colony.[168] In this it reflected a process that had been in operation in colonial India at least since the eighteenth century. Bayly has described this process well in his recent work on North Indian society in the early colonial period. The economic and social changes brought about by British rule, says Bayly, "had not really initiated a free market or undermined the headman system."

> What occurred was that the commercialisation of "shares" in the perquisites of authority, which had been a marked feature of the eighteenth century, was progressing at a local level. Almost every right or perquisite . . . was now up for sale. But what made the sale worthwhile was that *within* the "little domain" which was being put on the market, competition and the free market were still excluded. Here political muscle, the authority of the headman and rights of caste rank continued to operate to produce cash, labour or commodities. Thus [for example] while the right to engage in scavenging came on the market, it did not mean that outsiders could employ their own labour in this area without first submitting to the authority of the neighbourhood leaders of the Chamars.[169]

The *sardar* then embodied contradictory elements of authority. He owed his formal position of foreman to the managers and owners of capital and, in that sense, was a functionary in the capitalist production system of the jute mills. He was also different from the traditional village headman of North India in that "*sardar*-ships" could be bought and sold on the market. Yet he was not quite the industrial foreman of nineteenth-century Western Europe, whose role "became increasingly technical" as time passed.[170] *Sardars* were selected, not for any tech-

---

[167] This information comes both from my field investigations and from K.C.R.P., Bengali diary no. 3, entries for 25 August 1929 to 28 November 1929.

[168] *RCLI*, vol. 1, pp. 22–24, describes jobbery as the ubiquitous form of labor recruitment and control in Indian industrialization.

[169] C. A. Bayly, *Rulers, Townsmen and Bazaars: North Indian Society in the Age of British Expansion 1770–1870* (Cambridge, 1983), pp. 316–317.

[170] Michelle Perrot, "The Three Ages of Industrial Discipline in Nineteenth Century

nical ability, but for "the authority which they display[ed] over their fellowmen" even before becoming sardars.[171] *"Tumko āpnā sardār kā hukum mānnā hogā"* (You will have to obey the orders of your own *sardar*) was one sentence that the Scottish managers and assistants in the mills were expected to learn in order to use it in dealing with a refractory worker.[172] The sentence brings out the ambiguity of the *sardar*'s authority. His *hukum* "order" was obviously subordinate to yet another imperative ("You will have to"), that of the manager, the representative of capital. But the word *hukum* (with connotations of *hukumat* "sovereignty")—once again an ancient word familiar to the North Indian peasant—would have had long and deep resonances within the worker's consciousness and culture.

In this situation, legally required factory documents on working-class conditions were largely irrelevant to the exercise of the *sardar*'s authority, which was rooted not in capitalist but in precapitalist modes of domination. The *sardar* ensured obedience to his *hukum* through means that were either "illegal" or fell outside the rule of law. His was not the "disciplinary authority" that Marx outlined in his argument. When the Government of India grafted a disciplinary apparatus of documentation on the culture that supported (and sometimes resisted) the *sardar*'s domination, these documents found their own place and meaning within that culture: as additional vehicles of the *sardar*'s power and authority. The *sardar* now proved his power by bending rules and falsifying documents. Hence the phenomenon of "false fines," "cooked up charges," "wrongful dismissals," and the like. The very nature of this authority entailed, that is, "unreliable" documents.

WE MAY thus repeat our principal argument. An attempt to write a history of the conditions of the jute-mill workers of Calcutta on the basis of documents coming from the state and the owners of capital invariably reveals certain gaps in our knowledge of these conditions. Insofar as that knowledge has a history, the gaps have a history too. It was the same history that produced both the knowledge—enshrined in archival documents—and the gaps, which the same documents reveal. An examination of this history (with the aid of an argument borrowed from Marx) takes us into a closer study of the political economy of the

---

France," in John M. Merriman, ed., *Consciousness and Class Experience in Nineteenth Century Europe* (New York, 1979), p. 159.

[171] *RCLI*, vol. 5, pt. 1, pp. 280, 298. "Capability, efficiency, services" were the other qualifications required.

[172] Mohiuddin Ahmed, *Essentials of Colloquial Hindustani for Jute Mills and Workshops* (Calcutta, 1932), p. 89.

industry and the nature of the "industrial discipline" operating within the mills. Questions relating to the latter lead us to investigate the issues of "supervision" and working-class notions of "authority," and hence into the realm of culture and consciousness. We shall pursue these notions further in the chapters that follow. The problems of organization, militancy, and solidarity in the history of the jute-mill working class will bring us back to these very questions.

· 4 ·

THE PARADOX OF
ORGANIZATION

Most observers of labor conditions in the jute industry agreed that there was an urgent need for working-class organization. Even the government of Bengal, which could hardly be suspected of prolabor sympathies, was moved to remark in 1929 that the industry was "full of anomalies, which could never exist were there a properly organized jute workers' union."[1] Besides, with the jute mills situated in close proximity to one another, the industry often seemed to provide an ideal basis for a strong trade union movement. The government described this labor force in 1933 as "perhaps the largest and the most compact group of workers with identical interests in the world."[2] The Bengal labor commissioner wrote in the same vein in 1935: "Nowhere in the world are there better territorial conditions for labour organisation than round about Calcutta. The jute mills are concentrated in a narrow range of, say, 20 miles north and south of Calcutta . . . [and] employ about 300,000 persons."[3]

Yet a striking feature of the history of the jute workers' movement was the absence, relatively speaking, of strong and enduring trade unions. A government inquiry in 1945 revealed that only about 18 percent of the workers—some 47,697 of a total of 267,193—were members of unions.[4] This was an uncertain estimate: "it is important to remember," cautioned the author of the report, "that membership figures of Trade Unions are not always very reliable."[5] An important trade union leader was to sound an even more cautionary note a few years later. Speaking to a convention of the All India Trade Union Congress (AITUC) held in Calcutta in 1952, Indrajit Gupta, the general secretary of the Communist-dominated Bengal Chatkal Mazdoor Union, reminded his comrades of "the harsh reality that the *overwhelming majority* of them [the jute-mill workers], perhaps 95%, [were] not organized in any trade union" at all.[6] Both Gupta's conclu-

[1] RCLI, vol. 5, pt. 1, p. 159.

[2] W.B.S.A., Com. Dept. Com. Br., December 1933, A14–39.

[3] W.B.S.A., Home Poll. Confdl. no. 392 (1–3)/1935.

[4] S. R. Deshpande, *Report on an Enquiry into Conditions of Labour in the Jute Mill Industry in India* (Delhi, 1946), pp. 6, 34–35.

[5] Ibid., p. 34.

[6] Indrajit Gupta, *Capital and Labour in the Jute Industry* (Bombay, 1953), p. 50. Emphasis in original.

116

sion and that drawn in the official report of 1946 were the same. "There is no doubt," the latter said, "that Trade Unionism in the jute mill industry . . . is in an extremely weak condition."[7] "No healthy tradition of trade unionism has yet developed among the jute workers" was the view put forward by Gupta.[8]

THE PERSISTENT WEAKNESS of jute workers' organization has been seen as somewhat paradoxical, given the history of their longstanding grievances and their tradition of militant and sometimes well-organized strikes.[9] This militancy was especially marked in the 1920s and afterward when strikes became much more frequent than before. In analyzing some eighty-nine strikes—twenty-seven of them in jute mills alone—that occurred in the Calcutta industrial area during the second half of 1920, the Committee on Industrial Unrest did not think it necessary "to go back further than the 1st July 1920," since strikes were much less common in the past. "Before that time [1920]," said the committee, "a certain amount of industrial unrest had been evident in Bengal as in other parts of India, but in Bengal strikes had not been resorted to on any large scale as a means of enforcing the demands of the workers."[10] Their opinion was echoed by the director of industries in Bengal, in an article he wrote in 1921. He described the "epidemic of strikes" that broke out in Bengal in 1920 as "unprecedented in the history of the province," because strikes "had appeared only in isolated cases" in the earlier period when "the demands had more commonly been non-economic in character."[11] Between 1921 and 30 June 1929, there were 201 recorded strikes in the jute industry, far surpassing the numbers in the preceding decades.[12]

It was not just the higher frequency of strikes, however, that made the authorities take notice of them; the authorities were also some-

[7] Deshpande, *Report*, p. 35.

[8] Gupta, *Capital and Labour*, p. 51.

[9] This is how the problem has been formulated in a recent study of left politics in Bengal. See Tanika Sarkar, "National Movement and Popular Protest in Bengal, 1928–1934," Ph.D. thesis, University of Delhi, 1980. The "paradox in working-class organization" is seen here in "the absence of regular unions and the workers' indifference to long-standing joint work on the one hand and the remarkable discipline and organizational ability in the face of tremendous odds of the short-term strike committees on the other" (pp. 155–156). It is also said in this work that the "conditions of jute workers explain the long tradition of militancy and conflict with the management" (pp. 144–145).

[10] W.B.S.A., Com. Dept. Com. Br., July 1921, A40–42.

[11] [D. B. Meek?], "Trade Disputes in Bengal," *Journal of Indian Industries and Labour*, pt. 1, Feb. 1921, p. 71.

[12] RCLI, vol. 5, pt. 1, p. 126.

times worried by their longer duration. A strike in the Fort Gloster Jute Mill in 1928 was described by the government as "the most protracted strike in the industry" till then. It lasted from 17 July to 31 December 1928 and was soon followed by a general strike that began in July 1929 and ran till the end of September. One "notable" feature of this strike, the government thought, was its "magnitude": "never before in the history of the jute mills in Bengal had anything of the nature of a general strike been attempted."[13] The strike presaged the shape of things to come. After a temporary lull—1930 to 1933—working-class militancy reached a peak once again in the mid-1930s, culminating in a second general strike in 1937.

What this militancy reflected in the first place was certainly a heightened sense of grievance on the part of the jute-mill worker. The Royal Commission on Labour (1929) was told by a jute-mill manager who had been around for about thirty years that "there was not so much discontent [before] as there is today."[14] A. C. Roy Chowdhury, who carried out, on behalf of the commission, an inquiry into the standard of living of the jute-mill workers, reported that he had heard "much discontented talk on the subject of low wages and lack of accommodation."[15] Further, the commission itself came across some particularly sharp expressions of workers' grievances over wages and living conditions. "Upon this [wage]," said Kamala, an Oriya woman employed by the Howrah Jute Mill, "two people cannot live."[16] Mangrul, a young boy from Patna working at the Titaghur Jute Mill, was equally forthright. "Formerly I was well fleshed," he said, "but now I am weak as I do not get enough food."[17]

What made for such "discontented talk" by the workers? Partly, no doubt, their conditions, which seem to have taken a turn for the worse in the late twenties and thirties. From about the mid-1920s, as the industry experienced the beginnings of a trade depression, it moved toward a policy of reducing its wage bill. An early "sign of the change" was the decision of the Reliance Jute Mill in 1923 to switch over to the single-shift system of work, resulting in the dismissal of "over 2,000 workmen" and an important strike. "There is no doubt whatsoever," wrote R. N. Gilchrist, the labor intelligence officer of Bengal, "that the condition of the industry at the moment is giving the Managing Agents furiously to think," and some of them were now "coming round to the

[13] Ibid.
[14] Ibid., pt. 2, p. 188.
[15] W.B.S.A., Com. Dept. Com. Br., April 1931, A8–13.
[16] RCLI, vol. 11, p. 361.
[17] Ibid., vol. 5, pt. 1, p. 77.

view that perhaps it would be more economical to work 5 or 5½ days a week on the single shift in preference to the multiple shift system."[18] By 1927, the workers had begun to feel the pinch of the employers' policies. About one-third of the recorded strikes in the jute mills that year were because of "the recently introduced change in the system of shifts." The government of Bengal informed the Government of India that "in each of these disputes there invariably was a complaint on the part of the workmen concerned that the change, which was accompanied by the lengthening of the working week, resulted in a decrease in their weekly earnings."[19] The same complaint provided the "economic basis" to the general strike in 1929. When the employers tried to explain the strike away be attributing it to "the machinations of [political] agitators financed by Marwari 'Hessian' merchants," Sir David Petrie of the Government of India's Intelligence Bureau retorted by pointing to the "economic basis" of the strike, which "did not seem to be disputed by anyone"; this basis lay, in Petrie's words, in "an increase in the weekly working hours without any corresponding adjustment of wages."[20] To these grievances were added those of unemployment and actual reduction in the wage rates in the 1930s. About sixty thousand workers were laid off in 1930–31.[21] This was followed by wage cuts. As one government official wrote in August 1932,

> The majority of the mills are working for 40 hours a week spread over four or five days. Many operatives are now paid as little as from Re 1-10 to Rs 2-1 a week. In the present economic depression of the industry there is no possibility of any increase in the rates of wages.[22]

The decline in the bargaining position of the working class in these years is reflected in the stagnant money-wage figures for the industry. They are in strong contrast to an apparent increase in productivity. In addition, the figures for the remittances (money orders) sent by the workers to their villages suggest a significant drop in their earnings. The average value of such money orders fell by nearly 17 percent in

[18] National Archives of India [hereafter NAI], Department of Industries and Labour [hereafter Ind. and Lab.] no. L-881 (4) of 1923.

[19] NAI, Ind. and Lab. no. L-881 (18) of 1927.

[20] NAI, Home Poll. Confdl. no. 257/I and K.W. of 1930. I owe this reference to Mridula Mahajan.

[21] See W.B.S.A., Home Poll. Confdl. no. 150/1931.

[22] W.B.S.A., Com. Dept. Com. Br., February 1933, A5–37. See also Com. Dept. Com. Br., June 1935, A35–48.

the 1930s compared to the average for most of the 1920s (see Table 4.1).

There was thus enough in the jute-mill workers' conditions to make them feel discontented. But we should not fall into the trap of thinking that working-class militancy was rooted in conditions alone or that the conditions by themselves were sufficient to generate such militancy. The persistence and volume of labor unrest in the 1920s and 1930s have also to be understood as signaling a growing propensity on the part of the workers to protest and challenge the employer's authority. The 1929 general strike, for instance, surprised the government by the "apparent ease with which the jute mill workers were brought out" by the organizers of the strike.[23] "One thing is certain," Sir Edward Benthall privately remarked in his diary immediately after the strike, "the best paid labour struck as easily as the less well paid."[24] It is indeed this growing presence among the workers of a will to resist the employer that makes their lack of organization seem truly paradoxical.

Given the problems of documenting the consciousness of the jute-mill workers, their will to resist and question the authority of their employers can be read only in terms of the sense of crisis it produced among the people in authority. "Labour has come to a dim realisation of its own importance," discerned a concerned government official as early as 1924. "This is not yet overt," he said, "yet, as every mill manager will bear out, labour cannot be handled as it was in the old days. It now requires delicate management. Brutality, bullying, unfairness, all quickly lead to trouble—usually strikes."[25] The old argument of the government—that the strike was "a private matter between the masters and the men"[26]—was found no longer tenable as the force and magnitude of the general strike of 1929 compelled the government to abandon such fine considerations and intervene in settling the dispute.[27]

In the 1930s, the "private" authority of the individual mill manager was increasingly viewed as an inadequate agency for controlling working-class unrest. This may be seen in the direct and enlarged role given to the labor commissioner of the Bengal government in 1937 in moni-

[23] RCLI, vol. 5, pt. 1, p. 126.

[24] C.S.A.S., B.P., Box 7, diary for 1929–1933, entry for 10 September 1929.

[25] R. N. Gilchrist, *The Payment of Wages and Profit-Sharing* (Calcutta, 1924), pp. 236-237.

[26] W.B.S.A., Com. Dept. Com. Br., August 1925, A7–8.

[27] See RCLI, vol. 5, pt. 1, p. 133; NAI, Home Poll. Confdl. no. 257/1 and K.W. of 1930.

TABLE 4.1.
Average value (in Rs.) of money orders sent by jute-mill workers, 1922–37.

Post Office	Period I 1922–30	Period II 1931–37	Fall (%) from Period I to Period II	Average fall in value (%)
Angus	18.13	14.31	21.07	
Baidyabati	18.07	13.87	23.24	
Bally	15.23	12.87	15.50	
Bhatpara	18.84	15.37	18.42	
Baranagar	17.37	14.29	17.73	
Budge Budge	18.07	15.91	11.95	
Fort Gloster	17.01	12.56	26.16	
Garifa	18.47	15.20	17.70	
Garulia	17.59	14.58	17.11	
Ghusuri	16.18	13.68	15.45	
Kamarhatty	18.27	15.64	13.45	17.02
Kankinara	19.23	15.60	18.88	
Khardah	16.93	13.42	20.73	
Konnagar	15.41	13.92	9.67	
Naihati	18.86	15.18	16.41	
Ramkrishnapur	17.95	14.12	19.51	
Rishra	17.27	14.08	18.28	
Sankrail	19.23	15.34	20.23	
Serampore	16.77	13.79	17.77	
Samnugger	18.01	14.46	19.71	
Shibpore	18.47	15.61	15.48	
Sodepur	12.86	11.13	13.45	
Sonai	18.04	16.88	6.43	
Telinipara	17.17	14.83	13.63	
Titaghur	19.92	16.42	17.57	

SOURCE: IJMA, *Reports* for the respective years (except for 1927) and D. R. Wallace, *The Romance of Jute* (London, 1928), p. 108. The post offices selected here are those whose figures, according to Wallace, "may be taken [to represent] almost wholly jute employees' money."

toring labor disputes in individual jute mills.[28] The institution of labor officers that the IJMA created in 1937 was another attempt to create a new means of control.[29] In addition, the IJMA now set up its own Intelligence Service to receive timely "warnings of developments and of the general trend of opinion" among laborers.[30] "The idea . . . [was] to have paid spies in every mill or group of mills who [would] give information to the Intelligence Officers."[31] Some individual companies even created their own labor officers, and Benthall's description of the physical construction of the office proposed for their own man, Colonel Spain, bears a distinct imprint of the wariness with which the employers now viewed the mood of the workers. Spain's office was to be given a "bolt hole at the back in case labour control[led] him instead of the reverse."[32]

> We intend to provide him with an office in Titaghur Bazar on a piece of Kinnison land with an unobtrusive means of entry through the back into Titaghur [Mill] compound in case at any time a hasty retreat becomes desirable.[33]

"The average cooly," wrote an angry jute-mill manager in 1937, "has his point of view and thinks we are exploiting him all the time, which is borne out by the fact that they believe the most ridiculous things told to them by the outside agitators in spite of all we have done to try and convince them of the truth of affairs."[34] This naive but important statement can serve as a measure of the growing sense of hostility and distance that formed an important element of capital-labor relations in the 1930s. The intensity of this hostility is inscribed in the currency that the word *dalal* (an agent or stooge of the employer) acquired in the 1930s as a working-class term of abuse and in the strong emotions the word aroused. Some of the Muslim League trade unionists and workers who tried to combat the influence of the Communist leader A. M. A. Zaman among the jute-mill workers of Hooghly in 1937 learned this at much cost to themselves. Mohiuddin Khan, one of their leaders, bitterly complained to his mentor, H. S. Suhrawardy,

[28] C.S.A.S., B.P., Box 12, confidential record of an interview of the IJMA chairman with H. S. Suhrawardy, labor minister, with A. Hughes, labor commissioner, present, on 28 July 1937 at the Writers Buildings.
[29] IJMA, *Report, 1937* (Calcutta, 1938), pp. 43, 132.
[30] C.S.A.S., B.P., Box 12, "Paul" to Benthall, 11 August 1937.
[31] C.S.A.S., B.P., Box 13, "Paul" to Benthall, 1 September 1937.
[32] C.S.A.S., B.P., Box 13, Benthall to "Paul," 28 September 1937.
[33] C.S.A.S., B.P., Box 13, "Paul" to Benthall, 20 September 1937.
[34] C.S.A.S., B.P., Box 12, "Paul" to Benthall, 21 July 1937, enclosures.

that laborers belonging to his union had been "intimidated, threatened [and] molested" by the followers of Zaman. One of his "Dalhousie [Mill] Union worker[s]," he said, had been "assaulted by one Subhan of the Dalhousie Jute Mills"; his supporter, Mati Sardar of the Northbrook Jute Mills, had been "chased [away] by some mill-hands"; and his follower Syed Habibur Rahman's life was in such danger that "the poor man . . . slept inside [his] room bolted from within and was literally boiled in this oppressive weather." At the Champdany Jute Mill, an effigy of yet another worker of his union, Nurie, was "taken round the mill by the partisans of Mr. Zaman . . . [and was] spat on and beaten with shoes."[35] Interestingly, Khan's own explanation of what caused such working-class hatred an anger to be unleashed against his men suggests the strongly negative appeal of the word *dalal* to at least some of the laborers in the mills:

> The supporters of Mr. Zaman . . . abused and insulted us. [They] shouted that the Dallals had come and that nobody should listen to them [us] . . . [Zaman] incited the mob to beat the dallals if they ever set their feet in Champdany.[36]

If the mere labeling of someone a *dalal*, that is, an agent of the employer, could trigger such a violent response toward him, we can imagine how charged the atmosphere must have been, with a spirit of hostility toward the owners and the managers of the mills and a cordial hatred of anyone seen acting in their interests. To be sure, this does not fully describe the consciousness of the workers (if it did, proemployer Suhrawardy would not have had any followers at all), but for any understanding of the history of jute workers' organization, this aspect of the workers' consciousness cannot be overlooked.

WE CAN now formulate more clearly the apparent paradox in the history of the jute workers' trade union movement: so much militancy, yet so little organization. The "harsh reality" was not simply that the "overwhelming majority" of the workers had not been unionized. An even greater problem was that the unions that had been formed appeared inherently unstable. Throughout the 1920s and 1930s, the government continued to describe trade unionism in the jute mills as "still in its infancy."[37] Or, to slightly vary the mataphor, the trade union movement in the jute mills appeared to have been born spastic.

[35] W.B.S.A., Home Poll. Confdl. no. 326/1937.
[36] Ibid.
[37] W.B.S.A., Com. Dept. Com. Br., August 1922, A32–51; January 1925, A183–227; December 1933, A14–39; February 1937, A50–81.

One important symptom of this "spasticity" was the spasmodic formation of jute-mill unions. Each outburst of labor protest, especially from the 1920s, resulted in some kind of organization. Once the outburst spent itself, however, the organization as a rule disintegrated. As the government of Bengal put it to the Royal Commission on Labour, "in almost every strike some sort of labour body was formed, usually after the strike broke out," but such unions remained entirely ephemeral.[38] The Kankinarrah Labour Union, one of the oldest (1922) in the jute industry, complained in its submission to the commission that even though membership of the union "grew very rapidly during strikes or temporary excitements," it also fell "equally rapidly after the termination of disputes."[39]

The pattern can be traced for the entire period under study. The "widespread unrest" among the jute workers during the antipartition (or *swadeshi*) movement in Bengal (1905–08) coincided with the founding of the Indian Mill-Hands Union, organized by the *swadeshi* leader A. C. Banerjee. As the unrest continued, the union "gradually extended the field of its activities, and by the end of 1907 . . . was coming to be known by the more ambitious name of Indian Labour Union."[40] The enthusiasm it generated among the workers is revealed in the letters they wrote to Banerjee during these years. In these letters they expressed their feelings of "undying gratitude" to Banerjee for the "infinite good" he had done them by establishing this trade union.[41] But the organization faded away once the period of working-class unrest came to an end. To quote the historian of the *swadeshi* movement: "When the labour movement [in Bengal] revived immediately after the [1914] war, it was led by men of a new generation, and its Swadeshi pre-history was hardly ever recalled."[42]

An idea of "progress" obviously stirs within that optimistic word, "pre-history," but we would be wrong to suppose that the *swadeshi* experience of trade unionism was superseded and made irrelevant by a future that embodied "progress." A longer view of jute workers' trade unionism would produce a distinctly contrary impression. The *swadeshi* experience would then appear to have only foreshadowed the

[38] RCLI, vol. 5, pt. 1, p. 143.
[39] Ibid., p. 273.
[40] Sumit Sarkar, *The Swadeshi Movement in Bengal 1903–1908* (Delhi, 1973), pp. 227, 234.
[41] Sumit Sarkar, "Swadeshi Yuger Sramik Andolan: Kayekti Aprakashita Dalil," *Itihas*, vol. 4, no. 2, Bhadra-Agrahayan 1376 (1969), pp. 113–115; also Sarkar's *Swadeshi Movement*, pp. 233–235.
[42] Sarkar, *Swadeshi Movement*, p. 241.

future developments. For example, twenty-odd jute-mill unions were formed by the Khilafatists during the industrial unrest of 1920–21; six of these were "abolished" outright within a few months of their formation.[43] The rest were described by the government in August 1921 as "rather nebulous concerns."[44] The newly formed Bengal Labour Federation, which controlled some of these unions, was said to be "collapsing" by the middle of 1921.[45] The Howrah Labour Union and the Central Jute Mill Association (Howrah) were two unions whose "existence and activities [had been] deposed to by their respective Secretaries before the recent [1921] Committee on Industrial Unrest," yet in a few months' time the district magistrate advised the government that "the local police report that the associations [were] both dead and [had] no members [was] correct."[46] Trade unions had also been established among the jute workers of Barrackpore and Garden Reach (24 Parganas) in 1920. In 1921, the police described them as being "in a moribund state," and Donald Gladding, an official in the Industries Department of the government of Bengal, was reluctant to include them in his list of trade unions for that year "because they are almost certainly of a very frail and nebulous character."[47]

The groundswell of labor protest in the jute industry during the two general strikes of 1929 and 1937 was accompanied by the same phenomenon: quick flourishing and wilting of trade union organization. The strike of 1929 was preceded, as we have seen, by a growing volume of unrest in the mills over changes in working hours and wages.[48] This unrest surely helped in the establishment of trade unions in some of the jute mills in the Chengail-Bauria region of the Howrah District. It also helped to revitalize the Bengal Jute Workers Association at Bhatpara (24 Parganas) that had been formed in 1925.[49] In both these areas, the leadership of the unions was in the hands of a group of young Bengalis, committed by their ideology to the cause of the working class. With the strike movement gathering momentum in the jute mills,

> the organizations at Bhatpara under Kali[das] Bhattacharjee and
> Gopen Chakravarti and those at Chengail and Bauria under Rad-

[43] W.B.S.A., Com. Dept. Com. Br., July 1921, A34–72.
[44] W.B.S.A., Com. Dept. Com. Br., September 1921, A54–55.
[45] W.B.S.A., Com. Dept. Com. Br., July 1921, A34–72.
[46] W.B.S.A., Com. Dept. Com. Br., September 1921, A54–55.
[47] Ibid.
[48] For details, see W.B.S.A., Com. Dept. Com. Br., July 1927, A6–8.
[49] For details, see Gautam Chattopadhyay, *Communism and Bengal's Freedom Movement*, vol. 1 (Delhi, 1970).

haraman Mitra, Bankim Mukherjee and later Kishori[lal] Ghose amalgamated under a central organization called the Bengal Jute Workers' Union with its head office in Calcutta.[50]

The Bengal Jute Workers Union (BJWU) gave leadership to the general strike of 1929. As the strike began, and while it lasted, the organization of BJWU "began to extend" and branches were opened at Bhatpara, Champdany, Shibpore, Chengail, Budge Budge, and Titaghur.[51] The popularity and fame of the union spread fast among the working classes of Calcutta. In the words of one of the organizers of the union:

> The Bengal Jute Workers' Union stood right at the centre of working-class movement in Bengal at this time [April 1930]. Its success in leading the general strike of three and a half lakhs of jute mill workers in 1929 had awakened the entire working class to a new state of consciousness and generated a new enthusiasm among them . . . it [BJWU] enjoyed such fame that workers from any factory would rush to this union to seek advice regarding their own struggles. It was under the leadership of the organisers of this union [BJWU] that strikes were conducted by the workers of the ice factories in Calcutta, of the Gramophone Company and of Stuart Motor Company.[52]

Such popularity and spread notwithstanding, the Bengal Jute Workers Union was to lose its vitality very soon. An intelligence report of 1934 said:

> After the strike [of 1929] a split occurred between Miss Prabhabati Das Gupta [the acknowledged leader of the strike] on the one hand and Kali Sen on the other. . . . Two unions came into existence; one controlled by Miss Prabhabati Das Gupta which *gradually died out* and the other controlled by the communists under Bankim Mukherjee and Kali Sen. . . . *It is not a powerful organisation.*[53]

When sixty thousand jute-mill workers were "rendered idle" (to use the euphemism of the IJMA) in 1930–31, the jute workers' lack of any organization strong enough to resist the onslaught was painfully clear.

[50] W.B.S.A., Home Poll. Confdl. no. 161(29–67)/1934.

[51] Ibid.; RCLI, vol. 5, pt. 1, p. 161.

[52] Abdul Momin, "Kolkatay Gadowan Dharmaghater Chardin," *Mulyayan*, Pous-Magh (1977), pp. 11–12.

[53] W.B.S.A., Home Poll. Confdl. no. 161(29–67)/1934. Emphasis added.

The most that the retrenched workers could do was to go back to their villages.[54]

The thirties do not fall outside the pattern. The police authorities of Calcutta reported in 1934 "a steady flow of communist teaching . . . by leaders of trade unions," many of whom were now using "Communist slogans and . . . language characteristic of that movement."[55] In May the next year, the labor commissioner of Bengal drew the attention of the government to "the rapid development of labour organisations in the last few months."[56] The following few years saw another round of confrontation between labor and capital in the jute industry, the high point of which was the general strike of 1937 that lasted from "early February until the middle of May" and involved a good majority of the work force—about 77 percent.[57]

Once again, trade union organization flourished dramatically and sixty-seven jute-mill unions were registered with the government in the years 1937–38.[58] During the general strike of 1937, many of these unions formed themselves into one central executive body, the Bengal Chatkal Mazdoor Union, which was affiliated to the AITUC.[59] Although the outburst of trade union activity of the 1930s may look like a "definite advance" over the previous situation, the similarities with the past are too strong to be ignored.[60] The Bengal Chatkal Mazdoor Union, formed to function as "a single, centralised union," was described by one of its organizers in 1952 as "never [having] functioned as such."[61] When the AITUC leaders returned to trade union work among jute workers in 1943, they had only sixteen unions with a meager strength of 3,000 members altogether, an insubstantial minority in a 250,000-strong labor force. Abdul Momin, an important Communist trade union leader to whom we owe this information, admitted to his comrades in 1943 that none of the Communist-led trade unions formed "before the war" could be considered "powerful."[62] The situation remained unchanged for some time to come. Both Gupta and

[54] See W.B.S.A., Home Poll. Confdl. no. 150/1931.
[55] W.B.S.A., Home Poll. Confdl. no. 161(13–16)/1934.
[56] W.B.S.A., Home Poll. Confdl. no. 392(1–3)/1935.
[57] IJMA, *Report, 1937* (Calcutta, 1938), p. 41.
[58] W.B.S.A., Com. and Labour, April 1939, A14–16.
[59] Gupta, *Capital and Labour*, p. 45.
[60] See Sarkar, "National Movement," pp. 161–162.
[61] Gupta, *Capital and Labour*, p. 45.
[62] Abdul Momin, *Bharater Communist Partir Bangla Pradesher Tritiya Sammelane Grihita Pradeshik Trade Union Front Report* (Report on the Trade Union Front, accepted at the Third Bengal Provincial Conference of the Communist Party of India), Calcutta, 18–21 March 1943, pp. 7–8, 30.

Deshpande, as we have seen, have discussed the languishing state of the trade union movement among the jute workers even after the war and the coming of independence.

THE PARADOX of "strong militancy but weak organization" has been usually resolved by an implicit or explicit argument about the workers' lack of education. Organization was weak, or so the argument has run, because the structural and other features of the workers' conditions deprived them of any opportunity to acquire an understanding of trade union discipline and functioning. The effort, therefore, has been to understand why the workers remained "ignorant," and persistently so, in spite of two or three decades of attempts to educate and organize them. Depending on their convictions, various authors have emphasized different factors—economic, social, or political—to explain this "ignorance." Obviously, the answers differ in terms of their ideological contents and emphases, but one broad fundamental agreement runs through the entire body of the existing discourse on jute workers' organization: that to organize was to educate.

To the politically conservative trade unionist, this was simply a question of making the workers literate. K. C. Roy Chowdhury, the president of the Kankinarrah Labour Union, once cited the "widespread illiteracy of the [Indian] working class" as an important reason why "unions [had] failed to satisfy."[63] His unions told the Royal Commission on Labour that "illiteracy [was] the main cause of labour's helplessness":

> It is the conviction of the organizers of this union . . . that the plant of constructive trade unionism will not take root for many years to come until and unless the soil is weeded and workers receive primary instruction.[64]

Almost identical were the views of government officials. If "the Indian labourer" was "notoriously difficult to organise in trade unions," as R. N. Gilchrist put it in 1924, the reason lay in their lack of education, without which no permanent unity of working men was ever possible. "Only education," wrote Gilchrist, "and the mutual tolerance bred of education will soften the differences" of language, religion, and so on. "Living in close contiguity in circumscribed areas, and service under one master, may lead to temporary unity . . . but continuous and

[63] K. C. Roy Chowdh[u]ry, "Some Thoughts on Indian Labour," *Journal of Indian Industries and Labour*, vol. 3, pt. 1, Feb. 1923, pp. 23–28.
[64] RCLI, vol. 5, pt. 1, pp. 262–263.

sustained common action is as yet out of the question."[65] The government of Bengal pointed to the same relationship between education and organization in a memorandum to the Royal Commission in 1929:

> On the [jute-mill] employees' side, the organization at present is in an infantile stage, and little more can be expected till the workers have some measure of education. . . . With education and proper guidance he [the mill worker] will inevitably build up an organ to express his obvious community of interest with his fellows. . . . It is in the interest of employers and community at large that the basis of this organization should be well and truly laid.[66]

To the more radical authors, however, "education" has meant the "political education" of the worker and not simply the question of his literacy. Santosh Kumari Gupta, who in collaboration with Bankim Mukherjee and Kalidas Bhattacharya founded the Gouripore Labour Union in the mid-1920s, started several night schools where "newspapers were read out to educate the [mill] hands on the political situation" in the country.[67] She believed that it was the "ignorance" of the laborers that exposed them to harsh treatment from the bosses.[68] One of the earliest Bengali language tracts on trade unionism, *Trade Unioner Godar Katha* (The fundamentals of trade unionism), published in 1934, had as its aim the correction and improvement of the prevalent ideas of the laboring classes. "So many rival ideas have now entered the field of trade unionism [in Bengal] that the workers have problems in discovering the correct path, and the friends of the rich can come along and put all kinds of ideas into their heads." Hence, the author said,

> Every worker must read this book and explain its contents to ten others. He should organize his friends into a study-circle and meet three times a week to discuss in depth such issues as the sufferings of the labourers, the ways of the exploiters etc.[69]

True to this spirit, the Bengali communists who went about organizing jute workers in the 1920s, 1930s, and 1940s told them stories about

[65] Gilchrist, *The Payment of Wages*, pp. 232, 250.

[66] *RCLI*, vol. 5, pt. 1, pp. 153–154.

[67] Parimal Ghosh, "Emergence of an Industrial Labour Force in Bengal: A Study of the Conflicts of the Jute Mill-Hands with the State, 1880–1930," Ph.D. thesis, Jadavpur University, Calcutta, 1984, pp. 259–260.

[68] Manju Chattopadhyay, *Sramik Netri Santoshkumari Debi* (Calcutta, 1984?), p. 18.

[69] Saroj Mukherjee, ed., *Trade Unioner Godar Katha* (Calcutta, 1934), p. 3.

Lenin and the Russian revolution,[70] read out to them radical journals,[71] and started conducting "study circles" among them.[72] Imparting "political education" to the worker was seen as the key to a strong trade union movement. Indrajit Gupta's suggestion in 1952 that "serious attention" be given by communists "to cultural and social activity" among jute-mill workers "through libraries, night schools, schools for workers' children, drama and music groups" was inspired by the same consideration.[73]

The figure of the "ignorant" worker (even if this "ignorance" is defined in strictly political terms) has thus been central to all existing explanations of the problems of working-class organization in the jute mills. Factors such as the "linguistic heterogeneity" of the jute workers (or the absence of "a single means of communication" among them),[74] their "linguistic separation" from the Bengali community,[75] the "structural peculiarities" of this labor force, their "amorphous, undefined and generally unskilled nature,"[76] their "half-pastoralist, half-proletarian" outlook,[77] as well as the suppression of left-wing trade unions by the state,[78] have all been mentioned with varying degrees of justification to explain why the jute-mill workers never grew out of their "ignorance," political or otherwise.

It is not our purpose to contest the validity of these individual propositions, though some are obviously more true than others. The "linguistic separation of the majority of workers from the surrounding Bengali community," for instance, was indeed a problem that trade unionists had to reckon with. Abdul Momin writes in his reminiscences of the 1929 general strike that even when the strike spread from Alambazar to Titaghur with "lightning speed" and several people volunteered to help in the organization of the strike, language remained an important problem: "Not all our volunteers could speak Hindi and in no other language could propaganda in favour of the strike be car-

[70] See W.B.S.A., Home Poll. Confdl. nos. 161(29–67)/1934 and 33/1940.

[71] See Chattopadhyay, *Communism*, p. 135.

[72] W.B.S.A., Home Poll. Confdl. nos. W-40/1940.

[73] Gupta, *Capital and Labour*, p. 61.

[74] See Bagchi, *Private Investment*, p. 142; RCLI, vol. 5, pt. 1, p. 154; Deshpande, *Report*, p. 35, and Gupta, *Capital and Labour*, p. 142; Sarkar, "National Movement," pp. 156–157, 161–162.

[75] Bagchi, *Private Investment*, p. 142; Gupta, *Capital and Labour*, p. 42.

[76] Sarkar, "National Movement," pp. 156, 158.

[77] Gupta, *Capital and Labour*, pp. 56–57; Roy Chowdhury, "Thoughts," pp. 23–28, and his letter of 10 November 1924 in W.B.S.A., Com. Dept. Com. Br., January 1925, A183–227.

[78] Momin, *Report*, p. 8; Sarkar, "National Movement," p. 159.

ried out in most of the [mill] areas."[79] Given the necessary will, however, a solution was soon found to the problem. Before long, many trade unionists mastered the art of speaking Hindi. Momin mentions the following among the leaders of the 1929 strike who could make speeches in fluent Hindi: Bankim Mukherjee, Kali Sen, Bakr Ali Mirza, Prabhabati Das Gupta, Sachidananda Chatterjee, Moni Singh, Swami Biswanand, Shroff Nand Kishore Sharma, and himself.[80] Besides we should also remember that the leaflets distributed by BJWU during the strike were after all printed in "several languages."[81]

A more seriously crippling factor for the left-wing trade unions were the repressive measures that the state often adopted in dealing with them. The frequent use by the government of section 144 of the Indian Penal Code to expel leftist leaders from their areas of activity was clearly aimed at minimizing the level of their contact with the working class. The common sense of purpose that united the mill managers and government officials in this effort proved a particularly formidable obstacle to trade union activity. P. D. Martyn of the Indian Civil Service saw "something of life as it [was] lived in the huge jute mill suburbs" when he served as a subdivisional officer at Barrackpore early in the 1930s.

> While there [he wrote] I played my part in coping with a strike with 60,000 operatives out of work. Coping with the situation included the passing of orders prohibiting the entry of certain agitators from Calcutta into the area. What struck me at the time was how helpful the jute mill managers (Scots to a man) were during these troubles.[82]

For us, then, the question is not one of disputing the statements made by individual scholars who have attempted to explain the weakness of jute workers' organization. Taken by themselves these statements contain a certain measure of truth and many of them do point to important factors that may have retarded the growth of unions in the jute industry. What we are concerned with here is the point at which these different and apparently diverse statements meet. In the final analysis, they all seek to explain why the workers remained ignorant of "trade union discipline and functioning" and enumerate the factors that supposedly deprived them of such education. The task of

[79] Abdul Momin, "Chatkal Sramiker Pratham Sadharan Dharmaghat," *Kalantar*, 11 August 1970.
[80] Ibid.
[81] RCLI, vol. 5, pt. 1, p. 144.
[82] IOL, Memoirs of P. D. Martyn, MSS. Eur. F180/13, p. 6.

organizing is then seen in this entire discussion as essentially an exercise in making certain types of knowledge (literacy, self-awareness, etc.) available to the workers, that is, in educating them.

It is here that I feel we can use the current understanding of the "paradox" of jute workers' organization to open up a deeper paradox that is usually overlooked. There is something fundamentally problematic about viewing organization simply as a matter of political education for the worker. To do this is to sidestep certain important issues of culture and consciousness that are raised when we examine more closely the problem of working-class organization. Even within the framework of Marxist theory it is now recognized that the Leninist project of inserting a body of "intellectuals" between the working class and the "theory" is fraught with ambiguities.[83] This is only more so in a society entangled in a variety of precapitalist relationships. Besides, it would surely be a very elitist view of working-class history that did not ask if the "educators" themselves needed some educating as well.

THE CULTURAL ISSUES alluded to in the previous paragraph are fundamentally questions of power and authority. Indeed, it may be argued that to raise the point about the jute-mill worker's ignorance of "trade union functioning and discipline" is to raise these very issues. For what is "organizational discipline" if not a way of resolving questions of power and authority within organizations?

For the purpose of analysis here, the important point is that there are certain assumptions about culture—not just of the workers alone but of their leaders as well—inherent in the concept of "trade union discipline." Ideally speaking, the proper functioning of a stable, broad-based trade union requires a bourgeois culture. As Gramsci once said, trade unions are organizations based on "voluntary" and "contractual" relationships; their emphasis on membership, subscription, and other procedures of organizational discipline is based on the assumed existence of such relations.[84] Trade unions also embody a principle of representation that manifests itself in elections. The trade union, properly conceived, is thus a bourgeois-democratic organization and is organized in the image of the bourgeois-democratic government. In the

---

[83] Antonio Gramsci, *Selections from the Prison Notebooks*, trans. and ed. Q. Hoare and G. N. Smith (New York, 1973), pp. 9, 198–199; Christine Buci-Glucksmann, *Gramsci and the State* (London, 1980), pp. 29–30.

[84] Antonio Gramsci, "The Turin Workers' Council" (trans. from the *Ordine Nuovo*, 1919–20), in Robin Blackburn, ed., *Revolution and Class Struggle: A Reader in Marxist Politics* (Glasgow, 1977), p. 378.

same way as the latter represents the "people"—through "voluntary" and "contractual" relationships—the trade union represents its members and, through them, the class. Gramsci made the point clearly and forcefully while discussing the nature of trade unions and political parties: "These are organisations born on the terrain of bourgeois democracy and political liberty, as an affirmation and development of political freedom. . . . They do not supersede the bourgeois state."[85]

In theory, then, the elected representative of the worker is his equal and is chosen as a representative precisely because he stands in a relationship of "equality"—the equality of the "contract"—to those represented. He does not owe his capacity to represent to any prior position of privilege and authority; his is not, in other words, the figure of the master. This is the crucial question on which trade union democracy turns and it must be set in contrast to that other kind of political representation that Marx once talked about with respect to the peasantry: "They cannot represent themselves, they must be represented. Their representative must at the same time appear as their master, as an authority over them."[86]

If all this seems too theoretical and too much to expect in concrete historical situations, let me make two points. The model is always a useful measure of the reality. Second, and this is perhaps a more important point for the historian, the concept of trade union democracy explained above was precisely what all organizers of labor aspired to realize. The notion of democratic representation was fundamental to all discussions on the question of organizing the jute workers. Listen, for example, to the anticommunist, proemployer labor minister H. S. Suhrawardy arguing to the jute-mill owners in 1937 that the "mere availability" of mill managers was not enough to ensure sufficient contact with the working class:

> Contact between employer and employee should be made through the medium of the *elected* representative of *organised* labour and so that this might be possible the existence of trade unions was absolutely necessary.[87]

[85] Ibid. See also his remarks in Antonio Gramsci, *Selections from Political Writings 1910–1920*, ed. Quintin Hoare and trans. J. Matthews, (New York, 1977), pp. 98–113.

[86] Karl Marx, *The Eighteenth Brumaire of Louis Bonaparte*, in K. Marx and F. Engels, *Selected Works*, vol. 1 (Moscow, 1969), p. 479.

[87] C.S.A.S., B.P., Box 12, confidential records of an interview of the IJMA chairman and H. S. Suhrawardy, labour minister, on 28 July 1937 at the Writers Buildings. Emphasis added.

And now to the Communist Indrajit Gupta in 1952:

> Of course, organisation [of jute workers] must mean something
> more than mere formal enrolment of union membership. . . . The
> point is to function the unions democratically.

and

> the essence of trade union democracy . . . means, concretely, that
> the executive committee of the unions must be regularly function-
> ing bodies, *properly elected* by the members, participating in the
> day to day life of the union.
>
> Democratic functioning ensures that the unions will never suf-
> fer from a "shortage" of cadres, nor become dependent on a
> handful of leading officials or "organizers". On the contrary, it
> will encourage a regular flow of rank and file militants to come
> forward to discharge the multifarious jobs, ranging from manning
> the union office and collecting subscriptions to distributing leaf-
> lets, pasting up posters, addressing meetings etc.[88]

This ideal, however, was hardly ever approximated in reality. Trade
union organization in the jute mills remained extremely inchoate all
through the years under consideration. By *inchoate* I do not simply
mean the "traditional gap" or tension that exists in "every political
party or trade-union . . . between the rank-and-file . . . and the leaders."[89] Such tension existed in the jute-mill unions too. For example,
despite their claims "to represent all jute mill workers on the river,"
the Bengal Jute Workers Union "was unable [in 1929] to control workers in some important areas."[90] The "excellent intelligence service and
organisation" that the "agitators" displayed during the general strike
of 1937 was impressive enough to win praise in the most unlikely
places.[91] But the leaders nevertheless found it difficult to contain the
militancy of their followers in every case. "The result was," wrote a
government official, "that the Shibpore Mills came out much earlier
than . . . was wanted and proved a great embarrassment to the plans
[of the leaders]."[92]

By themselves, these cases do not exhaust the definition of *inchoate*,
since it is possible for organizations to maintain a certain degree of
coherence and discipline in spite of such tension between the leaders

[88] Gupta, *Capital and Labour*, pp. 51, 55. Emphasis added.
[89] Frantz Fanon, *The Wretched of the Earth* (Harmondsworth, 1974), p. 85.
[90] RCLI, vol. 5, pt. 1, p. 127.
[91] C.S.A.S., B.P., Box 11, M. P. Thomas to Benthall, 30 June 1937.
[92] W.B.S.A., Home Poll. Confdl. no. 60/1937.

and the rank and file. In our case the problem of incoherence went much deeper, for even at their liveliest, unions of jute-mill labor were never organizations based on a relatively disciplined body of workers subject to such institutional controls as membership rights and obligations, subscription rules, union constitutions, or even regular meetings. "The very sight of a subscription book," wrote K. C. Roy Chowdhury in his diary, made the workers feel "uneasy and suspicious."[93] In his submission to the Royal Commission in 1929 as the president of the Kankinarrah Labour Union he further added that "the constitution[al] aspect of the union [was] unknown to them [the workers]."[94] Roy Chowdhury's comments are confirmed in a report by Thomas Johnston and John F. Sime, who visited the Calcutta mills in 1925 on behalf of the Joint Committee of Dundee Jute Trade Unions to "enquire into the conditions of the Jute Workers in India." The authors found the Calcutta jute-mill unions seriously crippled by acute financial and other problems of organization.

> There are, on paper, some three or four Unions among the [Calcutta] jute workers, but with one exception they are quite useless, have no paying membership, and serve no purpose unless to advertise some politician as honorary president. The honorary presidents, we believe, pay for the notepaper and headings, and that is all there is to the Unions.[95]

The "one exception" that Johnston and Sime mentioned was the Jute Workers Association founded at Bhatpara by Kalidas Bhattacharya. Bhattacharya was a Bengali *bhadralok* with terrorist connections who had lost his employment with a jute mill for organizing and encouraging strikes.[96] He was described by the Dundee delegation as "an able, intelligent workman who . . . [had] the root of the matter [trade unionism] in him," and his association, it was said, was "definitely making an effort to remedy workers' grievances."[97] Yet of a nominal membership of "only 3000," not more than 400 to 500 paid any subscriptions and, despite low union fees, the organization suffered from severe "monetary limitations." It was "largely financed and inspired . . . by an interesting and self-sacrificing little lady, Mrs. San-

[93] K.C.R.P., diary no. 3, entry for 25 August 1929.
[94] RCLI, vol. 5, pt. 1, p. 273.
[95] Thomas Johnston and John F. Sime, *Exploitation in India* (Dundee, 1926?), p. 15.
[96] Sibnath Banerjee, "Labour Problems in Jute Industry," unpublished typescript, p. 3.
[97] Johnston and Sime, *Exploitation*, p. 15.

tosh Kumari Gupta."[98] The monetary problems of the Bengal Jute Workers Association were to continue in the future when the union reportedly received financial aid "in the shape of a monthly donation of Rs 100 from the Dundee Jute Workers Association" up to 1927 and perhaps even a bit later.[99] In the 1920s, Sime often received letters from trade unionists in India requesting monetary help during strikes in the jute mills. "We had an appeal from Kalidas Bhattacharji in November last year and sent a donation of thirty pounds (£30) to him," mentioned Sime while responding to another request for help during a "prolonged stoppage in the Howrah district" in February 1929.[100] That this "appeal" from Bhattacharya in November 1928 was not the first one of its kind is further suggested by a letter that Sime wrote to him in June that year:

> Your cablegram duly received was placed before my Committee and I am instructed to cable at once a grant of Twenty five pounds (£25) towards the Wellington Jute Mills strike fund. . . . Enclosed please find copy of the "Dundee Free Press" to which I gave the contents of your cablegram thereby giving the matter publicity.[101]

This persisting problem of finances, caused partly by the absence of a subscription-paying rank and file, was only an index—though perhaps the most obvious one—of the deep organizational maladies that afflicted the nature of trade unionism in the jute mills of Calcutta. After all, it is remarkable how the general strike of 1929 was conducted without the executive committee of the Bengal Jute Workers Union holding a meeting even once during the strike.[102] Moreover, no worker was ever a subscription-paying member of the union, as its leader, Prabhabati Das Gupta, was to admit later. She called it "a peculiar labour movement," for the union "never had any subscription or anything."[103] BJWU, however, was not unique in this respect; the govern-

[98] Ibid.

[99] David Petrie, *Communism in India 1924–1927* (Calcutta, 1972), p. 130.

[100] J. F. Sime to N. M. Joshi, 26 February 1929, in Sime's letter book, captioned "India," preserved in the archives of the Dundee and District Union of Jute and Flax Workers, Dundee. I am grateful to Dr. William Walker of the University of Dundee for bringing this letter book to my attention.

[101] Ibid.; Sime to Kalidas Bhattacharya, 13 June 1928.

[102] RCLI, vol. 5, pt. 1, p. 149.

[103] Nehru Memorial Museum and Library [hereafter NMML], Prabhabati Mirza (née Das Gupta), interviewed by K. P. Rangachary, 24 April 1968, Delhi. Transcript, pp. 10–11, 18–19.

ment of Bengal thus summed up the experience of trade unionism in the 1920s:

> After the war, unions of some kind developed with almost bewildering rapidity, because in every strike some sort of a labour body was formed. ... Such bodies had no constitution, no regular membership, and their power to control workers ... was extremely problematical.[104]

Although the thirties and later decades marked an advance in certain directions, seen mainly in the growing popularity of radical ideas in the political circles of Calcutta, a crucial problem remained unresolved. It was the trade union leaders' "failure," to use Indrajit Gupta's words, "to translate their growing mass influence into organisational terms."[105] This "failure" is well illustrated by the case of A.M.A. Zaman, the Communist labor organizer of Hooghly whose growing "mass influence" we have had occasion to document before. During the industrial unrest of 1936–37, Zaman formed a jute-mill union that got itself registered in 1936. In September 1937, however, the general secretary of the union went to court to complain of severe organizational irregularities. He described the union as a "great fraud" and said that even though as the general secretary he was responsible for "all correspondence," subscriptions, and depositing the subscriptions in a bank "in the name of the union," he found that in practice all of these rules were honored only in their violation. "Offices were opened and subscriptions ... raised through collectors but never deposited in any Bank." He was "shocked" to see "receipts being granted" by unauthorized persons while he was kept "in the dark." When he "insisted on accounts and explanation," "the accused No. 1 [i.e. Zaman] ... put it off on flimsy pretext from day to day ... and ... wanted your petitioner to resign from the post of the General Secretary giving a back date."[106] Such inchoateness of organization was to plague jute workers' trade unionism for a long time to come. To quote Indrajit Gupta once again, as he put it in his report of 1952:

> With one or two exceptions, the organisational structure of our unions also [i.e. in addition to those of other political parties] is most unsatisfactory. The pattern is common to jute—periodical

[104] RCLI, vol. 5, pt. 1, p. 143.
[105] Gupta, *Capital and Labour*, p. 51.
[106] W.B.S.A., Home Poll. Confdl. no. 326/1937.

mass meetings and bustee or gate propaganda, *irregular* collection of subscriptions, and *very nominal* office work.[107]

If the organization of jute workers' trade unions was so inchoate, how did they resolve questions of power and authority without the aid of organizational discipline? Or to put the question in another way, if it was not submission to organizational discipline that bound the rank and file of a union to itself, what did? The answer would seem to be: the power of the leader, the so-called representative who, as in Marx's description of the French peasantry, always turned out to be the "master" himself. The specific form in which this power expressed itself was to be seen in the personal loyalty, often temporary, that trade union organizers could elicit from the ordinary mill hands. In contemporary trade union parlance, the word used to describe this style of leadership was *zamindari*. Apparently, the style was endemic; Momin mentioned it to be so in a report to the Communist party in 1943.[108] Of the different political parties that came together to form the AITUC for the jute mills in 1937—"Congress, Socialist, Communist, Forward Bloc and other left labour workers"—it was said that "a sort of territorial division of 'spheres of influence' existed, with a particular leader exercising, as it were, 'zamindari rights' in his particular trade union area."[109]

One important characteristic of such power was, of course, its capacity to render organizational discipline redundant because this power was by nature independent of the niceties and rigors of any such discipline. This sometimes created serious problems for organizational unity, since factionalism at the top could easily split the followers. The Congress-sponsored Indian National Trade Union Congress (INTUC) experienced this in the early fifties when they failed to set up "a single central Congress-led [jute workers'] union because of the rivalries of the different groups within the West Bengal Congress itself." Their "individual unions (area-wise, mill-wise, and even more than one in the same mill) remained," wrote Gupta, "as the zamindaries of different leaders and groups," and could only be "loosely put together into the Jute Workers' Federation."[110]

Sometimes, however, the same force of loyalty allowed a particular leader to be influential even if that influence took no firm organizational shape. A good case in point is again that of Zaman, if only be-

107 Gupta, *Capital and Labour*, p. 50. Emphasis added.
108 Momin, *Report*, pp. 7–8.
109 Gupta, *Capital and Labour*, p. 45.
110 Ibid., pp. 45–46.

cause it is easier to document. As we have seen, Zaman's organization among the mill hands of Hooghly went to pieces at the height of his popularity. But in no way did this diminish his influence. In July 1937, Zaman was convicted "on charge of rioting during . . . [a] strike at the Wellington Jute Mill in Rishra." The workers, "about 4,800 in number," risked their employment and "came out on receipt of the news," such was Zaman's popularity with them.[111] Even in September 1937, when Zaman's union had suffered splits, mill managers, it was said, were "afraid of proceedings being drawn up against the miscreants [i.e. Zaman's followers] as they believe that under such circumstances their respective mills might go on strike."[112] The personal nature of Zaman's control over workers comes out in the following description of events:

> On 1.7.37 . . . a worker was surrounded in his house by Mr. Zaman's partisans who would have assaulted him had he not given in to . . . their demands. That very evening a meeting of Zaman's partisans was held and orders for getting all shops closed to those who had obeyed the orders of the Manager, Angus Jute Works, were passed as it was announced [that] *such was Mr. Zaman's wish.*[113]

Or consider the case of Sibnath Banerjee, the Socialist leader of workers in the Shibpore-Ghusury-Salkea areas of Howrah. After fifteen years of trade union work his authority still derived, according to Indrajit Gupta in 1952, from a display of "considerable personal initiative" and an exercise of "direct leadership."

> They have one central union—the Howrah Zilla Chatkal Mazdoor Union which has *no* organisational form. Its activities revolve entirely around the person of Sri Sibnath Banerjee, whose claim to renown rests on his long years of labour activity in Howrah. It is out and out a one man show.[114]

We must not see these as isolated examples or cases of individual failures. The tradition of *zamindari* leadership was strong and old. A. C. Banerjee, the *swadeshi* trade unionist active around 1905, was a good example of this spirit. Even though his trade union activity spanned only two or three years, Banerjee felt that his "influence with the millhands was so great and discipline so complete that he could

[111] W.B.S.A., Home Poll. Confdl. no. 484/1937.
[112] W.B.S.A., Home Poll. Confdl. no. 326/1937.
[113] Ibid. Emphasis added.
[114] Gupta, *Capital and Labour*, pp. 47, 48. Emphasis added.

CHAPTER 4

make them do whatever he liked."[115] During the 1929 strike, a "Barrackpore pleader, Babu Narendra Chatterjee . . . very quickly gained
ascendancy over the workers" of the Alliance, Craig, Waverley, and
Meghna mills. "The managing agents . . . said that after they had
granted the concessions which the workers had demanded, the workers refused to go back to work, unless they received a definite order
from this pleader."[116] Chatterjee was soon made the vice-president of
the Bengal Jute Workers Union even though "his name had never previously been mentioned in any labour connection whatsoever."

> He had no knowledge of the jute industry and had never previ-
> ously been known to have any business connections in Bhatpara,
> yet certainly for no [ascertainable] reason . . . and without any
> official position in any union . . . he seemed to get control over a
> considerable body of men.[117]

The "Naren Babu incident," the government pointed out, "is not uncommon in local labour politics." Not infrequently it happened that
"some persons entirely unknown . . . even to the majority of workers
suddenly assume[d] leadership during a dispute."[118]

The truth of the government's statement is borne out by the case of
Prabhabati Das Gupta, the most important leader of the 1929 strike.
When the strike began, "Miss Das Gupta was entirely unknown" to
the "average jute mill worker."[119] Soon afterward, however, the government described her control over workers as "absolute." The workers called her "Mataji" or "Maiji" (Mother) and would go by whatever her wishes were. Das Gupta herself was only too aware of this. As
she once put it to the government, "she only has to lift her little finger
and the workers would obey." The government had "no doubt" that
this was true.[120] Das Gupta herself later recalled that "wherever I went
I was welcomed by the slogan *Mataji ki jai, Mataji ki jai* [Hail the
mother]. That was my reward."[121] And her rival trade unionist K. C.
Roy Chowdhury admitted in his diary that

> both male and female workers—at least those living in Kankinara,
> Titagarh and Champdany—looked upon Miss Das Gupta as their
> "Maiji" [mother]. They would do anything to carry out her or-

[115] Sarkar, *Swadeshi Movement*, p. 237.
[116] RCLI, vol. 5, pt. 1, p. 144.
[117] Ibid., pp. 144, 149, 276.
[118] Ibid., p. 144.
[119] Ibid., p. 150.
[120] Ibid., p. 149.
[121] Prabhabati Mirza (née Das Gupta), "Interview," p. 19.

ders, and would not even listen to any other organisers of her union.[122]

Mark how independent such authority was of "discipline" or organization; these principles would appear to be irrelevant to its mode of functioning. Indeed, one of the aphorisms that Das Gupta's friends sought to popularize among mill workers was, "Unions may come and unions may go but Dr. Prabhabati will remain for ever."[123] This is the important point for us: what has so far been viewed simply as an absence of trade union discipline or training reveals on closer inspection the presence of alternative systems of power and authority.

THE IDEAL, democratic principle of representation based on "voluntary" and "contractual" relationships was thus never realized in the trade unions of the Calcutta jute-mill workers, and representatives instead became masters. Unions were run as though they were the leaders' *zamindaris*. One could in fact go further and argue that in the eyes of the mill workers, being a master was a condition of being a representative. Only masters could represent. To see this purely as a function of the worker's ignorance is to overlook the necessarily two-sided character of the relationship. One is reminded of Hegel's discussion (in his *Phenomenology*) of the master-slave relationship, in which the master's dominance is dependent on the slave recognizing him as the master, that is to say, on the slave's will to serve. In referring to the *bhadralok* trade union leaders as "masters," then, we do not intend to portray the working class as a passive instrument of the leaders' will. At issue is the question of the worker's own will, his own consciousness, his shrewd realization that under the circumstances he could sometimes best exercise his power by choosing to serve. The relation, therefore, was pregnant with tension and had its own moments of resistance as well. One only has to remember that for all the loyalty the leaders could elicit from the workers, Prabhabati Das Gupta was once "abused and insulted" by a number of jute workers toward the end of the first general strike, that Latafat Hossain once had his union office burned down by a group of angry workers, and that Sibnath Banerjee was greeted by the workers in Howrah with suspicion and insults when he first approached them for votes in 1937.[124] These are only three instances of overt tension between the workers and their leaders.

[122] K.C.R.P., diary no. 3, entry under 25 August 1929 to 28 November 1929.
[123] RCLI, vol. 5, pt. 1, p. 148.
[124] See RCLI, vol. 5, pt. 1, p. 132; Momin, "Chatkal Sramiker," *Kalantar*, 10–12 August 1970; Sibnath Banerjee, unpublished memoirs.

Sumit Sarkar has rescued from the private papers of the *swadeshi* labor organizer A. C. Banerjee a very instructive letter that gives us some insight into the nature of the leader-worker relationship and tells us how the workers perceived the "oppression" they faced at work. Twenty-eight workers of the Budge Budge Jute Mills wrote to Banerjee in December 1906.[125] They had to "pay bribes to the babu and the sardar . . . every month and also when the Durga Puja season approache[d]"; refusal to pay bribes led to unjust fines or dismissal "on false charges of bad workmanship."

> Till recently [they added] we felt compelled to meet their unjust demands. But as prices ran very high last year at the time of Durga Puja, we expressed our intention to pay them a little less than in earlier years. At this the Head Sardar Haricharan Khanra has been going around instigating the Assistant Babu Atul Chandra Chattopadhyay to collect even more *parbani* [customary gifts] than usual. The two of them have even advised the in-charge Panchanan Ghose, a nice gentleman otherwise, to force us to pay a much larger *parbani* this year. When [in protest] we stopped paying any *parbani* whatsoever, they got the sahib to fine us on cooked up charges. . . . But, in truth, we are not guilty.

We have used this letter in the last chapter to document the nature of supervision in jute mills. I quote it once again to draw attention to some additional interesting features of this statement. It is clearly a statement of protest, expressing the workers' resentment of the oppression they suffered at work and their wish to see their oppressors punished. The "citation of names, exact locations, and people's . . . status" perform here the function of lending "an aura of verisimilitude" and empirical verifiability to the workers' complaints.[126]

The statement is also a long and detailed list of sufferings that the workers were keen to bring to the attention of a *bhadralok* trade unionist like Aswini Banerjee. Significantly, however, the workers who wrote the letter called it only "a brief description" and expressed their "desire to describe in even greater detail" their sufferings to Banerjee, if and when they met him in person. It is important to understand this "desire," for in it lies the nature of the relationship we are seeking to explore. Why did the workers want to display their sufferings to men

[125] Sumit Sarkar, "Swadeshi Yuger Sramik Andolan," pp. 113–115.

[126] Cf. La Fleur's discussion on the use of such details in medieval Japanese Buddhist texts. William R. La Fleur, *The Karma of Words: Buddhism and the Literary Arts in Medieval Japan* (Berkeley, 1983), p. 47. My attention was drawn to this book by Rajyashree Pandey.

like Banerjee, to give such "cruel publicity" to the pains their bosses inflicted on them? What is the relationship invoked, and indeed established, by such a display?

The poor man making a spectacle of his sufferings, and thus obtaining the compassion and assistance of the rich, was, and still is, a familiar sight in societies marked by precapitalist cultures.[127] This was true of medieval Europe, where, as Huizinga said, "lepers sounded their rattles and went about in procession, [and] beggars exhibited their deformities."[128] And it is still so in Calcutta today.[129] The Budge Budge Jute Mills workers quoted above were engaged in a similar exercise. The long and detailed description of their sufferings was at once a manipulative act and a statement of helplessness, aimed at securing the support and aid of resourceful others in their struggle against poverty and oppression. They obviously saw Aswini Banerjee, a barrister and trade unionist, as a powerful *babu* who would respond to the plight of the "coolie" only if his compassion was sufficiently aroused. Characteristically, therefore, this is how they ended their letter to Banerjee: "We write to you about the oppressive acts of our superiors at work and pray for an urgent redress. We hope you will save us soon from their despotism."

This general aspect of the precapitalist relationship between the rich and the poor would thus appear to have constituted an important strand in the tradition that molded the culture of trade unionism in colonial Calcutta. In the absence of a better name, let us call this the "*babu*-coolie" relationship insofar as it could be seen to exist in the practice of trade unionism. One is indeed struck by the number of

[127] Cf. Michel Foucault, *The Birth of the Clinic: An Archaeology of Medical Perception*, trans A. M. Sheridan Smith (New York, 1975), p. 84: "Can pain be a spectacle? Not only can it be, but it must be, by virtue of a subtle right that resides in the fact that no one is alone, the poor man less so than others, so that he can obtain assistance only through the mediation of the rich . . . if others intervene with their knowledge, their resources, their pity."

[128] H. Huizinga, *The Waning of the Middle Ages* (London, 1949), p. 1.

[129] See, for instance, Jan Breman, "The Bottom of the Urban Order in Asia: Impressions of Calcutta," *Development and Change*, vol. 14, no. 2, April 1983, p. 159: "The cripples of all kinds who appear with great regularity in this scenario strengthen the Brecht-like effect. The procession of the limping, the hunchbacked, the hydrocephalitic, of those with paralysed or other deformed limbs, will not be entirely unknown to those who grew up before the coming of the welfare state. But even they will never have encountered creatures who, with hardly more than half a body and with only the most primitive means of support, crawl or trundle themselves through the streets, Brecht making place for Breughel. It is a bewildering spectacle from which it is impossible to escape." See also Claude Lévi-Strauss, *Tristes Tropiques* (Harmondsworth, 1973), pp. 169–170.

times the relationship surfaces in the middle of working-class protest
and trade union activities. The terrain is admittedly difficult for the
historian, and not only because the jute workers were predominantly
nonliterate. The written word that the historian relies on is in itself a
rather poor conveyor of this relationship, since it usually presents only
a fragment of reality.[130] In real life, however, as any Bengali would
know, the *babu*-coolie relationship would have been represented many
times over in many different ways: in manners of speech and dress, in
body language expressive of hierarchy, indeed, in the entire range of
the semiotics of domination and subordination (and hence resistance)
that the culture would have made available to both the jute-mill
worker and his *bhadralok* trade union representative. Although much
of this would normally escape the historian's attention, a careful inter-
rogation of the available documents yields considerable evidence of the
existence of this feudal bond between the *babu* and the coolie.

The historian, for instance, does not have to strain his ears to catch
"the voice of the poor" in the clamor of protests that went up in the
Calcutta jute mills from time to time. Echoes reverberate even in the
most elitist of sources. "In those days, i.e. about 1922–23," writes
K. C. Roy Chowdhury in his diaries,

> the workers preferred rich people as their [trade union] leaders.
> They were pleased to see the leaders come to meetings in their own
> motor cars. They had the mistaken idea that only the rich could
> successfully fight [for them] with the wealthy and big millowners.
> The *sardars* thought that trade union leaders who were themselves
> big advocates or barristers would fight for them in the court of
> law, free of charge.[131]

K. C. Roy Chowdhury called himself in his diaries "A Friend of the
Workers," but it is interesting to see how in his imagination the figure
of the worker merged with that of the poor. For all his enthusiasm for
socialism and strikes,[132] the working class is often transformed in his
prose into *daridra Narayan*, the Hindu god Narayan in the shape of

[130] "Writing is inescapably distinct" is how Roland Barthes put it in his *Image-Music-Text*, trans. S. Heath (Glasgow, 1979), p. 89, n. 2. See also the interesting discussion on analog and digital processes of communication in Anthony Wilden, *System and Structure: Essays in Communication and Exchange* (London, 1972).

[131] K.C.R.P., Bengali diary no. 3, entry under 7 April 1923.

[132] Roy Chowdhury wrote a Bengali play called *Dharmaghat* (The strike) in 1926 and thus described it in his old age when he considered making it into a film: "Kindly read it and note its objective—Socialistic propaganda, 21 years before Independence when very vew people had any idea of the subject." K.C.R.P., letter to J. P. Banerjee, 27 June 1959.

the poor.[133] The working class or even "socialism" could all be served from the standpoint of "pity." The sentiment was well expressed by a fictitious character called Mrs. Guha (presumably modeled on the contemporary trade unionist Santosh Kumari Gupta) in Roy Chowdhury's play *Dharmaghat* (The strike) when she remarked, "Poor workers! There is not a single soul to listen to their complaints and tales of woe."[134]

"After all it was helping the poor people," said Prabhabati Das Gupta, reminiscing in old age about the first general strike of jute-mill workers, which forced the mill owners and the state alike in 1929 to recognize her as the workers' representative. "We were not doing trade union movement, we were helping the poor people." "So," she asked, explaining the absence of trade union membership and subscription, "why should we have money from them?"[135] One may choose to dismiss this evidence as rationalization with hindsight, or see it only as an instance of the mellowing, with age, of a once-radical spirit. But what does one do when the *babu*-coolie relationship comes refracting through the practice of trade unionism even at the height of working-class protest? The leaflets put out by the leaders of the Bengal Jute Workers Union during the 1929 strike illustrate the point. True, they spoke of "oppression in the jute mills," of the worker's labor filling "the bellies of the rich," described "truth and right" as being on the worker's side, and recommended organization and unity.[136] Yet their language was densely inhabited by the *babu*'s stereotype and assumptions regarding the coolie's helplessness and ignorance.

Brethren—This is a very critical time.... So beware! It is said that some pleader has advised to the effect that your wages would be realized by action in the court. You are very simple folks, so you have been enmeshed in the plan of an ordinary pleader.... Ask the pleader to mention this matter to us, we shall give him the right answer.[137]

Necessarily, then, at the other end of the relationship stood the leader in her larger-than-life-size appearance: "Mother Provabati," "Mataji," "the father and mother of the poor," as she was described in her

[133] Even a casual reading of his diaries would confirm this point.
[134] K. C. Roy Chowdhury, *Dharmaghat* (Calcutta, 1926), p. 45; Chattopadhyay, *Santoshkumari*, p. 16.
[135] Prabhabati Mirza (née Das Gupta), "Interview," pp. 18–19.
[136] RCLI, vol. 5, pt. 1, pp. 159–160.
[137] Ibid.

union's pamphlets.[138] Wherever she went she was "welcomed by the slogan *Mataji ki jai.*" "That was my reward," she said, the reward of the dominant: "Practically, the whole of labour was under *my* control."[139] By now we know this voice: the representative invariably turned out to be a master, since only masters could represent.

"INVARIABLY?" one may still object. "Your examples so far have been A. C. Banerjee, K. C. Roy Chowdhury, and Prabhabati Das Gupta, people who were themselves somewhat elitist in their own minds. What about the generation of socialists and communists who followed them, men who tried to become one with the workers instead of wanting to dominate them, men who won the leadership of the jute workers' struggles in the 1930s and the 1940s, and whose faith in socialist ideologies remained unflinching to the very end of their lives?"

Before proceeding to answer our hypothetical interlocutor, let us fully acknowledge the transformation that socialist ideologies brought about in the Bangali *bhadralok*'s understanding of the problems of the working classes in Bengal. In the nineteenth century the *bhadralok* viewed the working classes as a problem of morality, and the blame for some of the social problems created by the growth of factories fell squarely on the workers themselves. This moralism had two expressions, one kind and concerned, the other cruel and indifferent toward the working poor. More often than not, workers experienced only the latter version of middle-class morality. A notable exception to this, however, was the Brahmo Samaj social reformer Sasipada Banerjee, active in Baranagar between the years 1866 and 1875. Banerjee reflected a middle-class desire to see an improvement in working-class morals. Significant among his achievements were a night school for workers that he opened in 1869, a workingmen's club started in 1870, a savings bank and an anna bank (modeled on penny banks in England) established in 1871, and the launching in 1874 of *Bharat Shramajibi* (The Indian workingman), often regarded as the first labor journal produced in India. Banerjee was also active in the temperance movement of the 1860s and 1870s.[140]

Underlying all of Banerjee's efforts was a kind but morally self-righteous attitude. His aim was to develop among the laboring poor the

[138] Ibid., p. 411.

[139] Prabhabati Mirza (née Das Gupta), "Interview," pp. 11–12, 18–19. Emphasis added.

[140] For a detailed discussion of Banerjee's activities, see my "Sasipada Banerjee: A Study in the Nature of the First Contact of the Bengali Bhadralok with the Working Classes of Bengal," *Indian Historical Review*, January 1976, pp. 339–364.

habits of thrift, industry, and temperance, the vitues of which were constantly preached in the *Bharat Shramajibi*, which itself was seen by Banerjee as a "means of improving the moral and intellectual conditions of the working classes."[141] To Banerjee, or his mentor, Miss Mary Carpenter of Bristol, the worker's poverty, ill health, or inadequate housing always pointed to the weakness of the worker's moral fabric, for did not "good and regular wages"—as Mary Carpenter was to put it to her Indian followers in 1866—always lead the poor to "vicious indulgences" unless checked by the efforts of those "who desire[d] to advance social reform"?[142] Writing to Carpenter in 1867, Banerjee expressed his own wish to see "the workingmen develop into good husbands, affectionate fathers and peaceful neighbours" (attributes they obviously lacked in the eyes of the *bhadralok*) and later measured the success of his activities in these morally loaded terms. An article published in 1880 in *Bharat Shramajibi* described a group of workers as "former bad characters" who had been transformed into "complete gentlemen [*bhadralok*] by the care which Babu Sasipada Bandyopadhyay took of them."[143]

The influence of mid-Victorian ideas on Brahmo Samaj social reformers like Banerjee are obvious and I have discussed the point in greater detail in my article mentioned above. These ideas, however, did not survive the process of transplantation and took no root in the Bengali soil. The institutions Banerjee built up were reduced to an ephemeral existence during his own lifetime. Banerjee, and the narrow band of social reformers to which he belonged, thus represented the kinder, but also the rarer, side of the moralism that colored the *bhadralok*'s perception of the laboring classes. It was far more common in the nineteenth century to see laborers simply as a social nuisance, an "annoyance," as a police report of 1896 put it, to "the quiet people" of the middle classes. The same report carried several references to *bhadralok* complaints regarding the "unruly," "noisy," and "rowdy" character of the mill workers.[144] Toward the end of the century, as industries expanded and Bengali laborers were replaced by migrants from Bihar and the United Provinces, the middle-class moral view of the working class was reinforced by the addition of the traditional contempt that the *bhadralok* had for the *merua*, a derisive Bengali term for any native speaker of Hindi. A poem written about the turn of the century by a Bengali Brahman schoolteacher—who lived in Bhatpara and saw that

[141] Kuladaprasad Mullick, *Nabajuger Sadhana* (Calcutta, 1913), pp. 186–187.
[142] Chakrabarty, "Sasipada Banerjee," p. 347.
[143] Ibid., p. 358.
[144] W.B.S.A., Judicial Dept. Police Br., January 1896, A6–11.

sleepy village change beyond recognition with the establishment of jute
mills and municipal offices, and with the influx of migrant laborers—
will illustrate this well. The poem is unremarkable for its literary qualities but captures in its bluntness the essence of the *bhadralok* perception of an immigrant and indigent working class:

> Well done, Bhatpara Municipality!
> Gone are the old jungles and bamboo-groves
> Of Kankinara and Jagaddal,
> Their places taken by palaces and bazars,
> Slums of *meruas*, factories and their sprouting
>   chimneys.
> The bazars now bustle with the ghostly *meruas*
> Buying and selling in their strange Hindi.
> On holidays,
> They loaf about the town in groups,
> Drunk,
> Singing songs that sound like the howl of dogs.[145]

It would be tedious and unrewarding to list here the racial and social
prejudices of the Bengali *bhadralok*; suffice it to say that the importation of socialist ideas, however vague, did much to change many of
these consciously held attitudes. There developed a new ideological interest in the working people in the 1920s, and it became a common
practice to use words like *worker* or *labor* (or their Bengali or Hindi
translations *sramajibi, sramik, mazdur*) in naming middle-class organizations and journals. The existence in the 1920s and later of parties
like the Labour Swaraj party (1925), the Workers and Peasants party
(1928), and the Labour party (1932) testifies to this new ideological
development in the *bhadralok* political scene.[146] By the late 1920s
some of this spirit had even spilled over into the sacred world of Bengali literature. Tagore's irritated comment in 1928–29—"Do we enter
a 'new era' in literature simply because so many writers [today] write
about the coal-miner or the *panwali*?"—celebrates this new presence
of the working class, if only negatively.[147]

[145] Ramanuja Vidyarnava, "Bhattapalli Gatha," in his *Kanthamala* (Bhatpara, c. 1913).

[146] The straightforward history of these parties and the journals (e.g., *Sramik, Sra-majibi,* and *Naya Mazdur*) they brought out is relatively well known and well docu-mented. Two interesting analytical accounts of the period are Roger Stuart, "The For-mation of the Communist Party of India, 1927–1937: The Dilemma of the Indian Left," Ph.D. thesis, Australian National University, 1978, and Sarkar, "National Movement."

[147] Tagore quoted in Sajanikanta Das, *Atmasmriti* (Calcutta, 1978), p. 197.

To the Bengali *bhadralok*, the workers still presented a picture of moral degeneration, but in contrast to the nineteenth-century view, this "degeneration" was now assigned a cause (largely economic) outside the worker's own morality and consciousness. The jute-mill worker, the *Amrita Bazar Patrika* said in 1928, was "something less than a human being," but this condition was not of his own doing. This was a significant departure from the point of view of, say, Sasipada Banerjee. "The modern industrial system" and the greed of the capitalist were now seen as the "cause" of the worker's moral problems:

> Condemned to life in slums . . . working long hours in closed and stuffy atmosphere and victims of all allurements held out by easily available grog and drug shops, and . . . deprived of the humanising influence of family life, he [the jute worker] is converted into something less than a human being. . . . [This] condition of life . . . is incidental to the modern industrial system generally but . . . in very few industries the disproportion between profits and wages is so striking as in this [the jute industry].[148]

The same understanding informed K. C. Roy Chowdhury's play *Dharmaghat* (The strike), which was staged in Calcutta in 1926. The "moral degradation" of the worker and the "stinking, unhealthy hovels around the jute mills at Naihati" are explained in this play in terms of capitalist neglect and exploitation. "It is in the interests of the rich capitalist to treat the workers like beasts," says Shirish, who is by no means a radical character in the play.[149]

On this ideological ground was bred in the twenties and thirties a generation of *bhadralok* politicians whose commitment to their own ideological construct, the working class, was beyond question. Gopen Chakravarty, a Moscow-returned communist, gave a dramatic demonstration of the commitment in 1926 when he joined a jute mill in Bhatpara "as a machineman in the steam room at Rs 14 a month."

> Even this was not enough [he said in an interview]—so I rented a small cubicle in the jute line and lived with the workers . . . and told [them] . . . stories about [the] Russian revolution, Lenin and workers' raj, I also read out news from *Pratap* run by Ganesh Shankar Vidyarthi and also from our *Ganavani*.[150]

[148] *Amrita Bazar Patrika*, 31 October 1928.
[149] Roy Chowdhury, *Dharmaghat*, p. 6.
[150] "Interview," in Chattopadhyay, *Communism*, vol. 1, p. 135.

Gopen Chakravarty was not alone in showing such exemplary zeal for organizing the working class. Much of the political experience of the Bengali left in the 1930s and afterward can be written up—and indeed it has been—as stories of the heroism and courage of men like Chakravarty. The impact of their commitment and activities is to be felt in the politics of West Bengal even today. "The memory haunts," as a sensitive Bengali intellectual has recently written,

> the memory of early dreams, oaths devoutly undertaken, careers forsaken, temptations thrust aside. For those who took to socialism, there was . . . a question of acute choice, one's convictions cut athwart one's class interests. They gladly made the transition. Forsaking homes and old loyalties, they fanned into the countryside to organise the poor peasants [and] pioneered the trade union movement in Greater Calcutta's jute belt.[151]

Yet I will insist that even these people, for all their sacrifice and commitment, remained imprisoned in the *babu*-coolie relationship insofar as the nature of their contract with the working class was concerned. Let me demonstrate this by analyzing a document that was authored by the very same people as our hypothetical interlocutor referred to, the committed, self-sacrificing, socialist-minded organizers of labor.

In January 1937 the manager of the Fort Gloster Jute Mill came upon a leaflet going around among his workers who were soon to vote in the coming provincial elections.[152] This was the first time that the Bengal Legislative Assembly would have its labor members elected and not nominated. The leaflet in question aimed at persuading the workers to vote for Sibnath Banerjee. Banerjee, a Socialist, was then the president of the All India Trade Union Congress. His candidacy was supported by the Communist party and the Congress, and he actually won the election.

The document, therefore, was about representation. It asked the workers to elect *their* representative. A crucial task before the authors of the leaflet was to prove this identity of the representative with the class he would represent. Here, of course, there was an obvious problem. Banerjee was a member of the *bhadralok* community and therefore a *babu*. And so were the other contestants. How then could he represent the "coolies," and why was his claim in this regard better than anybody else's?

---

[151] Ashok Mitra, "The Burnt-Out Cases," in his *Calcutta Diary* (London, 1976), p. 9.
[152] The leaflet is reproduced in W.B.S.A., Home Poll. Confdl. no. 484/1937.

Faced with these problems, the leaflet began by introducing a real/false distinction between "representatives" of labor.

> Friends, if we are to have [our] . . . grievances redressed, we must make, on the one hand, all the labour organisations more powerful, and on the other . . . see that the *real* labour representatives are sent to the Council. . . . Friends, you will be glad to know that there are eight seats for the Labour constituency. For these eight seats, if we can send *real* representatives of labour . . . then their interests are safeguarded.

But how could a *babu* become a "real" representative of the "coolie"? More important, how would he make this "reality" *visible* to the worker when all the usual signs of *bhadralok* existence set him apart from the working class? Our leaflet's answer was this: by suffering himself, by making "sacrifices" in the interests of the workers. "Real" representatives are "men who have *devoted* their lives for the welfare of labourers."

> To safeguard the interest of labourers, Comrade Banerjee has been to prison for many times. He was one of the accused in the Meerut Conspiracy case, and was in the lock-up for 2½ years, but [was] afterwards honorably acquitted. A few days back he was fined Rs. 200/- by the . . . High Court for delivering speeches to the Calcutta Corporation workers. From the above facts it is evident that there is nobody like Comrade Banerjee for upholding the cause of the labourers. If there is any man with *real* sympathy for the labourers, then it is . . . Comrade Banerjee.

The point was also made in another leaflet published on behalf of Sibnath Banerjee. The second leaflet too "quoted and glorified the sentences of imprisonment and fines that had been passed on him," and then asked the laborers, "I have been prepared to suffer this for your sake, am I not the man for you?"[153]

So the display of "sacrifice," a demonstration of the willingness to share the poor man's suffering, was what made Banerjee better qualified to represent the workers. The claim to being a "real" representative of the working class was thus based, in this argument, on the respect traditionally given in Indian society to the figure of the renouncer. It was a moral claim that arose from an ancient system of morality. The rhetoric of Indian politics, irrespective of political ideology, is replete with instances of this notion of "sacrifice" (or "renun-

---

[153] W.B.S.A., Home Poll. Confdl. no. 72/1937. Emphasis added throughout.

ciation") acting as the source of a moral claim on popular allegiance. Consider, for example, a piece of journalism written in 1920 in support of Gandhi. Its similarities to the "socialist" leaflet we have discussed above are obvious:

> Oh you voters of the Gorakhpur Division! . . . Who is your genuine well wisher? Gandhi . . . or those who are now . . . begging your votes? . . . Cast your eyes towards Mahatma Gandhi. This pure soul has sacrificed everything for you. . . . He has taken the vow of renunciation, gone to jail and [endured] . . . many a difficulty and suffering.[154]

There was in fact very little in common between this morality of "renunciation" and the "rationality" inherent in the Leninist theory of representation. As would be well known to any reader of *What Is to Be Done?* (1902), the Leninist "representative" based his claim to represent the working class, not on moral grounds, but on his (supposed) access to superior, "scientific" knowledge (i.e. theory) that was denied to workers by their own conditions.

Besides, an appeal to the idea of sacrifice was really an appeal to the power that flowed from inequality. In order to be able to make sacrifices, one needed to possess; he who did not possess could not sacrifice. The glory of the renouncer belonged to the "possessor." To talk of sacrifice was thus to talk of possessions, and hence of power. In the leaflet under discussion, the authors needed to underscore as it were just "how much" Banerjee had given up to become a "real" representative of the workers. So they told the workers:

> Sibnath is an educated man and has been to Europe, and for the last ten years he has been serving the labourers, leaving many high posts formerly occupied by him. Friends, please vote for Sibnath without any hesitation.

But an "educated man" who "has been to Europe" and had held "many high posts" was not a coolie or a worker but a *babu*. And the logic of identification-through-sacrifice ends up making this clear. The discourse thus silently subverted from within its own claims about democratic representation, and the *babu*-coolie relationship reap-

---

[154] *Swadesh*, 11 November 1920, cited in Shahid Amin, "Gandhi as Mahatma: Gorakhpur District, Eastern U.P., 1921–22," in Ranajit Guha, ed., *Subaltern Studies III: Writings on South Asian History and Society* (Delhi, 1984), p. 15. See also Partha Chatterjee, "Gandhi and the Critique of Civil Society," ibid., pp. 153–195. On *renunciation* see Louis Dumont, "World Renunciation in Indian Religion," *Contributions to Indian Sociology*, no. 4, 1960, pp. 33–62.

peared in the very act meant to cause its disappearance. Gopen Chakravarty, the Moscow-returned Communist mentioned earlier, may have thought that the workers accepted him as "one of them," but they still called him the "Union *Babu*."[155] So it is not surprising that in spite of his ideology and sacrifices—in fact precisely because of his sacrifices—Sibnath Banerjee's union assumed no "organisational form" for years and remained an "out and out one man show," his *zamindari*. Even a "real" representative turned out to be a master.

SINCE we do not mean to suggest that the Bengali followers of Lenin were insincere people who made cynical use of the concept of "sacrifice" only in order to manipulate the "ignorant" workers, we need to ask another question: Why was a hierarchical idea steeped in precapitalist morality so central to a discourse that was self-consciously socialist?

There was clearly more at work here than historians have cared to admit or explore. The solution to the paradox of jute workers' organization is usually sought in economic (or "structural") explanations or in arguments about political repression by the colonial state. Yet, surely, no amount of economic reasoning or evidence of state repression will ever explain why even the socialist message of democratic representation was ultimately translated and assimilated into the undemocratic, hierarchical terms of the *babu*-coolie relationship; nor will they tell us why Banerjee's pamphlet addressed to the working class spoke so compulsively of his education, overseas trips, and "successful" career.

Perhaps a helpful distinction to make here would be between political ideology, a body of conscious ideas (like Marxism), and culture, the "signifying system through which necessarily a social order is communicated, reproduced, experienced and explored."[156] Ideologically, the Bengali left was committed to developing trade unions based on the democratic, contractual, and voluntary procedures of organization that their theory of trade unionism entailed. In the culture of everyday life, however, they, as *babus*, related to the coolies through a hierarchy of status. Their education, their appearance, the language they spoke, the work they did, could all act as indicators of their authority and superiority over the coolies. The deployment of a system of *visible* markers that divided people into hierarchical categories of status and

---

[155] Chakravorty, "Interview," p. 135.

[156] Raymond Williams, *Culture* (Glasgow, 1981), p. 10. I may mention that I find Göran Therborn's attempt to do away with this distinction rather unhelpful. See Göran Therborn, *The Ideology of Power and the Power of Ideology* (London, 1980).

power had always been an important function of the culture to which they, the *bhadralok*, and the workers belonged. "The working people," said Sasipada Banerjee in the nineteenth century, "are in this country held as low, and as not important members of the society."[157] Years later, a young Sibnath Banerjee was to find the "tattered clothes, bare feet, dirty appearance and the foul language" of the jute-mill workers positively offensive to his *bhadralok* sensibilities.[158] The *bhadralok* clerks of the Burn Iron Works in Howrah staged a historic walkout in September 1905 when the management asked them to record their attendance by the same "new mechanical system" as the coolies were required to use.[159] An attempt in 1923 by the Scottish manager of the Anglo-Indian Jute Mill to hold a meeting of all of his employees to discuss a welfare scheme met with a similar fate. "The babus . . . refused to come to the same meeting as coolies, even if the latter sat on the floor."[160]

It was these culturally given relationships of power that entered the field of trade unionism. In terms of their theory, the Bengali trade unionists no doubt aspired to build bourgeois-democratic organizations. In reality, however, they formed organizations based on "loyalty," where authority did not flow through a grid of rules and procedures but derived directly from hierarchy and status. Indrajit Gupta, the CPI trade unionist, was honest enough to admit this in 1952. "Ever since he can remember," said Gupta, "the jute worker has understood by 'union' nothing more than an office situated outside the mill and some union '*babus*' whose job is to write occasional petitions and hold gate, bustee or mass meetings."[161]

By refusing to see these obvious signs of the feudal concerns of their own, everyday culture, and by seeing the cultural only as an instance of the economic, the Bengali left remained trapped, ironically enough, within the same culture they would have liked to have seen destroyed. Ideology, in this case, was not enough to erase the ties of power encoded in the culture. These ties derived from an older paradigm of power, and if we are to talk about a paradox in the history of jute workers' organization, then this is where the paradox has to be located: at the disjuncture between a radical ideology and a hierarchical culture.

[157] Chakrabarty, "Sasipada Banerjee," p. 346.
[158] Centre for Studies in Social Sciences, Calcutta, S. Banerjee, Interview transcript dated 19 July 1975, p. 1.
[159] Sarkar, *Swadeshi Movement*, pp. 200, 202.
[160] W.B.S.A., Com. Dept. Com. Br., April 1923, B77.
[161] Gupta, *Capital and Labour*, p. 54.

· 5 ·

PROTEST AND
AUTHORITY

"There was no organization. Yet there was a great struggle. How indeed could that ever happen?" Abdul Momin reflected on this question in 1970 as he thought back to the stormy days of 1929 when he, as a young radical trade unionist, took a prominent role in conducting the first general strike of the Calcutta jute workers.[1] In asking this question, Momin raised an important issue: How indeed does one understand a case of working-class militancy that does not flow from, or result in, organization? Historians often seek to answer this question in terms of the material conditions of the workers. "Grievances," "demands," and "living standards" form the stuff of their analyses. I, however, shall argue here that to understand the nature of jute workers' militancy, one will have to look at the relationships of power and authority within the mills, for it was in these relationships that "the will to protest" was rooted. This becomes clear if we examine an important feature of jute workers' protest: the ever-present tendency toward physical and personal violence directed against the authorities.

By *authorities*, I refer to the managers and their European superintendents, called assistants or European assistants, in the jute mills. They, as we know, were mostly Scotsmen from Dundee and its neighborhood; a *Handbook and Guide to Dundee and District* published in 1912 reported that "the overseers, managers and mechanics in the Indian jute mills [were] almost wholly recruited from Dundee."[2] I overlook here whatever complexities may have characterized relationships *within* the managerial hierarchy in a mill. I also overlook, in this chapter, the special role of the *sardars*, who occupied a gray zone between management and labor. I include them in my category of "workers," and thus ignore the complex relations between the *sardars* and ordinary workers below them (see chapter 3). One reason for doing this is that in instances of protests the workers were often led by the *sardars* themselves.

[1] Abdul Momin, "Chatkal Sramiker Pratham Sadharan Dharmaghat," *Kalantar*, 10 August 1970.
[2] British Association, Dundee, *Handbook and Guide to Dundee and District* (Dundee, 1912), p. 118. See also, *RCLI*, vol. 5, pt. 1, p. 265.

CHAPTER 5

Let me begin with some typical cases of working-class protest in the 1890s.

In 1895 there was a riot at the Kankinara Jute Mill after the manager had refused a wage increase. The manager "narrowly escaped," though "Iron bolts &c., were thrown at him and his house was attacked." Next year in the Baranagar Jute Mill, spinners, demanding increased wages, "surrounded the Manager and the Spinning Master . . . assaulted an Indian clerk and showered brickbats into the mill premises."[3] Muslim "coolies" at the Kamarhatty Jute Mill were refused leave on the Id day in 1895. They responded by striking the "Manager and the durwans" (gatekeepers, armed retainers) by throwing brickbats at them.[4] The same year Hindu workers of a mill at Titaghur protested in a similar way when they were not allowed leave on the day of the Annapurna Puja (a Hindu religious festival). The manager was beaten up, as well as the police who came to save him.[5]

Two very well known instances of labor protest in these years were an 1895 strike at the Budge Budge Jute Mill and an 1899 strike at the Bauria Cotton Mill. Regarding the former, an *Amrita Bazar Patrika* report ran as follows:

> On Tuesday last [June 1895] . . . a serious riot took place at Budge Budge. Nearly seven thousand labourers of the Budge Budge Jute Mills mustered in the vicinity of the bungalow, where European employees of the mill reside. It appears that the labourers fell out with their Sirdar and proposed to strike if his services were not dispensed with. The mill authorities declining to accede to the prayer, the labourers in a body assembled and broke down the panels of the bungalow by pelting stones and brickbats. The Europeans fired on the mob . . . along with two police constables . . . a durwan of the mills . . . has been assaulted by the mob.[6]

The Bauria Cotton Mill disturbance was caused by the reelers, who for some time past had been pressing for a wage increase. This refused, the reelers struck work and the manager issued a notice closing down the mill. The events that followed are described by the manager, A. M. Downs.

---

[3] W.B.S.A., Judicial Dept. Police Br., January 1896 A6–11.

[4] See Ranajit Das Gupta, "Material Conditions and Behavioural Aspects of Calcutta Working Class, 1875-1899," Occasional Paper 22, Centre for Studies in Social Sciences, Calcutta, January 1979, p. 97.

[5] *Indian Daily News*, 5 April 1895, quoted in ibid., p. 97.

[6] Quoted in Sukomal Sen, *Working Class of India: History of Emergence and Movement, 1830–1970* (Calcutta, 1977), p. 83.

Soon after the reelers to the number of 2-300 surrounded the mill office with threats to murder me . . . [Downs quickly collected four European officers around him]. I told them [the officers] that . . . being 5 Europeans together they [workers] would leave us alone. I immediately left the office. We were surrounded and one man took me by the shirt front and demanded his wage. I . . . told him to clear out. I then had a blow on the right shoulder. When this took place I clubbed my umbrella and cleared a space around me, and one man received the blow on the body and smashed the umbrella. This was the only weapon in the hands of the Europeans. We were attacked by bamboos, brickbats and parts of the machines broken by workers for this purpose.[7]

The manager and the assistants eventually used gunfire but were themselves also rather badly hurt: "One of my Assistants [Downs said] had his topi smashed; another lost his; mine was knocked off and my head cut open with a brickbat, the blood covering my clothes."

The details of such incidents are obviously bloodstained, but they help to underscore one point. Irrespective of their demands, working-class protest against mill authorities frequently contained a strong element of vengeance in it. In many of these protests, violence was directed personally at the manager, his European assistants, the *durwans*, and when they were inaccessible, their houses and mill property.

It is this element of personal violence that has prompted the author of a recent study of the nineteenth-century Calcutta working class to describe these protests as exhibiting "a somewhat primitive defiance of authority."[8] The operative word here is *primitive* and a little reflection on it may help us in defining the perspective of this chapter. In what sense was the jute-mill workers' defiance of authority "primitive?" Destruction of mill property and "physical violence against the employers," it is said in the study in question, "reminds us in some ways of the Luddites."[9] This reference to the Luddites suggests two connotations for the word *primitive*. It could refer to a particular period in the history of working-class protest in Bengal (presumably the early years of industrialization). On the other hand, it may have an ahistorical status and could refer to an implicit (since this is never spelt out in the text under consideration) and a priori classification of forms of protest into some "lower" and "higher" types. In fact a conflation of both

[7] W.B.S.A., Judicial Dept. Police Br., December 1899 A22–9.
[8] Das Gupta, "Material Conditions," p. 141.
[9] Ibid., pp. 30, 32.

these senses—the old-new and the lower-higher oppositions—is suggested in the way the study contrasts the working-class protests of the 1890s with those of the 1870s and 1880s. Note for instance the use of words like *transcend* and *new*: "the miniature-scale deputations, 'mobbings', strikes, violent troubles [of the 1890s] . . . revealed that they [the workers] were trying to *transcend* the blind, individualistic, instinctive forms of reaction and to find *new*, more powerful and effective forms of protest."[10] *Primitive* then also seems to imply here "blind, individualistic, instinctive forms of reaction."

Now there are serious historical and theoretical problems involved in looking at the history of working-class protest in Bengal in terms of a preconceived hierarchy of "stages," based essentially on the peculiar historical experience of England. Space will not permit a fuller treatment of the question here.[11] But this chapter will seek to demonstrate that the metaphors of "primitiveness," "instinct," and "blindness" are unfortunate in the present context. They do not help us to understand *why* working-class protest in the Calcutta jute mills was frequently marked by a strong degree of physical violence or personal vengeance. It will be argued here that we do not understand a particular expression of defiance until we have examined the particular forms of manifestation of the "authority" that is under challenge. The way the mill worker chose to register his protest had something to do with the way he related to authority. Far from being "blind," it depended on how he actually saw authority.

Employment of personal violence and vengeance against managers was not just a nineteenth-century phenomenon in Calcutta. It characterized much of working-class protest in the twentieth century as well. For instance, at the Birla Jute Mill in Budge Budge, one day in March 1937, when strikers from a neighboring mill came in a procession, waving red flags, and "paraded in front of the mill," the spinners got out "in a body" and "assaulted the European Engineer."[12] The manager of the Kankinara Jute Mill was "assaulted" in another case of labor protest in January 1937.[13] Later in the year in June, again, as he was "remonstrating" with the spinners for "disobeying mill regula-

[10] Ibid., p. 149. Emphasis added.

[11] I have discussed some of these problems in a larger critique of Das Gupta's paper. My critique and Das Gupta's reply are available in "Some Aspects of Labour History in Bengal in the Nineteenth Century: Two Views," Occasional Paper 40, Centre for Studies in Social Sciences, Calcutta, October 1981. See also chap. 7.

[12] W.B.S.A., Home Poll. Confdl. no. 128/1937, Pt. 3.

[13] Ibid.

tions," he was "suddenly hit by a bobbin."[14] A note from the district magistrate of the 24 Parganas said:

> Yesterday's trouble arose when an Assistant Manager warned one of the operatives for bad work. He refused to obey the Assistant Manager's orders and [said that] he must have the Manager's orders. The Manager then came to the spot and upheld the Assistant Manager's orders. The man refused to obey and was then asked to leave. He refused to do so and struck the Manager on the head with a bobbin. A number of other operatives also threw bobbins at the Manager and [the] Assistant Manager.[15]

A strike caused by a reduction of staff at the Northbrook Jute Mill in December 1937 featured a similar kind of violence. "The mill hands," a government report said, "were excited." They "became rowdy . . . and indulged in rough play by throwing bobbins—one spinner being rather badly hurt."[16] In July 1939 the weavers of the Samnugger Jute Mill "attacked the European Officers inside the mill in a body" over what the police thought was "a trifling matter" and assaulted them, damaging some mill property too in the process.[17] In August of the same year the weavers of the India Jute Mill "assaulted the manager and two European Assistants," according to the police report, "without any provocation."[18] Earlier in 1936, a strike in Hukumchand Jute Mill on 9 April was marked by working-class violence, whereby "four Europeans were injured" and a *durwan* killed.[19] Even when there was no actual physical violence against the manager, there was always a possibility of this occurring. There was a strike in May 1937 at the Khardah Jute Mill, caused by the dismissal of a few spinners. No violence was seen in this case, but the management handed over to the police "some iron bars" that had been found with the spinners and the police thought that "this trouble . . . might [have] led to an outbreak of violence."[20]

In case all my illustrations should appear to come from the 1930s, here is the text of a telegram that the Bengal government sent to Delhi, regarding a "riot" at Anglo-Indian Jute Mill on 18 May 1926:

[14] W.B.S.A., Home Poll. Confdl. no. 484/1937.
[15] W.B.S.A., Home Poll. Confdl. no. 128/1937.
[16] W.B.S.A., Home Poll. Confdl. no. 60/1937.
[17] W.B.S.A., Home Poll. Confdl. no. 446/1939.
[18] Ibid.
[19] W.B.S.A., Government of Bengal, "Fortnightly Confidential Reports on Political Situation in Bengal, First Half of January to Second Half of June 1936."
[20] W.B.S.A., Home Poll. Confdl. no. 128/1937, Pt 3.

Mill hands demanded increased wages and attacked [Manager's] office. Outside crowd broke in mill gates and pushed European Assistants to their quarters. The European Assistants who are members of auxiliary force fired nine shots in air with service rifles and dispersed crowd.[21]

Such examples could be multiplied. The manager of the Bally Jute Mill "went to surprise the workers of the weaving department" one day in June 1926. He was immediately "attacked by 260 to 300 weavers and asssaulted by many of them who threw shuttles, bobbins and other missiles at him causing injuries." The manager thought that his decision to suspend "the wages of four sirdars of the department . . . [had] led them to organise an attack on him."[22] During the 1920–21 phase of "industrial unrest" in Bengal, certain similar incidents occurred. The strike of 6 July 1920 at the New Central Jute Mill, Howrah, occurred over the arrest of some weavers accused of "a serious assault upon [a] European Assistant."[23] Labor protests in the Wellington Jute Mill or the Union South Jute Mill in early 1921 exhibited very similar features: "assaults, on managers or assistants."[24]

Even the so-called blind, individualistic form of protest was quite in evidence in the twentieth century. In November 1926, Razak, a mill hand belonging to the Hooghly Jute Mill, was "charged with having assaulted seriously the Mill manager, Mr Wilson."

It is alleged [a newspaper report said] that the accused was having a chat with some coolies and the mill manager took him to task for it. The accused grew furious and struck the manager with a lathi which separated the thumb from the forefinger of his hand.[25]

What does such protest signify? Why did defiance of authority take the expression of personal vengeance? To answer these questions we need to examine the mode of functioning of authority in the mills. The next two sections focus on this aspect of the problem.

THE NATURE of managerial authority in the Calcutta jute mills comes out very clearly in some of the documents pertaining to the mid-1930s, when, as seen in the last chapter, this authority was challenged by a massive upsurge of labor protest and strikes, organized under Com-

[21] NAI, Ind. and Lab. no. L-881(15) of 1926.

[22] *Amrita Bazar Patrika*, 1 December 1926, carried a report on this case.

[23] W.B.S.A., Com. Dept. Com. Br., July 1921, A 40–2, contains the *Report of the Committee on Industrial Unrest in Bengal* (hereafter *Report IUC*). See Appendix.

[24] Ibid.

[25] *Amrita Bazar Patrika*, 3 November 1926.

munist leadership. The captains of the industry, the government of Bengal, and the Indian Jute Mills Association then set about introducing certain "reforms" in jute-mill labor-management practices. Sir Edward Benthall tried at this time to get his managers to accept "reforms" like Whitley councils or works committees, labor officers and welfare officers, alongside "healthy" (which meant employer-promoted, anti-Communist) trade unions. He advised his brother "Paul" to "encourage all the men to establish closer contact with labor" and thus explained the move:

> I am quite sure that we shall never have any labour trouble of a really dangerous nature so long as our labourers are fairly treated and get a square deal. . . . Organised trouble there may be, but labour will not get nasty so long as they have no real grievances.[26]

"A policy of welfare work" and "regular touch with actual workers" through works committees, Benthall emphasized in his letters to his colleagues, were absolutely essential to counteracting the Communists.[27]

It is interesting to note that Benthall's proposals met with strong opposition from the mangers. He was quickly warned against doing anything that undermined the authority of the manager in the eyes of the workers.[28] Two of his managers objected to the idea of a works committee on the ground that the workers would read this only as a sign of the manager's weakness.[29] Indeed, managerial indifference led to the failure of some of the works committees set up under pressure from Benthall. One such committee at the Howrah Jute Mill soon ran out of topics to discuss when managers could not find issues on which consulting the workers could be considered worthwhile.

> At first [wrote Benthall's correspondent] they used to discuss the prospects of Mohammedan Sporting in the [soccer] league but after Mohammedan Sporting had won the League, subjects for discussion were difficult to find and the Mills staff consider the committee a complete frost.[30]

Even the subject of workers' welfare, which Benthall thought needed urgent attention in the fight against communism, was dealt with by the managers only in bad faith. Policing the workers with the help of pri-

---

[26] C.S.A.S., B.P., Box 12, Benthall to "Paul," 14 July 1937.
[27] C.S.A.S., B.P., Box 13, Benthall to McKerrow, 9 November 1937; Box 12, Benthall to "Paul," 1 August 1937.
[28] C.S.A.S., Box 11, "Paul" to Benthall, 7 July 1937.
[29] C.S.A.S., B.P., Box 12, "Paul" to Benthall, 21 July 1937.
[30] C.S.A.S., B.P., Box 11, "Paul" to Benthall, 19 July 1937.

vately appointed "intelligence officers" seemed to them to be a more effective instrument of control than welfare work. "Of course," commented Benthall's brother "Paul," writing about the idea of "intelligence officers,"

> it will be necessary not to allow the Intelligence Officers to be confused with the Labour Officers [proposed by the IJMA] although the Intelligence Officer will have to have some official designation other than "Intelligence Officer" which will justify their existence and give them access to the Mill areas without undue comment. Possibly they will be designated "Welfare Officers" and will be nominally in charge of the welfare of labour, e.g., quarters, lights, drains etc."[31]

Benthall recognized the nature and strength of the opposition to his ideas, and the jute-mill manager's point of view was soon accommodated within his general strategy for containing labor unrest. He gave up the idea of purely western-style Whitley councils or even "healthy" trade unions, in which workers and managers sat as supposedly equal partners and made decisions jointly on matters affecting production and the worker's life. Such equality would be too un-Indian. If managers and workers were to get closer together through an institutional arrangement, then that arrangement had better be a *panchayat* (traditional Indian village council), which was "indigenous," and Benthall's idea of the works council was gradually assimilated into the supposedly Indian idea of the *panchayat*:

> I do think [wrote Benthall] we might try out in one or two mills the experiments of Works Committees comprising three or four workers' representatives. . . . They may prove to be suitable for India where things are more primitive and where such committees would take the form of a panchayat. The natural leaders, mouth piece or *mukhis* of the workers would come to the fore. . . . [This] would do a great deal more than Trade Unions.[32]

What made this idea of the *panchayat* more acceptable to the managers is revealed in a letter that Benthall wrote to a partner in 1941:[33]

> Can you picture as possible any change which is likely to make a genuine Trade Union movement possible in India in our time? All

[31] C.S.A.S., B.P., Box 12, "Paul" to Benthall, 11 August 1937.

[32] C.S.A.S., B.P., Box 11, Benthall to "George," 26 June 1937.

[33] See C.S.A.S., B.P., Box 16, "Paul" to Benthall, 26 November 1940 for evidence of such acceptance.

the bad features will be developed but the good ones will not. . . . There is still much in Man[sic]-bap and I am real glad to see panchayats developing.[34]

Benthall had thus come round to the manager's point of view. The proposed works committee-cum-*panchayat* was more desirable than other forms of consultation because the *panchayat* was seen as an extension of the traditional *Ma-Baap* relationship that was supposed to exist between managers and workers in jute mills.

Ma-Baap literally refers to both parents. Managers obviously claimed that they were *in loco parentis* to the workers.[35] The worker was a "child" and was thought incapable of "rational," "adult" behavior. He could be easily led astray; strikes, for instance, were always seen as the handiwork of "ringleaders" or "outsiders."[36] He was unreasoning and unpredictable; managers often expressed surprise at the "suddenness" of working-class protest.[37] The worker was therefore childlike. A typically parental statement, which Sir Alexander Murray (whom we have met in earlier chapters) introduced into the body of the report of the Committee on Industrial Unrest (1921), ran as follows. Note the key words: "Labour, in its *ignorance*, is certain to make *unreasonable* demands which could not be granted without destroying industry, but *firmness* in refusing such demands needs to be mingled with much *patience* and *consideration*."[38]

This statement encapsulates the two necessary aspects of a *Ma-Baap* authority. On the one hand, managers had to be seen as dispensers of "parental" justice (showing the "patience" and "consideration" that Murray mentioned). Approaching the manager with complaints about an oppressive *sardar* was obviously an indication that managers were seen and even partly accepted in this role. Even in some of the Communist-led jute-mill strikes of 1937, workers frequently demanded that there should be "no dismissals except by the manager or a European," an obvious reference to the oppression the workers suffered at

[34] C.S.A.S., B.P., Box 16, Benthall to "George," 5 April 1941.
[35] Interview with Mr. G. D. Butchart, Dundee, October 1979.
[36] Even a casual reading of the weekly reports on strikes available in the Home Poll. Confdl. series (W.B.S.A.) will bear this out.
[37] See, for example, W.B.S.A., Home Poll. Confdl. no. 818/1936, Govt. of Bengal letter no. 522 Com[merce] of 1936.
[38] W.B.S.A., Com. Dept. Com. Br., July 1921, nos 40–2. Emphasis added. A note by J. H. Kerr says: "This was Sir A. Murray's own idea." Compare the advice given by the Bengal government to jute-mill managers in 1937: "It should be realized that the workers are crude and ignorant but appreciate kindness"; see IJMA, *Report, 1937* (Calcutta, 1938), p. 126.

the hands of the *sardars* or their accomplices, the Bengali mill clerks.[39] But, on the other hand, being seen as patient and kind was not enough; managers also needed to be seen as disproportionately powerful figures, embodying the "firmness" of Murray's prescription. The power relationship between the manager and the worker had to be visibly as asymmetric as that between an adult and a child.

The exemplary manager was someone whom the workers would "look up to . . . *as a sort of God.*" This is how John Finlay, the manager of the Hastings Jute Mill, was described in 1894 by a visitor from Dundee:

> John Finlay . . . is the Nestor among the mill men now. . . . [He] has tact, mother-wit, and common sense in the management of the workers. He is intimately acquainted with their language and character, and the consequence is that things go on smoothly. There are no better workers in the world than those in the Indian jute mills. A *paternal despotism* suits them exactly. Whenever they get to believe in their manager as one who will be kind though firm with them, who, while demanding absolute obedience, will give them absolute fairplay, their loyalty is secure. They look up to him as a sort of God.[40]

This quotation overestimates the importance the manager normally attached to learning the worker's language or about his character. According to an official report of 1906, the average jute-mill manager, "usually a kindly Scot from Dundee," knew "but little of the language which his employees talk[ed] . . . [and] often [could not] freely communicate with them." He did not have "much acquaintance with their manners and habits" either.[41] This description seems closer to reality and is borne out by the evidence of the Benthall papers. One persistent complaint of Benthall and his partners during the frequent jute-mill strikes of 1937 related to the absolute lack of managers and supervisors who knew the language of the workers well enough to be able to act as mediators between labor and capital, especially at moments of increased tension and hostility. "There is . . . no doubt," wrote "Paul" to his brother on 26 July 1937, "that we have no man in our Jute Mills organisation who is altogether suitable to undertake the work of a Labour Officer either in one mill or in a group of mills, chiefly for the reason that there is not one man in the organisation who has sufficient

[39] See W.B.S.A., Home Poll. Confdl. no. 484/1937 and no. 60/1937.
[40] "The Calcutta Jute Mills," in *Dundee Year Book*, 1894 (Dundee, 1895), p. 95. Emphasis added.
[41] B. Foley, *Report on Labour in Bengal* (Calcutta, 1906), par. 23.

knowledge of the [worker's] language. This may be a confession of weakness, but I think it is the truth." Benthall agreed with his analysis: "We have really got to the heart of the question when we find that none of our men can talk the language sufficiently well to handle the position." "I can't preach myself," he added in a note of self-criticism, "I do always regret that I didn't do more at the language when I first came out."[42]

But a detailed knowledge of workers, their languages or customs, had never been considered relevant to the task of managing labor. The shallowness of the manager's knowledge of the worker's language was never seen to stand in the way of his *Ma-Baap* authority. In 1923, a female doctor investigating the conditions of women workers in the jute mills came across typical instances of assumed "deification" of the manager. The manager of the Baranagar Jute Mills told her how the "temporary wives [of workers] go over to other men, upon which there is trouble, and then the manager is required to give a decision. . . . [He] said his Sunday mornings were often given up to such work." At the Lothian Jute Mill, the manager pointed out to the doctor a Bengali woman worker. "Once when one of her 'husbands' had been beating her when she was pregnant, she appealed to Mr. Macnab [the manager] who, when he found the offence was proved, dismissed the man from the mill." Another instructive case was the manager of the Fort Gloster Jute Mill:

The manager of this mill succeeded his father, and has himself been here 20 years. . . . I noticed as we went round the mill *he did not hesitate to hit workers lightly with his cane.* He himself settles disputes among the workers, gives divorces etc. He allows a wine shop and toddy shop inside the workers' village, says there is less "budmasheri" and he has more control over his workers if they get drunk inside the village than out.[43]

Such appropriation by the manager of absolute authority to himself was obviously dependent on the worker seeing him as absolutely powerful, through in reality the manager's powers were often quite limited.[44] For the *Ma-Baap* relationship to work, it was necessary for the

[42] C.S.A.S., B.P., Box 12, "Paul" to Benthall, 26 July 1937, and Benthall's reply of 5 August 1937. See also Benthall to "Paul," letters of 1 and 21 August 1937, and "Paul" to Benthall, 11 August 1937.

[43] W.B.S.A., Com. Dept. Com. Br., April 1923, B no. 77. Emphasis added.

[44] Raising wages, for example, was often not within the manager's power. Even orders for lockouts at times came from the managing agent's head office. B. C. Roy Papers, held

CHAPTER 5

manager to have an overpowering presence, and for the worker to be made to feel it. If this were not so, no manager would have dared to walk among his workers, alone, flicking his cane about, hitting them casually, as the Fort Gloster Mill manager did in the incident mentioned above.

What made the manager appear so powerful and big, and the worker powerless and small? What was the technology, so to speak, of such magnification?

IT IS when we touch on this question of "magnification" that we realize that the manager's authority was essentially colonial. It derived more from the colonial situation than from technology or any other factor internal to the production process. The word *colonial* is meant here to include what was indigenous to Indian society. There is no denying that the authority of the mill manager was bolstered by his position as a member of the ruling race. But, in some respects, one also cannot help noticing the "Indian" elements of this authority. Hence the close resemblance—often commented upon in the nationalist press—of the jute-mill manager's authority to that of the nineteenth-century indigo planter in Bengal, who in turn modeled himself on the Bengali (or North Indian) landlord.[45]

The Scottish manager in a Calcutta jute mill was something that he could never have been at home. Our 1894 visitor observed: "The jute mill manager in India is a much more important personage than his brother in Dundee. . . . He lives in a spacious bungalow, beautifully furnished, and has quite a retinue of servants to attend to him."[46] Thus it was the typical signs of ostentatious colonial power that made the manager more important than he would have been in Dundee: "spacious bungalow," lavishly furnished, a large "retinue of servants." The works speak of plenitude and excess, which marked the life style of the Scottish assistant as well. The Scotsmen in Calcutta presented such a novel spectacle to the Dundee gentleman whom we have been quoting so far that he proceeded to record this life style in utmost detail. To an

at the Nehru Memorial Library, New Delhi, have some correspondence (from the early 1920s) bearing on the problem. See also W.B.S.A., Home Poll. Confdl. no. 215/1930.

[45] For evidence regarding the nationalist press, see Sumit Sarkar, *The Swadeshi Movement in Bengal 1903–1908* (Delhi, 1973), p. 227, and P. Saha, *History of the Working Class Movement in Bengal* (Delhi, 1978), p. 111. For evidence of similarities between the indigo planter's tyrannical authority and that of the Bengali landlord see Blair B. Kling, *The Blue Mutiny: Indigo Disturbance in Bengal 1859–1862* (Philadelphia, 1966), and Ranajit Guha, "Neel Darpan: The Image of a Peasant Revolt in a Liberal Mirror," *Journal of Peasant Studies*, vol. 2, no. 1, Oct. 1974, pp. 1–46.

[46] "The Calcutta Jute Mills," p. 104.

166

Indian reader, many of the details would seem obvious and trivial, but their presence in the pages of the *Dundee Year Book* goes to show how strange and exotic they must have appeared to the readers in Dundee. The Scottish jute-mill assistant, it was reported, "lives well." "[He has] a bearer, a Mahomedan, who helps off and on with his clothes, takes charge of his room, attends him at table, stirs his tea, lights his pipe." And this is how the assistant spent his days:

> When a mill man gets up in the morning . . . his attendant brings him a cup of tea with some toast and sometimes a couple of eggs. This is called *chota haziri* (little breakfast). When the real breakfast time comes, he sits down to *several* courses, consisting of fish, stewed steak and onions, eggs, curried fowl and rice, with the usual addenda of tea or coffee, with bread, butter and jam. Instead of the tea, some prefer beer or iced water, while others take a peg. The "peg" is a great Indian institution. . . . It consists of a glass of whisky, a bottle of soda water, and a lump of ice all tumbled into a tall glass. . . . The "peg" is responsible for the downfall and early death of many a fine promising young man. . . . The tiffin (luncheon) . . . is less elaborate than the morning meal . . . and when the day's work is over, and bathing and dressing accomplished, the whole chummery sit down together to their evening meal consisting of a soup, fish, joint, side dishes, pudding and fruit. The various fruits in season are on the table at every meal. A plentiful supply of ice is provided by the Company.[47]

Nutrition was obviously not at the center of such an eating routine—the reference to the "peg" makes that clear. Eating was a ritualized expression of a colonial ruling-class culture, a well-defined culture with its own vocabulary—*chota haziri*, "peg," "tiffin"—signifying, again, excess and plentitude.[48] In his collection of excerpts from reminiscences about the "ways of the British in India," Hilton Brown introduces the chapter on food and drink with a comment on the "appalling appetites" of "our forefathers" and thus cautions the reader: "it is well to remember that only a fraction of what appeared on the table was actually consumed: the rest was waste."[49] An American gentleman

[47] Ibid., pp. 100–102.

[48] See R. Pearson, *Eastern Interlude: A Social History of the European Community in Calcutta* (Calcutta, 1954), pp. 20, 202.

[49] Hilton Brown, ed., *The Sahibs: The Life and Ways of the British in India as Recorded by Themselves* (London, 1948), p. 49. Cf. also Claude Lévi-Strauss: "The English . . . realized that the surest way to give the impression of being supermen was to convince

who lived and worked in the jute-manufacturing circles of Calcutta in
the 1920s noted with interest the emphasis his European colleagues
placed on their living styles. He wrote:

> Europeans in India must keep up a certain standard of living. In
> fact, this is so vital to the white man's prestige that most of the big
> firms will not allow their juniors to marry on less than a thousand
> rupees a month. And this did not go far when I was in Calcutta.
> Take the servants alone, a married couple must keep. . . . Ten ser-
> vants seem a lot for a couple with modest means, but there is no
> way of cutting down.[50]

There was an irony of history in all this. For the mill managers and
assistants were often themselves of working-class origin.[51] But out in
the colony, they were transformed overnight into members of the ruling class and the ruling race. They sat on municipal committees, were
made honorary magistrates, and socialized with the British civil servants in the colonial bureaucracy.[52] The private and public statements
of the civil servants sometimes bore unintended testimony to the close-
ness and warmth of this relationship. "Social life in Hooghly was
brisk," reminisced T. G. Holman, an ICS officer serving in Bengal in
the 1920s and 1930s. "Alethea and I had many happy times with the
gentlemen in jute at Angus [Mill]. They had a delightful swimming
bath and a very well kept nine-hole golf course, where I had the good
luck to win the Chinsura Challenge Trophy."[53] A note written by
N.V.H. Symons, the district magistrate of Howrah, in June 1937 on
the occasion of a strike at the Belvedere Jute Mills reveals the same
element of solidarity:

---

the natives that they need a much greater quantity of food than is required by an ordinary man." *Tristes Tropiques* (Harmondsworth, 1973), p. 178.

[50] D. W. King, *Living East* (New York, 1929), p. 40.

[51] "The overseers, managers and mechanics in the Indian jute mills are almost wholly
recruited from Dundee. There are hundreds of such men who have passed through Dundee's technical classes, and a certificate of attendance at the technical college has come
to be regarded as proving that the holder has been willing . . . to acquire a knowledge of
the principles of jute manufacture." British Association, Dundee, *Handbook and Guide*,
pp. 118–120.

[52] See W.B.S.A., Home Poll. Confdl. nos. 307(1–32)/1920 and 22/1930, P. D. Martyn,
of the subdivision of Barrackpore in the early 1930s, later recalled: "When in Barrackpore I inspected the honorary magistrates' courts in the various jute mill areas—mostly
mill managers from Dundee or Aberdeen on the Benches. . . . Justice may have been done
but it was surprisingly rough." IOL, Memoirs of P. D. Martyn, MSS. Eur. F180/13, p.
18.

[53] IOL, T. G. H. Holman Papers, MSS. Eur. D884, "Bengal Diary," p. 306.

McKay, the manager of the mill is a very decent fellow, youngish and on perfectly good terms with his labour, and I should say competent and conscientious. It is very bad luck on him that he should keep on having these troubles and I am sure he has done nothing to deserve them.[54]

In short, the managers became the bearers of the colonial rule in *mufassil* Bengal. Even *bhadralok* enterprise and social reform movements in the mill areas often depended crucially on their patronage.[55] An interesting example of such colonial transformation is the career of James Robertson of Dundee, who went out to Bengal in 1874 as the manager of Samnugger Jute Mill. A certificate from the Douglas Foundry, Dundee, dated 25 January 1866, described him as one who "has served a regular apprenticeship of 5 years to us as a machine maker and has been with us as a journeyman for some months."[56] But two farewell addresses that he received in 1885 when he retired from Samnugger Jute Mill show him in a very different light. One address, from the local residents, mentioned how "mill employees and the villagers . . . looked upon him as the promoter of their welfare and happiness." Another, from the secretary of a local school, was even more supplicatory in its tone:

Mr. James Robertson . . . the worthy gentleman, whose good feelings towards the natives . . . induced him to commiserate the want of an English School. . . . It is he, who favoured [the school] with a donation and . . . took a lively interest in the Examination and distribution of prizes. . . . To preserve his memory hereafter, we beg of him for [a] miniature in photograph . . . to be suspended in the school.[57]

The effect of such colonial "magnification" of one's power and status was not lost on the mill manager or his assistant. To quote the 1894 visitor again:

When the mill assistant arrives out in Calcutta his circumstances undergo a change. He may have been known in Dundee as Sandy

[54] W.B.S.A., Home Poll. Confdl. no. 60/1937.
[55] See my "Sasipada Banerjee: A Study in the Nature of the First Contact of the Bengali Bhadralok with the Working Classes of Bengal," *Indian Historical Review*, January 1976, pp. 339-364.
[56] TDA, bundle on James Robertson.
[57] TDA, the bundle on Robertson contains these addresses.

Tamson: but out here he is changed at once into Alexander Thomson, Esquire, weaving master, and all his letters are so addressed.[58]

The effect was not lost on the worker either. This was the context for K. C. Roy Chowdhury's statement, mentioned earlier, that the jute-mill workers always preferred a "rich" Indian as their spokesman when it came to dealing with the *sahibs*, and that they were very pleased to see trade union leaders come to attend meetings in their own motor cars.[59] In other words, the worker registered the signs of managerial authority and wanted his leader to match up to them.

In the jute mills of Bengal, then, managerial power worked more by making a spectacle of itself and less by the quiet mechanism of "discipline" that acts through the labor market, technology, and the organization of work.[60] In the "classic" case of metropolitan capitalism, to recall Marx's words once again, the "place of the slave-driver's lash is taken by the overlooker's book of penalties."[61] In the colonial capitalism of Bengal, as I shall now proceed to show, the lash remained more important than the fine book.

IF WE LOOK at the way the manager's authority was represented, three characteristics of his authority stand out. They are related but separable.

First, *authority was personalized*. Factory rules were seen as the manager's will. Issues like wage increases, wage cuts, dismissals, or lockouts were perceived as matters of his personal choice. A telling case was a riot that broke out at the Anglo-Indian Jute Mill on the morning of 18 May 1926. The mill had just laid off some workers. So the atmosphere in the mill was tense. It had also changed its working hours, as a result of which women workers expected a raise in their wages.

> In making his morning rounds at 6.30 in the mill a mob began following the Manager round and a few bobbins were thrown. The Manager then went into his office which was immediately surrounded by a crowd of 2000-3000 . . . deputations were sent to the Manager to ask him to increase the wages. On his saying

[58] "The Calcutta Jute Mills," p. 100.

[59] K.C.R.P., diary no. 3, entry for 7 April 1923.

[60] Michel Foucault, *Discipline and Punish: The Birth of the Prison*, trans. Alan Sheridan (Harmondsworth, 1979), p. 220.

[61] Karl Marx, *Capital*, vol. 1 (Moscow, n.d.), p. 424. See also the discussion in chapter 3, above.

that it was not in his power, bricks were thrown at the office windows and the windows . . . were smashed.[62]

Much violence followed. A later police report repeated that the raising of wages was indeed *not* within the manager's power: "Managers have no say in the matter of wages, which are controlled by the [Managing] Agents."[63] Why did the workers not believe this? Because they were used to seeing authority as an unrestrained expression of the manager's personal will. On the Friday preceding the riot, which was also their payday, the same manager had refused to pay them when he heard "some murmuring" among the workers. He had warned them instead that he would cancel all due wages unless workers (then on strike) joined work by the following Monday. In the absence of explicit service or wage regulations in the industry, such a warning could have only appeared to come from the manager personally.

Even in the course of daily, routine conversations with the workers, managers and assistants projected their authority not only in the imperative but often in the first person singular. A sample of "useful sentences" taken from a manual of spoken Hindi, put together for use in jute mills, will make that clear.[64] It should be noted that the word used to mean "I" was *hām* (or *hum*), which literally meant "we." The British in India used it often as a substitute for the royal "we." The sentences thus sought to impress upon the mind of the worker a sense of the manaer's (or the assistant's) "sovereignty," his unlimited power.

(a) Āgar tum kārkhānā men phir jhagrā karegā to hām tumko jawāb degā.

If you quarrel again inside the factory, I shall sack you.

(b) Tum do māhinā huā ghar gayā thā. Hām tumko ābhi jāne nahin degā.

It's now only a couple of months since you've been back from home [village]. I shall not allow you to go now.

(c) Tum ābhi ek māhinā talab bāghair kām karo. Āgar tumhārā kām āchchā hogā to hām tumko barābar rākhegā.

You work now for a month without any wages. If your work is satisfactory, I shall keep you permanently.

[62] For details, see W.B.S.A., Home Poll. Confdl. no. 286(1–4)/1926.
[63] Ibid.
[64] Mohiuddin Ahmed, *Essentials of Colloquial Hindustani for Jute Mills and Workshops*, 2d ed. (Calcutta, 1932), pp. 88–91.

(d) Jo ādmi kāl der se   I shall fine anyone who comes
    āegā hām uspar   in late tomorrow.
    jurmānā karegā.

(e) Hām jaise boltā hāi   Do as I say, or give up your
    waisā karo nahin to   job and leave.
    kām chhor do.

(f) Tum donon kā kasūr   You are both guilty. I
    hāi. Hām donon ko   shall sack you both.
    jawāb degā.

(g) Agar Barā Sāhib   Look, if the Bara [Chief]
    dekhegā to wuh   Sahib happens to see this, it
    bahut gussā hogā.   will make him very angry.

Small wonder, then, that authority was seen in personal terms. As A Bengal government report once said: "The ensuing of trouble on the appointment of a new Manager is not an infrequent occurrence."[65]

Second, apart from being personalized, *authority was excessive*. I use the word *excess* in opposition to the word *economy*. In Marx's (or Foucault's) discussion of capitalist discipline, managerial and supervisory authority is seen to operate through an articulated body of rules and legislation that have the effect of ensuring an economy in the use and exercise of managerial power.[66] In the jute mills of Calcutta, however, there prevailed the idea that the managers should be in complete and unchallenged control of their laborers.

It is arguable that the demonstration of excessive authority had some utility in retaining labor, since, in a highly imperfect labor market, there was always the fear of temporary but serious labor shortage. A report from 1918 brings this out:

> A manager . . . starting a new mill heard that a mill across the river was out on a strike and so he sent a sardar with a launch to get some of the labour. The sardar came back without the labour and was ordered to go back once more. But he again returned alone. To the manager's question he replied that there was a sahib with a gun standing on the ghat [steps leading from the river bank to the river] daring him to come near.[67]

[65] See NAI, Ind. and Lab. no. L-881(11) of 1921, and W.B.S.A., Home Poll. Confdl. no. 32/1940.

[66] See chapter 3.

[67] J. C. Kydd, "Industrial Labour in Bengal," *Bengal Economic Journal*, 1918, pp. 345–346. See also "The Calcutta Jute Mills," p. 95, for similar instances from the 1890s.

Underlying it all, however, was an idea of managerial absolutism. The worker had, according to A. P. Benthall, "a theoretical right to appeal to Head Office and even to the Partners of the Managing Agents, but in practice this right [was] seldom exercised." The managing agents themselves were "very anxious" in the strike-ridden year of 1937 that "nothing should be done which might weaken the authority of the Managers who have to deal with the numerous complaints and applications which are now reaching them from labour."[68]

The trade unionist or political organizer of labor who intervened in capital-labor relationships was always hated and resented by the managers. Long after trade unionism had become a respectable vocation in the country and had actually been given a fillip by the Indian Trade Unions Act of 1926, the trade unionist, especially of the left-wing variety, was seen by the mill manager as someone engaged in illegitimate activity, an interloper, a *badmash* (scoundrel) who only meant trouble. Even the strike wave of 1937 was described by managers as "the work of a few *badmashes* in each mill," since labor, after all, was "quite content to carry on and there was no trouble whatever until the usual *badmashes* got to work."[69] That this statement occurs in the private correspondence of employers and was not meant for public consumption only shows how strongly they believed it themselves.

The maintenance of industrial peace was thus directly predicated on jealously protecting the manager-worker relationship from any outside interference. We can see why the manager of the Fort Gloster Jute Mill lost his temper when, in October 1905, he saw some of his clerks and workers wearing *rakhees*.[70] The *rakhee* to him was a sign of the presence of the "outside agitator." He "struck a Bengali clerk and two or three Mohamedan mill-hands," which led to a strike.[71] During the Khilafat movement in 1920, the manager of the Union Jute Mill came across "a hartal [strike] leaflet posted up on the wall of the mill." In a dramatic demonstration of anger, he tore it off the wall and "trampled it under foot" before the watching eyes of his workers.[72] Managers' reaction was the same when the government of Bengal intervened to

[68] C.S.A.S., B.P., Box 11, "Paul" to Benthall, 7 July 1937.
[69] C.S.A.S., B.P., Box 14, Report from Bird and Company, Calcutta, to Benthall, 14 December 1937.
[70] A piece of thread worn around the wrist as a mark of brotherhood. A traditional Hindu rite. During the agitation against the partition of Bengal in 1905 Hindu Bengali leaders often exchanged *rakhees* with Muslims to indicate Hindu-Muslim unity. See Sarkar, *Swadeshi Movement*, p. 287.
[71] *Bengalee*, 18 October 1905.
[72] W.B.S.A., Home Poll. Confdl. no. 106(1–36)/1920.

settle the 1929 general strike. A deputation of employers to the governor bitterly complained how, as a result of such "unfortunate action . . . control of labour had . . . passed out of the hands of the employers."[73]

> [The] Government's interference [wrote Benthall in 1929] has led to a position entirely new to the trade. Government while pretending to refuse to recognise the so-called Bengal Jute Workers' Union negotiated with them and got their signature to a settlement. By doing so they virtually recognised the union leaders and put power into their hands. The result has been that the power has gone from the Managers and Managing Agents and there is no longer any discipline in the industry.[74]

Third, *authority bore marks of terror.* Excessive authority obviously depended on a certain use and demonstration of physical force. Managerial power had a necessary extralegal dimension to it.

There was the Voluntary Artillery Force, of which "nearly every jute mill assistant" and manager was a member.[75] The object of raising the force was to meet labor unrest "with arms."[76] As some of my examples will have shown, this was no empty threat. Besides, throughout the period under discussion, assaulting the worker physically was an extremely common practice—far too common, in fact, for it to be overlooked as any individual manager's personal failing. The nationalist press was always full of complaints about this aspect of managerial behavior. A report that appeared in the *Bengalee* of 2 August 1906 describing how the manager of the India Jute Mills once kicked one of his weavers while "using abusive language at the same time" was typical of the genre of such reports. Jute-mill workers, it is said, often compared their bosses to ill-tempered horses, because in dealing with both one faced the danger of getting kicked.[77] With the coming of the nationalist movement in the twentieth century such behavior on the part of European bosses received much adverse publicity, for it grievously wounded nationalist pride. There was, for example, an attempt in 1914 by some Bengali middle-class nationalists to murder a Mr. O'Brien, an engineer of the Alexandra Jute Mills of Jagaddal, "who had kicked to death an employee of the Mill and had received in

---

[73] NAI, Home Poll. Confdl. no. 257/1 and K.W. of 1930.

[74] C.S.A.S., B.P., Box 7, diary 1929–33, entry for 10 September 1929.

[75] "The Calcutta Jute Mills," p. 102; W.B.S.A., Home Poll. Confdl. no. 307(1–32)/ 1920.

[76] IJMA, *Report, 1895* (Calcutta, 1896), Appendix, pp. 76–80.

[77] Interview with Jyotish Ganguli, Calcutta, September 1979.

return a nominal fine of Rs 50."[78] Matters came to a head in 1926 when a Scottish assistant killed a weaver by kicking him in a fit of anger.[79] The ensuing scandal and uproar in the press, and mounting working-class grievance over physical "torture," forced IJMA to assure the government in 1929 that "there will be no corporal punishment" in the mills.[80] This was not a very effective assurance, for we hear of physical assaults by managers and assistants as late as 1938 or 1940.[81] By then the assumptions underlying the so-called *Ma-Baap* relationship had obviously become part of a strong managerial tradition in the jute mills.

Even more vicious, from the worker's point of view, was organized managerial terror (as distinct from sporadic physical assaults) that was unleashed on labor at moments of protest. In the flow of such excessive, organized managerial violence, the police, the *sardars*, and the *durwans* often acted as capillaries, aiding the flow.

Sumit Sarkar records in his aforementioned book an early instance of this. The workers of Fort Gloster Jute Mill had gone on strike in March 1906. "On the night of 12–13 March," Sarkar writes, "mill durwans, a mob of upcountry coolies and some police constables launched a violent attack on the neighbouring villages of Khajari, where many of the [striking] workers lived."[82] Abdul Momin, one of the organizers of the 1929 general strike, mentions the use by managers of hired Kabuli *goondas* when the strike was one.[83] During a strike at the Ludlow Jute Mill in May 1928, the manager one day let off "the blacklegs" (working in place of the strikers) "two hours before the usual time," and they, "assisted by the Jamadars [*durwans*] and other servants of the mill, armed with lathis, swords, sticks and daggers, set upon the [striking] workers in their quarters and inflicted serious injuries on them." A month later at the same factory, the women went out on strike. One day during the strike the manager "induced" (in the language of a newspaper report) the women leaders of the strike to come to his office:

> Thereafter the gates were locked up and strikers were threatened with prosecution if they failed to rejoin at once. The police and the Jamadars of the mill continued to intimidate them all along.

[78] Uma Mukherjee, *Two Great Indian Revolutionaries* (Calcutta, 1966), p. 47.

[79] For details, see W.B.S.A., Home Poll. Confdl. no. 177/1926.

[80] NAI, Ind. and Lab. no. L-881(24) of 1930.

[81] W.B.S.A., Home Poll. Confdl. nos. 381/1938 and 32/1940.

[82] Sarkar, *Swadeshi Movement*, p. 229.

[83] Abdul Momin, 'Chatkal Sramiker Pratham Sadharan Dharmaghat,' *Kalantar*, 12 August 1970.

On their refusal to resume work, several of the leaders were severely assaulted and immediately put under arrest. The rest of the women workers were . . . assaulted and dispersed, being forcibly dragged by their hair.[84]

It should be emphasized once again, however, that this projection of authority in personalized, excessive, and terrorizing terms was not a European invention on Indian soil. Nor was it a European monopoly. Even after making allowances for the haughtiness and arrogance of a ruling race, the evidence points to remarkable similarities between the managerial style described above and that obtaining in the Indian-managed cotton mills in Bengal. The Communist-run newspaper *Ganabani* published a report in 1928 that described how the workers of the Dhakeshwari Cotton Mill (near Dacca) had been treated by the mill management on demanding a raise in wages. The Bengali manager of the mill, who eventually forced them out of the factory with the help of his *durwans*, hurled a shower of abuse on the workers, using the Bengali equivalents of "bastard," "swine," and "son of a bitch."[85] The details of the following police report on a strike at the Indian-owned and Bengali-managed Bangoday Cotton Mill (on the outskirts of Calcutta) are also instructive:

On . . . 6.4.[19]37 in the afternoon one Kartic Ch. Dey, weaver, while working in the Bangoday Cotton Mill was assaulted by one Ganesh, Head Jobber of the weaving department. . . . At this other weavers of the department took objection and complained . . .to the weaving-in-charge Godu Babu who took no action but threatened with further assault and discharge. So these Bengali weavers determined not to work in the company and wanted their pay. As arranged by Godu Babu these weavers about 64 in number . . . went to the mill gate on 7.4.37 at 11.30 hrs to take their pay, when some Darwans and collies [coolies] came out of the mill gate with lathis and under the direction of Godu Babu and the mill manager Kunja Babu assaulted the . . . weavers . . . causing injuries.[86]

While consulting the private papers of Sibnath Banerjee, I came across the not untypical case of a Kariman Bibi, a female worker of the Indian-owned Shree Ganesh Jute Mill, who was "laid off" in 1956 when

[84] *Amrita Bazar Patrika*, 3 May and 10, 22 June 1928.

[85] *Ganabani*, 13 September 1928, excerpted in Gopal Haldar, ed., *Communist* (Calcutta, 1976?), p. 25.

[86] W.B.S.A., Home Poll. Confdl. no. 128/1937, Pt. 1.

she was found to be pregnant. She was not given any maternity benefits and, according to Banerjee's papers, her "wages for 1 week and 14 days' earned leave" were still due even a year later. When Kariman Bibi went back to the factory in 1956 to seek reemployment, after having been recommended by the labor commissioner's office as being fit for work, she was allegedly "beaten by Gana Babu (Barababu [head clerk]) and turned out."[87]

THE STRONG resemblances between the managerial styles of the Scottish jute-mill manager and the Bengali cotton-mill manager point to the existence in both cases of a culture obsessively concerned with the employment and maintenance of the visible signs of domination and subordination. However much the British in India may have improvised on it, this culture was also undeniably "Indian," and it refused to come to terms with the bourgeois notion of "contract" that, theoretically at least, underlay the wage relationship between labor and capital. Abusing the worker verbally or physically and addressing him in the disrespectful form *tum* (see the Hindi sentences quoted above) or the even more disrespectful *tui* (which was used by the Dhakeshwari Cotton Mill manager) were all signs of the worker's lowly social status and, insofar as he accepted them, of his subordination. The *Ma-Baap* relationship was thus the name that managers gave to their near-feudal domination. Up to a point, it must have worked. But as workers' protests show, the relationship broke down quite often. When exactly did such moments occur?

Let us go back to the case of the Anglo-Indian Jute Mill manager in 1926, the gentleman who was subject to much working-class violence when he pleaded his inability to grant a wage increase. As we know, the workers thought this to have been his personal choice. But that was to be expected; authority perceived as personalized could be only "arbitrary." But arbitrariness alone was not sufficient to provoke protest. If it were, jute mills in Bengal would never have known any moments of "peace." In this case, the manager was seen as not just "arbitrary" but also "unfair." He was arbitrary in an unfair way. The *combination* was explosive. The workers here believed—wrongly, but that does not matter—that other managers in the mills had already agreed to a wage increase, and the gentleman here was holding this back quite unreasonably.[88] The supposed agreement of the other managers had already made the demand reasonable and just. So in holding it back, the man-

[87] Private papers of Sibnath Banerjee, Banerjee's letters of 7 March 1956 and 8 September 1957.
[88] See W.B.S.A., Home Poll. Confdl. no. 286(1–4)/1026.

ager was withholding something that the workers thought was due to them. He was therefore unfair and deserving of punishment.

Time and again, through instances of working-class protest, we return to the worker's notions of "fairness" and "justice." The worker reacts when he sees himself being deprived of something that he thinks is justly his. Such an injured sense of fairness and complaints about the manager's unreasonableness permeate a petition that the workers of eight jute mills of the Titaghur area sent to the district magistrate in 1931. This was a time when the mills were laying off thousands of men. Managers, fearing trouble from outside workers, had ordered entries into or exits from the mills to be strictly controlled. The petition is indicative of the workers' view at a time of heightened tension:

> . . . at the time we are working in the mills we find ourselves imprisoned, as it were, with no liberty even to go to answer the calls of nature. If any of us pressed by an urgent call goes out his token is taken away and he is dismissed. If any of our relatives in our houses happen to fall ill or if any danger befalls any member of our family at the time we are working in the mills, we cannot get any information as the gates of the mill are kept closed and no one is allowed to go in or come out. We do not see why this rule should have been introduced, regarding closing of gates.[89]

The petition is quite clear on the working-class "logic" of protest: "when for many years in the past the gates were kept open during working hours there was no trouble whatsoever in the working of the mills." Thus it was not because there was trouble that the gates were shut, which would have been the managerial view, it was because the gates were shut that there was trouble. In point of fact, this was not a "true" explanation; there had been much trouble before even when "the gates were kept open." But the "truth" of the statement lay elsewhere: the closing of the gates symbolized the manager's unfairness, and it was this that called for protest.[90]

In the absence of more documents from the workers themselves,

[89] W.B.S.A., Home Poll. Confdl. no. 150/1931.

[90] The gate occupied a crucial position in the architectural plan of the mill, as far as the exercise of managerial power was concerned. It was a means of controlling entry and exit. It was also where workers were physically checked by *durwans* for possible "thefts" and other offenses. Scuffles between workers and *durwans* at the gate were quite common. Managers often ordered the gate to be closed as a demonstration of their will (as in the case of a lockout), hence, as a demonstration of a counterwill, there was gate-crashing by striking workers. See W.B.S.A., Home Poll. confdl. no. 128/1937, pt. 3, note dated 4 June 1937 by the inspector general of police; NAI, Ind. and Lab. nos. L-881(30) of 1931 and L–881(10) of 1924.

their notion of fairness or justice is difficult to unravel and analyze in depth. Yet some aspects of the question are clear. The worker's idea of fairness was related to his idea of what was customary (or *riwaz*). "Unfair" was what was not done. If attending to ailing relatives or "urgent calls" was his "duty" and therefore customary, even if it meant interrupting work, then that was fair. Whoever or whatever stopped him from doing so was unfair. Similar in import was the point about the closing of the gates. As the petition quoted above illustrates, the workers made little distinction between their own time—time when one could visit ailing relatives—and work time. This, however, was not entirely "unreasonable" of them. In their more prosperous days when they always carried an extra complement of labor, the mills themselves had shown little interest in inculcating in their workers ideas and habits of capitalist discipline. A sudden departure from this tradition felt like an unreasonable curbing of workers' "freedom," which they, the workers, now sought to protect in the name of fairness and customary practices.

Chitra Joshi, in her work on the Kanpur (in Uttar Pradesh) textile-mill workers, workers from the same cultural region as the jute-mill workers, has identified a notion of "fair wage" that the workers there had.[91] A similar notion can be discerned in the case of jute-mill workers too. A "fair" wage was what a laborer in a neighboring mill received (or what a neighbor working for a different mill did). In other words, fair was what was seen as "customary." Therefore, if one manager granted a wage increase (for whatever reasons) and another in a neighboring factory refused to do so (for whatever reasons, again), the latter was unfair, because he was denying workers what had become customary (in other mills) and thus rightfully theirs. The general strikes of 1929 and 1936–37 provide good illustrations of this. This was also at the heart of some of the important conflicts of 1920—the year of "industrial unrest." At the Hooghly Jute Mill in November 1920, the spinners asked the manager for a wage increase, "alleging other mills are getting it." The manager denied this, but—and this is significant—"says if others get it they shall also." The spinners went on strike, and the strike quickly spread to the mills in the town of Howrah: the Ganges, Fort William, and Howrah jute mills. The strikes broke out on the same day, ended on the same day, and made the same demand: a 25 percent wage increase. The only way the government

[91] Chitra Joshi, "Kanpur Textile Labour: Some Structural Characteristics and Aspects of Labour Movement," Ph.D. thesis, Jawaharlal Nehru University, 1982. I am grateful to Ms. Joshi for letting me read two of her chapters in draft.

could explain the spread of this strike, which originated in a single isolated mill on the other side of the river, was by pointing out that, though isolated, the Hooghly Jute Mill "belongs by intercourse to the Howrah group, quite a proportion of the labour of the Howrah mills living in its neighbourhood."[92]

To appear "just," however, an idea did not always require the force of real tradition behind it. The definition of what was "customary," and hence legitimate, was the subject of bargaining and struggle between managers and laborers. As the Genoveses have pointed out, the so-called customary always represents "a compromise hammered out in harsh class struggle":

> To speak of custom means to identify that range of activity, called privileges by the masters, assumed as rights by the slaves ... which flowed from the masters' knowledge that the violation of norms would carry an unacceptable level of risk.[93]

"Custom," "tradition," and "legitimacy" were thus open to interpretation. An arbitrary reference to the *kanoon* (law) of the land or to a superordinate authority, for example, was often sufficient to establish something as time honored or legitimate (and thus a matter of "right"), much the same way as insurgent peasants would invoke the authority of the *raj* against an oppressive landlord. In April 1936, for example, the workers of the Hooghly Jute Mill went on strike and the authorities issued notices asking them to vacate their rooms in the mill's coolie lines. Much violence resulted. But what preceded the violence is even more interesting. Debendra Nath Sen, a Communist leader, told the strikers: "as you pay rent and as you are employees in their Mills, the proprietors have no right to eject you all of a sudden." In a later meeting, another leader, Abdul Aziz, was even more forthright: "The notice given by the Sahib is *not lawful. He does not conform to the laws of the Government.*"[94] Both Sen and Aziz were wrong in their knowledge of the law, as a prolonged court case later proved. But the argument worked. When the manager went to the lines with his assistant and *durwans* to evict the workers, they were greeted by a very heavy dose of working-class anger and violence.[95]

The worker's notion of fairness was also bound up with his sense of

[92] *Report IUC*, Appendix.

[93] Elizabeth Fox Genovese and Eugene D. Genovese, *Fruits of Merchant Capital: Slavery and Bourgeois Property in the Rise and Expansion of Capitalism* (New York, 1983), pp. 144–145.

[94] *IJMA, Report, 1937*, pp. 136–137. Emphasis added.

[95] W.B.S.A., Home Poll. Confdl. no. 207/1937.

honor and dignity, notions that were themselves influenced by his perceptions of "tradition." This came out strongly in strikes over alleged acts of misbehavior toward women by assistants or *durwans*, where striking was a matter of protecting the women's *izzat* ("honor").[96] Another good example is the case we have cited earlier of the manager of the Union Jute Mill who tore up a Khilafat leaflet in 1920 and trampled it under his foot in the presence of his Muslim workers. He was "chased to his private quarters by a number of workmen who threw brickbats at the doors and windows." The workers later told the police that "as there were certain religious verses quoted in the notice, the trampling under foot was . . . insulting to their religion."[97] In other cases of protest, too, there always remained an element of the worker's dignity being at stake. In December 1905, when two "ringleaders" of the protesters at the Fort Gloster Jute Mill were arrested, workers "promptly went on strike, and . . . told the . . . police . . . that in arresting the two men they had all been insulted."[98] In January 1933, when the *burra sahib* of the Waverley Jute Mill "roughly handled some of the weavers whose production did not prove satisfactory," it was not just "bad yarn" that the weavers complained of. They actually "resented . . . this alleged bad behaviour and . . . severely assaulted him with shuttles and iron instruments, necessitating his removal to the hospital."[99]

Thus it was at points when the manager was not only arbitrary but both arbitrary and unfair (and thus unreasonable and insulting) that there was protest. At these moments the *Ma-Baap* relationship broke down. It not only broke down: more important, the terms of the relationship became instantaneously reversed.[100] The manager's view of the worker as a "child" was replaced by the worker's view of the manager as a "despot." Working-class vengeance took the place of managerial terror, and protest now bore marks of retaliation that the worker needed to stamp on the manager's body (since authority was personalized) or on the body of his assistant or *durwan* or on objects bearing a relationship of contiguity to them, such as their bungalows, quarters,

[96] See, for example, *Report IUC*, Appendix, and NAI, Ind. and Lab. no. L-881(10) of 1924.

[97] W.B.S.A., Home Poll. Confdl. no. 106(1–30)/1920.

[98] Sarkar, *Swadeshi Movement*, p. 228.

[99] *Amrita Bazar Patrika*, 14 January 1933.

[100] Cf. Foucault's discussion of the inversion of relationships that "normally" existed between the sovereign's terrorizing power and ordinary people, where violence became "instantaneously reversible." Foucault, *Discipline and Punish*, pp. 59–60, 63.

or offices (that is, mill property).[101] Using the anthropologist's language, we may schematize this "reversibility":

$$\frac{\text{Manager}}{\text{Worker}} \; : \; : \; \frac{\text{Unreasonable—Powerful}}{\text{Unreasonable—Powerless}}$$

$$: \; : \; \frac{\text{Despot}}{\text{Child}} \; : : \; \frac{\text{Terror}}{\text{Vengeance}} \; : \; : \; \frac{\text{Manager's Violence}}{\text{Worker's Violence}}$$

Protesting then became a ceremony of defiance. The rebel worker inverted the terms of his relationship with the manager or the supervisor, and overturned the two major everyday signs of his subordination: abusive language and physical violence. This inversion of relationships can be seen in most instances of working-class protest in the period under study. But an example from the nineteenth century would probably serve to show it in its elementary clarity. We reproduce here a letter that the authorities of the Alliance Jute Mill wrote to IJMA, reporting a "disturbance" at their mill on 6 July 1897:

We continued full working until about 10.30 A.M., when notice was brought that a large gang of men armed with *lathies* had attacked the gate, burst it open, and were surrounding the Mill. As things looked serious the engine was stopped, and the Europeans went off to their houses to arm themselves, but before they got back to the compound the Mill was surrounded by two to three thousand excited men all armed with *lathies*, and with their clothes tightly tied up, shouting all kinds of abusive language and making threatening gestures with their sticks. The engine, the governor gear was broken, and other damage done. It was only the prompt appearance of some of the Europeans with fire-arms that prevented the rioters from continuing their course of destruction and attacking the European quarters, upon which a body of men were marching. When asked to state their reason for causing the disturbance the only reply was a shout of defiance, with abusive language, a brandishing of their *lathies* and a shower of bricks. A few shots fired in the air, and a charge or two of snipe shot at their legs, got them to retire as far as the gate which they again attacked

[101] For the concept of contiguous (or metonymic) relationships, see Edmund R. Leach, *Culture and Communication: The Logic by Which Symbols Are Connected* (Cambridge, 1976); Roland Barthes, *Elements of Semiology* (New York, 1979), pp. 59-60.

with their sticks and broke to pieces. This and the throwing of bricks appeared to satisfy them for a time.[102]

The nationalist movement in the twentieth century introduced competing ideologies and organization into the field of industrial relations in Bengal. The whole scene of the labor movement became literally more colorful in the 1930s as the left in Bengal started celebrating such ceremonies as May Day, Lenin Day, and November Day.[103] "The [red] flag with the insignia of the hammer, sickle and star and revolutionary slogans are a common feature of most demonstrations in Calcutta and most of the speeches which are made at these . . . demonstrations advocate communism," noted the chief secretary of Bengal in 1937.[104] Along with this went a constant effort to undermine the authority of the British. A police report of 1939 gives a good description of the kind of "manuscript posters" that the Communists often circulated in mill areas, inciting the mill hands against the mill authorities and Europeans.

This poster exhibits a picture of a man calling himself . . . a revolutionary holding a revolver in his hand and with the other holding a rope tied to the neck of a man who has been styled . . . a two-footed monkey probably meaning [a] European.[105]

All this, of course, had a significant influence on the working class, as the scale and intensity of labor protests in the 1930s suggest. As the nationalist movement gained momentum and the legitimacy of the British presence suffered erosion, workers naturally felt more encouraged to challenge the authority of their superiors at work. Given the oppressive and arbitrary forms that authority assumed in the mills and factories of Bengal, even the moderate legal provisions of the 1920s and 1930s that allowed for some degree of unionization of the workers offended the pride of the managers. The trade union organizer Sibnath Banerjee mentions in his memoirs how the Workmen's Compensation Act of 1923 helped them undermine the prestige of factory managers, who found the idea of being cross-examined in front of their workers "very humiliating."[106] In the atmosphere of the time, the act of forming a trade union, or even a mere mention of the legal rights of the workers, amounted to questioning the hitherto "unchallenged" authority of

[102] IJMA, *Report, 1897* (Calcutta, 1898), Appendix.
[103] W.B.S.A., Home Poll. Confdl. no. 553/1934.
[104] W.B.S.A., Home Poll. Confdl. no. 68/1937.
[105] W.B.S.A., Home Poll. Confdl. no. 446/1939.
[106] NMML, Sibnath Banerjee, interviewed by A. K. Gupta, 10 February 1971. Transcript, p. 40.

the bosses. And, as the following description of a strike at a jute press in 1937 illustrates, trade unions sometimes sprouted up to reflect this very spirit of defiance. The following note was received by Benthall in November 1937 in connection with a strike at one of their jute presses:

> Labour generally is still very touchy and there have been several strikes in Press Houses. The cause of ours was ridiculous. One of the supervising babus had words with one of the contractor's foremen which developed into an exchange of abuse and apparently the babu . . . was the real offender. . . . A so-called labour leader at once appeared and the men were all enrolled as members [of a union] and it was suddenly found that it had become a matter affecting the whole of the staff. A public apology was demanded together with the punishment of the babu and full disclosure of the punishment meted out to the babu.[107]

It is possible, then, to recognize a continuing structure in the nature of working-class defiance of authority all through the history of the "political mobilization" of labor. There are, for this reason, uncanny similarities between the modes of labor mobilization of the *swadeshi* period (1905–8) and those, under Communist leadership, of the 1930s. The red badge replaced the *rakhee*, slogans like *Mazdur ki Jai* (Victory to the workers) replaced *Bande Mataram* (Glory to the motherland), but the "bourgeois" nationalism of the *swadeshi bhadralok* and the Marxism of the later *bhadralok* Communist often spoke to the worker with the same voice. Thus if the sight of the worker wearing the *swadeshi rakhee* angered the manager in 1905, then how much more so Zaman, a Communist leader, who exhorted the workers of a jute mill in 1938 "to enter the mill for work with red badges on and with lathis [and] gave them instructions to assault anybody objecting to their wearing badges."[108] In 1905 Aswini Banerjee, the *swadeshi* nationalist labor organizer, told his followers "that it was the slave who tempted, invited, nay compelled tyranny and that if they could return 2 blows for one, their burra sahibs . . . would begin to respect them."[109] Years later, in 1937, the Communist Niharendu Dutt Majumdar had the same message for the working class: "if any workman was assaulted by a manager, the workers should retaliate by hitting him back."[110] The particular ideological content of the preachings do not seem to have been crucial. *Bande Mataram* was as good as *Mazdur*

[107] C.S.A.S., B.P., Box 14, "George" to Benthall, 30 November 1937.
[108] W.B.S.A., Home Poll. Confdl. no. 31/1938.
[109] Sarkar, *Swadeshi Movement*, p. 237.
[110] W.B.S.A., Home Poll. Confdl. no. 128/1937.

ki Jai when it came to signifying defiance. At the Kamarhatty Jute Mill in June 1937, spinners charged with bad work defied the manager's order to leave, and "struck the manager on the head with a bobbin." "A number of other operatives also threw bobbins at the Manager and Assistant Manager," whereupon the police arrested "several of the rioters." "Immediately a crowd of about 1000 workmen assembled in front of the thana [police station] shouting slogans such as 'Mazdur ki Jai' " and demanded their release. When asked why, the "ringleaders" replied, *"it was their order."*[111] How similar to the incidents at the Fort Gloster Jute Mill in December 1905, where one day, when a "considerable amount of unrest" already existed in the workers' minds over a recently concluded strike, the cry of *Bande Mataram* was "taken up by one department after another," the European assistants "hustled about the place," and the police were told by the workers, on arresting two people, that they were "all brothers in the mill, all brothers in Bengal; that in arresting the two men they had all been insulted."[112]

These similarities across the separation of decades are not accidental. They arise from the fact that both the *swadeshi bhadralok* and his later Communist successor had to address themselves to the already existing working-class notions about defying authority. These notions were rooted deep in the worker's understanding of authority and in the manager's projection of it. Physical violence against the employer was not necessarily a "primitive" defiance of authority; it was rather an acknowledgment of the way authority was represented in the jute mills and elsewhere. In the very nature of defiance was mirrored the nature of authority.

[111] Ibid.
[112] *Amrita Bazar Patrika*, 18 December 1905; Sarkar, *Swadeshi Movement*, p. 228.

· 6 ·

CLASS AND
COMMUNITY

Their poverty gave the jute-mill workers a sense of identity and a certain sense of social stratification as well. Even when issues like religion divided them, there still remained, in their own minds, a fundamental distinction between themselves as "poor people" and others who seemed well-off. "We are poor people and [we] work in mills" is how a group of Muslim mill hands once described themselves in 1896 when requesting help from wealthier Muslims in fighting their Hindu fellow workers, who were just as poor and would have possibly described themselves in very much the same terms.[1] Overlapping with the rich-poor distinction was the distinction the workers made between themselves and their employers. During times of strikes and industrial tension, especially after the 1930s, the workers suspected any affluent-looking stranger moving about in their midst of being a "spy" working for the employers. For instance, a group of Bengali sociologists who had decided in 1944 to live in a working-class slum in Jagaddal in order to research the living conditions of the workers soon discovered that "the employment of a cook and servant promptly led to their being taken for agent of jute mill owners." It was only after they had "dismissed the servants," taken turns "at [the] cooking of their meals," and explained their mission to the workers that they were able to "disarm suspicion" and make "friendly contacts."[2]

If this was the one expression of an emergent, though elementary, class consciousness on the part of the jute worker, there were other expressions as well. The strike wave of 1937–38 was accompanied by some very impressive demonstrations of working-class solidarity. The government documents belonging to these years speak of the workers of the Naihati Jute Mills "receiving monetary assistance from the workers of certain other jute mills" while on strike in December 1937, or of some "530 spinners" of the Dalhousie Jute Mill striking work "in sympathy with workers on strike at the Northbrook Jute mill."[3] On 12 November 1937, to give yet another example, more than

[1] W.B.S.A., Judicial Dept. Police Br., July 1896 A55–56.

[2] K. P. Chattopadhyay and H. K. Chaturvedi, "How Jute Workers Live," *Science and Culture*, vol. 12, no. 8, Feb. 1947, p. 376.

[3] W.B.S.A., Home Poll. Confdl. no. 371/1938.

twenty-five hundred workers at the Cheviot Jute Mill stopped work in "sympathy with the workers on strike in the Caledonian Jute Mill"; they even made (unsuccessful) attempts "to bring out the workers of the Budge Budge Jute Mill" in support of the same cause.[4]

Much of this may seem understandable. Conditions in the jute mills were never inviting, and although the monetary benefits of employment in Calcutta may have had their attractions for a desperate peasantry, wage slavery, or *nokri* as it was called, often evoked a feeling of resentment caused by a sense of loss of honor and freedom.[5] Says a Bhojpuri song:

> Railways are not our enemy
> Nor are the steamships.
> Our real enemy is *nokaria* [*nokri*].[6]

When one adds to this the exposure that the workers would have had—at least since the 1920s—to the experience, however limited, of trade unionism and radical politics, one has, as it were, the standard formula for the emergence of "class consciousness," even if only of an elementary kind.[7]

Indeed, it appears that by the turn of the century the laboring poor of Calcutta, in spite of the diversity of their backgrounds and occupations, did show some important signs of being a "community": there had evolved in the working-class areas of the city a distinct variant of spoken Hindi that was not to be heard anywhere else in the country.[8] These ties of "community" were also in evidence during the so-called Talla riot that occurred in Calcutta on 29 June 1897 over the issue of

[4] Ibid.

[5] Cf. the Bhojpuri proverb: "One who gets a job in the East, can fill his house with gold." Cited in Gyanendra Pandey, "Community Consciousness and Communal Strife in Colonial North India," unpublished manuscript, chapter entitled "Economic Dislocation."

[6] Ibid. See also the discussion in Sridhar Misra, *Bhojpuri Lokasahitya: Sanskritic Adhyayan* (Allahabad, 1971), p. 183. Apparently, the term *coolie* was resented for its connotations of low status. "Why should we be called coolies," asked a protest song of Indian laborers in British Guiana, "we who were born in the clans and families of seers and saints?" Quoted in Brij V. Lal, "Approaches to the Study of Indian Indentured Emigration with Special Reference to Fiji." *Journal of Pacific History*, vol. 15, pt. 1, Jan. 1980, pp. 52–70.

[7] From very early on, the trade union literature directed at the working class concentrated on discussing the glaring disparities between "wages" and "profits." The language of this discourse would repay examination. For example, see Appendix B to Manju Chattopadhyay, *Sramik Netri Santoshkumari Debi* (Calcutta, 1984?), pp. 66–71.

[8] See Suniti Kumar Chatterjee, "Calcutta Hindusthani: A Study of a Jargon Dialect." in his *Select Papers*, vol. 1, (Delhi, 1972), pp. 204–256.

the eviction by court order of a Muslim mason named Himmat Khan
from a piece of land at Talla in north Calcutta. Himmat Khan, faced
with the court order, declared his hut to be "a *Musjid* of long standing." The "mosque" was subsequently demolished by the police, and
this sparked off a riot.[9] The riot blazed in the northern parts of the city
until 2 July; the mill hands in the outskirts were reported to be restive
as late as 6 July.[10] Eighty-seven people were ultimately sent up for trial
on charges of rioting, and eighty-one were convicted.[11]

What was the nature of the "community" that was involved in rioting? In the absence of court documents, it is indeed difficult to depict
the people who constituted the "crowd" in the Talla riot. Besides, motives for joining the riot varied widely.[12] But looking through newspaper reports we can identify some faces in an otherwise anonymous
crowd. The identifiable are no doubt few in number, but they may be
indicative of the social composition of the men who fought for saving
the demolished mosque. There was, for example, Sheikh Chadi, a fifty-
year-old rioter killed by the police, who was a "thatcher by profes-
sion." So was Gajadhar Kurmi, a fifteen-year-old boy, also killed by
police. Sheikh Chadi, the thatcher, had a son called Sheikh Abdul who
worked in the jute mill at Sealdah. At 2:00 P.M. on 30 June, when the
son heard that "his father had been shot by some *goras* [whites] at the
Moonshi Bazar," he left the mills "with 200 or 250 workmen and went
to the scene of the riot" to join the mob. Natra Abdul, another of the
rioters, was a "coolie" who declared in court that "he and several
others kept away from work" during the riot on 30 June. Another accused, Nanku Khan, "worked in Jetty" and lived in Subedarpara, an
area of rioting. One Nabijan was identified as having been among a
group of laborers accused of assaulting a certain Mr. Slotter, engineer
in the Ashcroft Jute Press at Chitpur, Chitpur and Kashipur (Cossi-
pore) being two places where many of the local jute presses were located. Himmat Khan, the man at the center of events in the Talla riot,
was himself a mason; the newspapers carried reports on the "hundreds

[9] W.B.S.A., Judicial Dept. Police Br., November 1897 A12–13, 39–43; *Amrita Bazar Patrika*, 2 July 1897; *RNPB*, 17 July 1897.

[10] W.B.S.A., Judicial Dept. Police Br., November 1897 A22.

[11] NAI, Home Public, January 1989, A 55–7; October 1897, A 150.

[12] There were the obvious hangers-on who were quick to join the rioting. One such person mentioned in the reports is a Jew called E. M. Cohen, who was unemployed and dependent on his father: *Amrita Bazar Patrika*, 6 July 1897. It was said that a part of the disturbance was also created by Marwari rain-gamblers, who gambled on whether or not it would rain on a particular day. They had an "old score to settle with the police," who were lately getting "strict" with the crime: NAI, Home Judl. March 1897, A 31–42; May 1897, B 297–308.

of masons and coolies" who fought a seesaw battle with the police throughout the two days of rioting. The commissioner of police later reported that the rioters were composed mostly of "low class" Muslim weavers, perhaps Jolahas, and "bricklayers, who were joined by bad characters of the disturbed area," and another newspaper identified the bulk of the rioters as "up-countrymen."[13]

It would be hasty, however, to understand the nature of this "community" in terms of an economic conception of "class." Most of the men who fought the demolition of a "mosque" were, naturally enough, Muslims and the events give some indication of the part religion played in defining their sense of "community." It is true that the physical involvement of Muslim mill hands in the Talla riot remained mostly marginal, being confined mainly to the few mills that were situated either within or very close to the city, including those at Sealdah, Garden Reach, and Baranagar.[14] But certain events that occurred after the riots had subsided in the city served to demonstrate how strongly mill workers saw themselves as members of wider religious communities. Babu G. C. Mukherjee, assistant superintendent of police, 24 Parganas, has left a graphic account of the impact that the Talla riot had on the jute-mill suburbs:

On the morning of the 6th ultimo [July] a letter in Bengali, purporting to be under the signature of Hazi Nur Mahomed [Zakaria] of Calcutta, reached some of the mill operatives of the Kankinara Jute Mill, requesting all true Muhammadans to join the Talla rioters in rescuing the Masjid-Ground and calling those, not complying, "sons of Muchis [cobblers]."

The letter . . . created great excitement, and the Muhammadan employees of the Jute Mill applied for and obtained leave from the Manager, Mr. Clark, for the day at 9:00 A.M. The mill hands struck work and marched downwards, shouting and beating a tomtom. Some had sticks. They numbered over a thousand. . . .

These operatives came down at the gate of the next mill, viz. the Kankinara Paper Factory, but as there were only 75 adult Mu-

[13] This description is based on *Amrita Bazar Patrika*, 2, 16, 22, and 25 July 1897; Indian Central Jute Committee, *Report on the Marketing of Jute and Jute Products* (Calcutta, 1952), pp. 166–167; *RNPB*, 17 and 31 July 1897; W.B.S.A., Judicial Dept. Police Br., November 1897, A39–43. For more specific references, see my "Communal Riots and Labour: Bengal's Jute Mill-Hands in the 1890s," *Past and Present*, no. 91, May 1891, pp. 159–160.

[14] This is partly to be explained by police precautions and military measures taken to prevent any mill hands from entering the city. W.B.S.A., Judicial Dept. Police Br., September 1897 A101–13; November 1897 A16–22.

hammadans . . . employed; the Manager Mr. Boon somehow managed to make them work on; and so this mill was not closed.

The Kankinara Jute Mill coolies next marched down to the Anglo-Indian Jute Mill, at Jag[ad]dal, a mile off.

The Manager, Mr. Thompson . . . allowed his coolies a holiday when asked for, and closed his mill for the day. There were 816 Muhammadan coolies here, including females and children.

The few Muhammadan coolies employed in the adjoining Jute Mills, also were allowed by the Asstt . . . to join their brethren of the Mills. At the Gordon only 76 Muhammadans were employed.

This large body, numbering about 1,500, arrived at the gate of the last mill at Jag[ad]dal, viz. the Alliance. The operatives inside, who had evidently been informed of the plans of the operatives of the other mills named above, applied for leave, but having been refused communicated . . . what had happened to the coolies who had collected outside the gate and been creating disturbances.[15]

"A row then occurred," in which the coolies used brickbats in response to the European assistants' opening fire on them, and a few were killed. The news of the disturbance spread to the two mills at Samnugger the Dunbar Cotton Mills and the Samnugger Jute Mills, where more than six thousand operatives were employed. The Muslims in the former struck work after midday, "evidently on receipt of information of the state of things at the other mills of Jag[ad]dal and Kankinara," and some of the two thousand Muslim coolies at Samnugger Mills came out and "collected on the road close to their bustis." The entire crowd of mill hands was later dispersed by the police.[16]

These Muslim mill hands thus shared a sense of identity with other indigent Muslim migrants in the city: the mason, the thatcher, the jetty worker, the coolie, and the jute-press worker of north Calcutta. Their communal bonds are reflected in the events described above as well as in the fact that on the first night of the Talla riot, Muslims came over from different places such as Chitpur, Kashipur, Baranager, and Nikaripara to fight the police.[17] In addition, mill hands at Garden Reach felt restive on the same night.[18]

An important aspect of this sense of religious "community" needs to be noted: its capacity to divide "class." The years immediately preceding 1897, the year of the Talla riot, had seen some bitter Hindu-Mus-

---

[15] Ibid., September 1897 A101–3.
[16] Ibid.
[17] NAI, Home Public, October 1897, A 124–47.
[18] W.B.S.A., Judicial Dept. Police Br., November 1897; A9.

lim conflicts break out among jute-mill laborers, in the middle of a rash of strikes over falling wages and worsening conditions.[19] It could not be without some significance, after all, that the first mill-hand organization formed in these years (1895), at Kankinara, should have given itself such a partisan name as the Mahomedan Association and have as its two principal objectives the recruiting of more Muslims to jute-mill work and the renovating of mosques.[20]

The strength and depth of workers' feelings over issues relating to their religion were revealed in three Hindu-Muslim riots that were to break out in 1896, involving mill hands from Titaghur, Garden Reach, and Serampore. The riots focused on the issue of cow killing—a reprehensible act in the eyes of the Hindus—during the Muslim festival of Bakr Id. In each of these riots, a notion of religious "community" was clearly at work. I summarize below the salient features of these riots.

The Bakr-Id riot at Titaghur in 1896 started when Mahomed Hossain, an upcountry bricklayer working at the construction site of the Standard Jute Mills, brought in a heifer to be sacrified. The heifer was stolen by a group of four Hindu workers who were opposed to the sacrifice of cows on Bakr Id.[21] In the ensuing riots, however, workers of the neighboring Titaghur Paper Mills and the Titaghur Jute Mills joined in, taking sides according to religious allegiance. Word had spread from the "Titaghur mosque," where about three hundred Muslims from neighboring areas congregated on the morning of Bakr Id and where Mahomed Hossain and other Muslim bricklayers had gone to say their prayers. About "300 or more Hindus and 180 Mahomedans" took part in the riot, and slogans like *Mar Hindu sala log* (Beat up the bloody Hindus!) were frequently shouted in frenzied outbursts.[22]

The Bakr Id riot at the Lower Hooghly Jute Mill also witnessed conflict between Hindu and Muslim immigrants. Here too on the day of Bakr Id, the Muslims sacrificed a cow, and in revenge some Chamars and Dosadhs (low-caste upcountry Hindus) killed a pig within the mill premises. The mill was short of yarn the next day, so the weavers—all Muslims, which was usual—were given a three-hour break. "During the interval the Muhammadans were talking together, and they asked the manager what he was going to do with the men who had killed the

[19] See my "Communal Riots and Labour" for details of these conflicts and those of the riots discussed below.

[20] *Report of the Indian Factory Labour Commission* (London, 1909), vol. 2, pp. 263–264.

[21] W.B.S.A., Judicial Dept. Police Br., August 1896 A4–5.

[22] Ibid., A13–14; *Englishman*, 2 June 1896.

pig." Passions rose and the Muslims refused to resume work "till the business of the pig had been settled." Thereafter the riot started, the Muslim mill hands aggrieved that whereas they had been forbidden to hold their sacrifice within the mill premises, the low-caste Hindus had actually been permitted to so so.

As in the Bakr Id riot at Titaghur, here also Muslim mill hands from neighboring areas showed a readiness to come to help their coreligionists. "Some outside Muhammadans" were reportedly already inside the mills, and made a demand jointly with the Muslim workers that the Chamars and Dosadhs be made over to them. On the evening of the same day, the Hindu employees raised the alarm, saying that a large Muslim force was coming down "to beat the Hindus at the mill." At the same time, about three hundred Muslims arrived, probably from the Garden Reach and Metiabruj area, in order to "protect their co-religionists living in the [coolie] lines," who feared a big Hindu attack on them. Finally, when "a number of Muhammadan employees of the Upper Hooghly Jute Mills at Garden Reach left work [on 26 June 1896] with the object of helping friends in the lower Mills," the managers made peace by dismissing some Hindu laborers. Work was resumed but communal discontent continued to smolder. A "large number of Mahomedans" of the Lower Hooghly Jute Mills appeared on 29 June before the joint magistrate of Alipore and complained against the Hindu employees, "charging them with killing a pig in their presence while they were engaged in their prayers on the occasion of the *Bakr-Id*, and thereby wounding their religious feelings."[23]

Communal passions were similarly aroused to a high pitch in the Bakr Id riot at Rishra (in Serampore, Hooghly District), where Hindu and Muslim employees of the Hastings Jute Mill were involved.[24] The Muslims had made it known in the locality that they would be sacrificing a cow that year, and a petition in protest of the sacrifice was made to Mr. Lister, the subdivisional officer, by Hindu mill hands as well as shopkeepers of the "Rishra *Bustee*," headed by a "rich Marwari shopkeeper." One of the petitioners said, "Eight days ago I heard Buna Mian, a worker in Hastings Mill, say that they would kill cows. I also heard Khuda Mian, a weaver, say [that] three days ago." This was on 18 May, six days before Bakr Id. On 21 May, Lister received a petition from Muslim workers, headed by one Multan Mian, asking for permission to kill cows, whereupon a counterpetition was submitted by

[23] The description of this riot is based on W.B.S.A., Judicial Dept. Police Br., July 1896 A36–8; *Englishman*, 2 May and 1 July 1896.

[24] This account is based on W.B.S.A., Judicial Dept. Police Br., July 1896 A52–7; *Englishman*, 29 May 1896; *RNPB*, 13 June 1896.

fifty Hindus saying that "*Korbani* [animal sacrifice] at Rishra should be forbidden."

Lister immediately arrested "some eight to ten persons who were heard to consult" on the question of sacrificing a cow "within [the Rishra] musjid [mosque]," and placed the building under police guard. Nazir Mian, the imam of the mosque, who was regarded by local Muslims as a fakir (holy man), had reportedly been to Barrackpore to organize help from the Muslim workers of Titaghur in case of any riot with the Hindus. He had also sent a letter to Calcutta asking for men to fight the Hindus. The letter was intercepted and Nazir Mian was arrested when he returned on the eve of Bakr Id. Cow sacrifice was forbidden. On 24 May, the first day of Bakr Id, the whole area was tense. Both Hindu and Muslim mill hands refused to go to work and spent the day in keeping an eye on each other. Only measures that included a strong police detachment near the mosque, forced stoppage of "ingress of Mahomedans into the town," and bands of constables patrolling all over the town succeeded in preventing a riot.

Nazir Mian's letter that the police intercepted is worth our attention. The letter ran as follows:

It is informed that in village Rishra, police station Serampore, district Hooghly, the Hindus are going to create a row during the *Bakr-Id* [cow] sacrifice; they say they do not sacrifice here, if you do so, we [Hindus] will create row. Therefore, I request that you all assist us. We are poor people and work in mills. You better give this information to Muhammadans in the Friday prayers that it is religious act and everybody should assist as possible.[25]

This statement both documents and appeals to a sense of religious "community." We would, however, be mistaken to see in this "community" any "unity of the poor against the rich," a unity mediated by religion. The poor knew themselves by their poverty, but the "community," as defined in this case, had no way of excluding the wealthy. Nazir Mian's letter was in fact addressed to Haji Noor Muhammad Zakaria, a very rich and influential Muslim trader and pan-Islamist of Calcutta.[26] The reference in the letter to the workers' poverty was thus as much a statement about their self-image as it was an attempt to secure help from the rich by evoking sentiments of pity and religion, a variation on a theme we have encountered before (see chapter 4).

[25] W.B.S.A., Judicial Dept. Police Br., July 1896 A55–6.
[26] The reader may recall that it was a letter purporting to be from the same Zakaria that caused unrest among the Muslim mill hands at the time of the Talla riot.

Yet we cannot ignore the point that even a religious or racial riot that seemingly divided the workers contained an element of rebellion as well. In 1894–95, for instance, some of the mill workers became extremely assertive about observing their religious festivals, including those of Id, Muharram, and Rath Jatra. The mills involved were some of those at Titaghur, Baranagar, Kamarhatty, Garden Reach, and Hooghly, where workers demanded and "forcibly" took holidays on these religious occasions by "threatening" to go out on strike. An assertion by the workers of their religious identity thus became, by the very nature of power relations in the mills, an act of self-assertion as well, and a very concerned IJMA hurriedly wrote to the Bengal government on 26 April 1895 asking for "additional police supervision" in jute-mill municipalities to help control the "riotous combination of mill-hands."[27]

The close and contradictory coexistence of a religious, and potentially divisive, outlook and an antiemployer, and hence potentially uniting, mentality was thus characteristic of the collective and public acts of the jute-mill work force. This observation will not surprise students of Indian labor history, but it deserves emphasis, since, for more than fifty years—that is, for the entire period under consideration—this remained a major characteristic of the jute workers' struggle. Their sense of identity as "workers" or "poor people" was always enmeshed in other narrower and conflicting identities such as those deriving from religion, language, and ethnicity. It is difficult, in other words, to write the history of the jute worker's consciousness in terms of a gradual evolution from an "elementary" to a "mature" stage of formation. The "gulf" that remained "between the . . . Hindustani [i.e. Hindi-speaking] and Bengali workers," and the lack of "strong fraternal ties" between them, always presented the trade union organizer with special problems of working-class unity.[28] Sometimes the "gulf" was so large that "the Bengali labourer [would] not bathe in the same tank with the Hindustani labourer" because the former considered the latter "dirty."[29] And there was, as we have already shown, the perpetual problem of what (in the language of Indian nationalism) is called the communal question, that is, the problem of antagonism between Hindu and Muslim laborers. Thus, its impressive manifestations notwithstanding, the class identity of the jute-mill workers remained re-

[27] *IJMA, Report, 1895* (Calcutta, 1896), pp. 4–6. For details see my "Communal Riots and Labour."

[28] Indrajit Gupta, *Capital and Labour in the Jute Industry* (Bombay, 1953), pp. 41–42.

[29] *RCLI*, vol. 5, pt. 2, p. 118.

markably fragile and easily gave way to the other identities created by race and religion.

This was most dramatically revealed in the 1930s and 1940s, when the workers' hostility toward their employers was matched by an equally strong sense of hostility between large sections of the workers themselves, resulting in a series of bitter feuds between Hindus and Muslims. There was, for example, a "serious" riot between Hindu and Muslim workers at Gourepore (24 Parganas) at the time of the Bakr Id festival in 1932.[30] Extreme feelings of hostility between the Hindu and the Muslim workers of the Oriental Jute Mill at Budge Budge were reported on the occasion of the Bakr Id festival in March 1934; "at Shyamgunge, at the site of the G. D. Birla Jute Mill to the south of Budge Budge," violence erupted between the two groups and "a very ugly situation likely to have resulted in bloodshed" was averted only by strong police action.[31] On 3 June of the following year the Muslim workmen at the India Jute Mills at Serampore abstained from work and fought with "brickbats and soda-water bottles" the attempts by local Hindus to demolish what they, the Muslims, regarded as a mosque.[32] "Tense feelings" and "a likelihood of a fracas" between Hindus and Muslims at Kamarhatty and Titaghur were reported to the police in 1938.[33] In Titaghur and Kankinara, the Hindus and the Muslims took turns in complaining to the government about each other's unfriendliness. In June 1938, the "Hindus of Kankinara" wrote to the government describing a riot between them and the Muslims "during the Holi festival day last" when "several" Hindus were injured and "one killed." Besides, "Hindu houses" and women were attacked "in front of the Kankinara big mosque." The news of this incident, said the Hindus, "ran into the city like . . . wildfire and Mussalmans began to assault Hindus wherever they found them lonely [sic]."[34] A petition from some sixty Muslims of Titaghur in October 1938 on the other hand complained of Hindu arrogance in playing music before Muslim mosques during the celebration of Hindu festivals. In his note on this petition, H. J. Twynam, the chief secretary to the government of Bengal, admitted that it was "unfortunately true that a state of communal tension exists at Titagarh at present," and pointed out that "numbers taking part in the Durga Puja procession [this year] were a good deal above normal."[35]

[30] W.B.S.A., Home Poll. Confdl. no. 117/1934.
[31] Ibid.
[32] Ibid., no. 578/1935, pts. 1 and 2.
[33] Ibid., no. 115/1938.
[34] Ibid., no. 260/1938.
[35] Ibid., no. 370/1938.

In March 1939, the situation turned ugly once again when the celebration of the Hindu festival of Holi was marred by an outbreak of Hindu-Muslim riots among the mill hands of Metiabruj, Titaghur, Khardah, Kamarhatty, Naihati, and Jagaddal, in which both lives and property were lost.[36] Tension between the two groups was evident again in 1940 when the government felt constrained to refuse permission to "the Hindus of Kamarhati" to take out a religious procession "at Kamarhati Agarpara Jute Mill [coolie] line." The government based its decision on the ground that "the processionists definitely refused to proceed unless allowed to go armed."[37] In March 1940, a communal riot at Bansberia in Hooghly was acknowledged by the government to have had "injurious reactions on Hindu-Muslim relationship in the Mill area generally."[38] The state of feelings can be gauged from the way the members of the two communities often proceeded to describe each other. On 11 March 1940 some Muslims of Gourepore wrote to the government asking for protection from attacks by Hindus. The letter described the upcountry Hindu workers of "the jute mill area in the suburb[s] of Calcutta" as "deadly enemies of Muslims," their "cherish[ed] desire . . . [being] to harass and oppress" the latter.[39] These antagonisms received an ultimate and gruesome expression in "the communal riots of 1946–47 and . . . the subsequent riots of 1950," which, to quote Indrajit Gupta, "particularly affected the jute mill areas of Barrackpore, Hooghly and Howrah."[40]

At first sight, these conflicts of race and religion among the workers may appear to reveal a totally different aspect of the workers' consciousness from that expressed through conflicts between the workers and the authorities (e.g., strikes). In every strike by jute workers, however, "there [was] *always* . . . the *possibility*," as the government put it in 1929, "of communal and even racial clashes."[41] At the very height of the general strike of 1937, the government noticed "acute comunal [i.e. Hindu-Muslim] tension" among the workers in the mill towns of Kankinara, Jagaddal, Khardah, and Kamarhatty. The tension had in fact been "augmented by the strikes," in which "the Muhammadans [were] very unwilling" to participate.

[36] Ibid., nos. 324/1934 and 11/1940.

[37] Ibid., no. 302/1940.

[38] Ibid., no. 157/1940.

[39] Ibid., no. 229/1940.

[40] Gupta, *Capital and Labour*, p. 43. See also IOL, Memoirs of P. D. Martyn, Mss. Eur. F180/3, Appendix, "Diary prepared from rough notes kept during the disturbance of August 16th-20th, 1946," entry for 16 August 1946.

[41] RCLI, vol. 5, pt. 1, p. 139. Emphasis added.

At Jagatdal [the government said], one Muhammadan Sardar of Meghna Mill—Mulla sardar—had kept Meghna running by bringing in his Muhammadan workers of the mill in a body. They were one day attacked by the Hindu strikers (Rajputs) of Anglo-India Middle Mill . . . and there is great ill-feeling over this on both sides.[42]

One can adduce more such instances of strikes turning into "communal" conflicts. In March 1937, a strike at the Birla Jute Mills ended in a race riot between the strikers and the "loyal" workers, the strikers being "local Bengalee men" and the loyal workers, Hindi-speaking up-country people.[43] A similar situation occurred at the National Jute Mill in December 1938 with the difference that here the lines of division between the "strikers" and the "nonstrikers" were based on religion and not language. The result was a Hindu-Muslim riot "on the morning of the 5th [December]" when the authorities tried to reopen the mill with the help of nonstrikers. A police report said:

About 400 workers attended [the mill]. Almost the whole of these men were Muhammadans. About 7 o'clock a crowd of about 300 men composed of recently dismissed workers and strikers attacked the cooly lines of the men who were working in the mill. The Muhammadan coolies working in the mill received . . . information [of this] and seizing weapons from the mill rushed out to defend their quarters . . . [and] a riot started between the two parties—the one party being mainly Muhammadan and the other mainly Hindu.[44]

Here is another example. Six Hindu spinners of the Standard Jute Mills were dismissed in November 1938 for assaulting the manager. Their dismissal caused a strike on 14 November and resulted soon in sympathetic strikes at a few other mills, forcing the closure of five of them, the strike thus affecting thirty thousand workers altogether. This was no doubt an impressive instance of workers' solidarity against the employers. On the night of 16 November, however, "a free fight" ensued between "the strikers and the loyal workers at Tittagarh," which, the government reported, "later took the form of a communal [Hindu-Muslim] riot [in which] one man was killed and several persons injured."[45] When the local authorities tried to arrange a peace-making

[42] W.B.S.A., Home Poll. Confdl. no. 128/1937, pt. 1.
[43] Ibid., no. 128/1937.
[44] Ibid., no. 403/1938.
[45] Ibid., no. 381/1938.

meeting of the leaders of the two communities, "it was found difficult to persuade the speakers to discuss the communal trouble without reference to the strike in the local mills." The Muslims resented "being out of work because the Hindus wish[ed] to strike." At this meeting, it was reported, "the Mahomedans continually referred to the fact that all the workers [were] without wages because 6 Hindus [had] a disagreement with the management."[46]

These strikes and the religious and racial riots discussed before help to isolate an important aspect of the jute workers' culture that we wish to emphasize here. This culture was undoubtedly capable of generating militant protests and an antiemployer outlook, as the discussion here and in the preceding two chapters will have made clear. It would appear that the workers did have an awareness of being poor and oppressed, and on occasion gave remarkable demonstrations of a sense of solidarity against their employers. Yet all collective public actions of the workers were marked by an inherent duality. An act of revolt against the authorities, such as a strike, always had the potential of turning into its opposite, a fight among the workers themselves, a religious riot; a religious or racial riot, on the other hand, contained a necessary element of rebellion against authority, an extreme manifestation of which were the strikes based on "religious" or "racial" demands.

This duality characteristic of the collective and public acts of the working class usually prompts explanations that are either political or political-economic in orientation. None of these explanations, we shall argue, gives us any clues to the nature of the consciousness that was expressed through the "duality" in question.

SYMPATHETIC OBSERVERS of the working class often explain the weakness of worker solidarity in terms of the seeds of division deliberately sown among workers by interested people from the ruling classes (naturally including the employers). We should listen carefully to their argument, especially as it applies to the present context, for it is not without some force to it. "The real gravity of this communal disruption," wrote Indrajit Gupta, referring to Hindu-Muslim riots in the jute-mill areas in the 1950s, "lies in the latent anti-Muslim sentiments *which have been fostered* among the non-Muslim workers . . . by the poisonous anti-Pakistan propaganda carried on by reactionary leaders." The workers had been "provoked and incited by communal reactionaries into regarding their . . . fellow workers as enemies."[47]

[46] Ibid., no. 370/1938.
[47] Gupta, *Capital and Labour*, p. 44.

Stated so baldly, this sounds like a crude theory of manipulation and conspiracy. Yet we could do worse than Gupta by ignoring altogether the existence of such "provocation" and "incitements" and the place these categories held in the explanation that sometimes the workers themselves gave of their own action. For example, in the same letter of 1940 in which the Muslim mill hands of Naihati described their up-country Hindu fellow workers as "deadly enemies to Muslims," they also made a pointed reference to the doings of the Arya Samaj, which, in their view, exacerbated such "enmity." Thanks to "the activities of the Arya Samaj" over "the last two years," the letter told the government, the Hindu workers' hostility had turned to "open violence." Their decision to take out procession on the day of the Holi festival—"with a large number of armed Hindu Gundas with exciting slogans full of abuse to Muslims and their faith," accompanied by "a lorry full of brickbats and soda–water bottles" that were hidden from view by "15 strong durwans of the Gouripur Jute Mill" sitting on them—was, according to the letter, quite a new feature in Hindu-Muslim relations in that area. So too, allegedly, was the Hindu demand that they be allowed to play music while passing by mosques. "This year," the authors warned, "the situation appears more grave [due to] the increased activities of the Arya Samajists combined with [those of] the disciples of Shyama Prasad and Mo[o]nje."[48]

On the side of the Muslim worker, too, much of the sensitivity he showed toward religious issues in the 1930s and 1940s had to do with the activities of the Muslim League, of politicians like H. S. Suhrawardy and the backing they received in these years from employers and the government. The strike wave of 1936–38, the prospect of India's self-rule, and the success of the Bengali left at the elections of 1937 (in which all eight labor seats were won by them) had unnerved the European employers and the British bureaucrats in Calcutta. To many of them "labour conditions" now looked like "becoming increasingly difficult."[49] Their nervousness was reflected in their reactions to the jute workers' general strike of 1937. Arguing from the premise that the strike could not have had a "real economic basis . . . [as] otherwise labour surely would have protested long before," the employers soon talked themselves into believing their own, imagined scenario of an imminent Bolshevik revolution.[50] The strike was "purely political," declared IJMA, "with the workers being exploited for communistic and

[48] W.B.S.A., Home Poll. Confdl. no. 229/1940.
[49] C.S.A.S., B.P.., Box 10, G. B. Morton to Benthall, 13 September 1935.
[50] C.S.A.S., B.P., Box 12, mimeographed note dated 27 April 1937: "Jute Strike Situation."

political purposes having as their object the overthrow of ordered government."[51] That this was not an act of empty grandstanding by IJMA is suggested by the following private note from Benthall to one of his colleagues in 1937:

> What we have to be careful about [wrote Benthall] is that congress or the Communists do not form proper Labour Unions— "proper" in the sense that they conform with the definitions of the [Trade Unions] Act and use those unions as the nuclei of revolution in accordance with the standard Communist method of working.[52]

The militant mood of the workers only confirmed some of the worst fears of the employers and the government. An official report entitled "Strikes in various jute mills in the district of 24 Parganas" in 1937 described the "general attitude which has been growing among mill workers" as "one of defiance" and concluded that "there is no doubt whatever that communistic ideas are rapidly spreading among them," producing "a contempt for and defiance of authority."[53] Understandably, therefore, the authorities were more than pleased to be assured by H. S. Suhrawardy, the labor minister in the new ministry, that his Muslim League unions were "the best antidote to communism," that his men were "at least taught two things," as he told Benthall over a private lunch in 1940: "respect for the employer and respect for the government."[54] Suhrawardy's strident advocacy of anticommunism had caught their attention even earlier and his success in weaning a substantial section of the Calcutta dockworkers away from the Communists during a strike of 1934 had won him praise from the government and the employers alike.[55] The bond between Muslim League ministers like Suhrawardy or Khwaja Nazimuddin and the European employers was reinforced by the fact that the new ministry depended for its survival on the support of the European bloc in the Bengal Legislative Assembly.[56] The ministry, therefore, as Nazimuddin was re-

[51] IJMA *Report 1937*, (Calcutta, 1938), pp. 41–42.

[52] C.S.A.S., B.P., Box 12, Benthall to McKerrow, 9 November 1937.

[53] W.B.S.A., Home Poll. Confdl. no. 128/1937.

[54] C.S.A.S., B.P., Box 19, diary entry for 19 March 1940; see also Box 12, synopsis of Suhrawardy; discussion with Chapman Mortimer on 5 June 1940.

[55] See, for instance, Godfrey Harrison, *Bird and Company of Calcutta* (Calcutta, 1964), p. 183, and IOL, Hoare Papers, Mss. Eur. E240, letter from Stanley Jackson, June 1935.

[56] See Shila Sen, *Muslim Politics in Bengal 1937–1947* (New Delhi, 1976), p. 96; also Humaira Momen, *Muslim Politics in Bengal: A Study of Krishak Praja Party and the Elections of 1937* (Dacca, 1972).

ported to have said to a colleague of Benthall's, was "particularly anxious ... to avoid a break with the Europeans, especially over labour policy."[57] The employers responded warmly to the gesture. Benthall advised his friends in Bird and Company to "go on keeping in close touch with Shaheed [Suhrawardy],"[58] and proceeded to congratulate "Fazl [sic] Huq, Shaheed and [Nazimuddin] ... on the capable way in which ... [they had] ... met the menace of communism that surrounded the [1937] jute mill strike."[59] This was followed by a round of lunches and dinners, and men like Suhrawardy were now allowed a degree of "familiarity" and "intimacy" with the European businessmen that surely would have been denied to most other Indians. Benthall's description of a private lunch he once hosted for Suhrawardy in 1940 ended in this way:

> My guest had two helpings of each course and finished off with a large cigar which by 3.30 PM. proved too much for him. After being revived with ice water, he decided it was time to get back to work and departed with many pleasant personal compliments.[60]

The support that the jute-mill owners gave to the Muslim League unions was not simply confined to dinners and lunches, however. Suhrawardy, on his part, clearly saw them as an important source of funds for his organizations. "To get these [White Flag] unions going," he told Chapman Mortimer in 1937, "we need money and my proposal is that the [jute] Mills should provide this." Asked if any possible public knowledge of such funding would not be embarrassing, his calculated reply was that "no one would know."[61] It is difficult to tell from the evidence of the Benthall papers to what extent Suhrawardy succeeded in achieving this objective, but we are left in no doubt about the active employer-support for his Muslim League unions. IJMA assured him in July 1937 that the "Association Mills had consistently refused to have anything to do with the self-styled labour leaders, to wit the communist agitators who were the cause of all trouble." Instead, they "would be prepared to recognize ... [Suhrawardy's unions] and deal with

[57] C.S.A.S., B.P., Box 12, "Strictly Private" letter from "David," 19 April 1937; see also the unsigned note (marked "Strictly Private") on discussion with Suhrawardy, dated 4 May 1937.
[58] C.S.A.S., B.P., Box 12, Benthall to "Mac," 21 May 1937.
[59] C.S.A.S., B.P., Box 12, Benthall to Nazimuddin, 11 May 1937.
[60] C.S.A.S., B.P., Box 19, diary entry for 19 March 1940.
[61] C.S.A.S., B.P., Box 12, synopsis of Suhrawardy's discussion with Chapman Mortimer on 5 June 1937; notes on "confidential" meeting between Suhrawardy and the IJMA chairman, H. H. Brown, on 28 July 1937; Box 16, unsigned note on "Mr. S[uhrawardy]," dated 9 December 1940.

them."[62] Once, when Suhrawardy complained to a high official of Bird and Company about the attitudes of some of their jute-mill officers toward his unions, the gentleman "asked Mr S., if he had any complaints of this nature, to ask Lewis or anyone else he pleases to send them *privately* to me so that I could investigate them."[63] Benthall offered him similar advice from time to time:

> I said that so far as building up Labour Unions is concerned, our greatest difficulty was the personnel that he [Suhrawardy] employed and the cases that he brought up. As regards personnel, if only he could establish *close* working conditions with the managers ... he would make wonderful progress with the Trade Unions. Further, I said that the mistake which his Unions made was to take up bad cases. . . . He could save himself much trouble and build up more quickly if he could instruct his chosen men to approach our organization *privately* to find out whether the case was good or not.[64]

Now, a major ingredient of the "antidote to communism" that Suhrawardy wanted to administer to the working class was an emphatic assertion of Hindu-Muslim differences. In the appeal to religion he found an answer to communism. The Communist trade unionist A.M.A. Zaman made the following complaint to the government in July 1937:

> One Mr. Mohiuddin of Howrah, in the name of the Hon'ble Labour Minister [Suhrawardy], is forming several unions on communal basis in Bhadreswar P[olice] S[tation] area and Serampore P.S. area. . . . [He] is carrying on his propaganda with some so-called Maulvis and religious heads against my lawful union.[65]

Zaman did not fabricate his complaint. On 23 August 1937 the police superintendent of Hooghly warned the district magistrate of the trends of "the last two months," which showed that there was "a danger that the rivalry between the unions of Zaman and Mohiuddin may develop on communal lines and that Mohiuddin has definitely been trying to detach the Muhammadans from Zaman's union by using the religious appeal."[66] He also quoted another Intelligence Branch report (of 8 Au-

[62] C.S.A.S., B.P., Box 12, notes on discussion with Suhrawardy, 28 July 1937.
[63] C.S.A.S., B.P., Box 16, unsigned note on Suhrawardy, 9 December 1940. Emphasis added.
[64] C.S.A.S., B.P., Box 19, diary entry for 19 March 1940. Emphasis added.
[65] W.B.S.A., Home Poll. Confdl. no. 326/1937.
[66] Ibid., no. 326/1937.

gust 1937), which described "the Maulana of the Dalhousie Jute Mill mosque [as having] indulged in enlisting members on behalf of Mohiuddin on communal basis by saying that Zaman was not a true Muhammadan . . . that no true Muslim could join it [Zaman's union] . . . [and] that the Muhammadan workers who helped the Hindu strikers with money etc. were *kafirs*."[67]

The activities of parties like the Arya Samaj and the Muslim League thus have to be taken into account in any attempt at a comprehensive historical understanding of religious conflict among the jute workers in the 1930s and later. But what made the Muslim League unions into a specially effective force in the 1930s was not simply their religious appeal but also the support they received from the employers. In their propaganda to the ordinary workers, Suhrawardy's men made a point of mentioning the fact of this support, thus adding to the heavenly rewards of being a "true Muslim" the promise of tangible, concrete and immediate material benefits as well. "Mohiuddin's party," we read in the police file mentioned above, enlisted members "[by] saying that his union [was] the true Muslim union and [that] it [was] being backed by the mill companies, Labour Minister and the government." Because of this, the report added, "many Muhammadans who were of Zaman's party were enlisting their names in Mohiuddin's office." Some of these new members even mentioned these considerations openly as their reasons for joining Suhrawardy's union (note especially points 2, 4, and 5):

1. That the union was the true union of the Muhammadans.
2. That the rents of the coolie lines will be removed.
3. That the sardars who . . . take bribes wil be discharged.
4. That all the appointments and discharge will be made by the companies according to the instructions of the Presidents and the Secretaries of the Unions.
5. That the union will be patronised by the ministers, it being a union of the Moslem League.[68]

Indrajit Gupta's argument, then, that the jute workers were "victim[s] of all sorts of fissiparious tendencies and disruptive propaganda" or that they were "always liable to be provoked and incited by communal reactionaries into regarding their . . . fellow workers as enemies" is not to be ridiculed. Yet the poverty of this formulation is obvious in the statement itself. One can turn Gupta's expression around

[67] Ibid.
[68] Ibid.

203

CHAPTER 6

and ask: Why were the workers "always liable" to be provoked into divisive conflicts?

The tradition of Hindu-Muslim riots predates even the formation of the Muslim League (1906) and cannot be explained by the latter's politics alone. We have already documented and analyzed some of the Hindu-Muslim riots of 1895–96. More riots were to follow. "A disturbance took place at Naihati at the *Bakr-i-Id* of 1898 with reference to the *kurbani* [animal (cow) sacrifice]," wrote the Commissioner of the presidency division in 1900. "The Muhammadan mill-hands of Gouripur wanted to sacrifice kine at Garifa, a village near Naihati, to which the Hindus objected," and this led to the disturbance.[69] Two years later, in 1900, the Hindu mill hands of Naihati were reported to be "still bitterly opposed to the slaughter of kine there." The district magistrate of the 24 Parganas wrote: "The feeling among the Hindu hands of the Gouripore Jute Mill is evidenced by the serious riots which broke out on the 12th April 1900 on the mere suspicion, which proved groundless, that a calf had been killed by the Muhammadans." "[An] excited crowd of Hindu mill-hands armed with *lathis* broke into the Muhammadan quarter and proceeded to wreck the houses and beat the occupants who were chiefly women and children."[70]

In the years that followed, Muslim and Hindu religious festivals like Bakr Id, Muharram, Holi, and Durga Puja continued to be the occasions when serious divisions surfaced between the two groups of mill hands, resulting sometimes in violent disputes. Bakr Id disturbances, for instance, were reported from Telinipara (Hooghly) in 1913. Another Hindu-Muslim riot among the workers of the Angus Jute Mill in the same year, during which "the Muhammadans of the Angus Mill went down to the Northbrook Mill to get help from their co-religionists," was explained by the authorities as "a relic of the Tittagarh riots many years ago."[71] Telinipara was to become a scene of "prolonged rioting" in 1922 and by 1926 the official practice of posting "a small force of military police" there "during important Muhammadan festivals," was considered a "customary" one. "A few men [were] also sent to Champdany and Rishra," the other important mill areas where violent conflicts between Hindus and Muslims were always a strong possibility.[72] Bakr Id riots occurred at the Garden Reach area in 1924 when "600 Hindus attacked a group of 300 Muslims who were . . .

[69] Ibid., no. 59/1900.
[70] Ibid.
[71] Ibid., no. 66/1913 K.W.
[72] Ibid., no. 77/1926.

performing *Korbani* [and] killed one and wounded 37."[73] In October 1926 the Hindu and the Muslim mill hands at Naihati fought each other with "lathis, bayonets and naked swords" after the Hindus placed "an idol on the ground near a mosque," allegedly to "insult" the Muslims.[74] In March 1927, to give another example, the Muslim laborers at Serampore began to assert their "right to kill cows" as a result of "Hindu Muslim tension regarding music before mosques."[75] Tension between the two communities was also reported in 1927 from Ramkrishnapur in Howrah (where "there was a disturbance during the last *Durga Puja* festival") and Rishra in Hooghly.[76] The issue of "music before mosques," especially at the time of Hindu religious festivals, often caused serious rioting at Titaghur and Kankinara till a "committee of Hindu [and] Muslim leaders was formed [at Kankinara in 1927] . . . [to] avoid rioting on the day of the immersion of Durga pratima [idol, image]."[77]

A more determined search would no doubt produce many more examples of such religious or racial conflicts in the jute workers' history. One could, of course, explore the individual and unique nature of the circumstances surrounding the origins of each of these outbreaks and stress the role played at different times by organizations like the Arya Samaj or the Muslim League (or their likes) in making the workers deviate from the path of class solidarity. But one could also question the fragile nature of this solidarity itself and inquire into the reasons for its fragility in the case of the Calcutta jute-mill workers. Narrowly political explanations emphasizing "provocations" and "incitements" do not throw any light on questions of underdeveloped class consciousness.

LET ME anticipate here an answer usually offered in response to these questions by scholars who expect "economic" factors to act as the ultimate limits on—if not as the determinants of—the course of human history. The very structure of the labor market in the jute industry, it will be said, created conditions conducive to the growth of racial and religious conflicts that were subversive of class solidarity. Two signifi-

[73] Kenneth McPherson, "The Muslims of Calcutta, 1918 to 1935: A Study of the Society and Politics of an Urban Minority Group in India," Ph.D. thesis, Australian National University, 1972, p. 146.

[74] W.B.S.A., Home Poll. Confdl. no. 516(1–14)/1926.

[75] Ibid., no. 117/1927.

[76] Ibid., no. 51/1927 and 327/1927.

[77] Ibid., no. 174(1–24)/1926 and K.C.R.P., English diary no. 2, entry for 25 August 1927, and Bengali diary no. 2, entry for 6 October 1927.

cant aspects of the labor market would be of crucial importance to this argument: the *sardari* method of recruitment and control, which emphasized the "primordial" ties of the worker, and the keen competition for employment inevitable in a market that was overstocked with unemployed laborers and where the unskilled nature of work made every single worker easily replaceable. These factors would seem to make it understandable that the workers should find their religious, linguistic, and geographical bonds useful in obtaining and retaining employment. Did not religious or racial clashes, then, ultimately reflect the competitive nature of the labor market, which, thanks to its organization, reinforced religious and racial solidarities? The problem of working-class unity and the question of class consciousness would then appear amenable to an explanation (and solution) that gave primacy to the economic.

It is undeniable that, in their concern to create and maintain a steady supply of cheap unskilled labor, the jute-mill owners developed a labor market in which a host of "informal" relations and methods came to acquire important economic functions necessary for the running of the industry (see chapter 3). For the mill workers, kinship and village connections often provided the network for the flow of information regarding the state of the market. One heard of and obtained employment through these connections. Foley, who investigated the labor market for the Calcutta industrial belt in 1905–6, noted this while traveling in the district of Saran (Bihar). "I believe," he said, "the rates and conditions of work in the Calcutta industries are well known in this district."

> There is a constant flow to and from the mills, and one man will inform a whole village as to what his earnings and his work have been. To test this I attended a chaukidari parade. Several chaukidars told me, as I thought correctly, what some weavers from their village had made in a Jute Mill, and a third seemed to know a good deal about jute presses.[78]

The importance of these family or village or other community ties was stressed in many of the interviews of individual jute workers, recorded for the Royal Commission on Labour in 1929. "My brother is working in the Standard [Jute] Mill; I got my job through my brother," said Prakash, a boy from U.P., who worked at the Titaghur Jute Mills. Kalil, a weaver from Ghazipur (U.P.) owed his job at the Anglo-Indian Jute Mills to his uncle, who did "weaving work in this mill." Jamrath,

---

[78] B. Foley, *Report on Labour in Bengal* (Calcutta, 1906), par. 83.

an "ordinary weaver" at Titaghur, "secured [his] employment through one of [his] village men who was working the mill." Lachanao, a migrant boy worker, had "heard from his father that there was work in the mill." Behari Rai, an upcountry spinner at the Angus Jute Mill, had heard about vacancies at the mill from "some of his village folks" who worked there. Noormahamad, a weaver at Titaghur who was born in Jaunpur (U.P.), was "only a boy . . . when his mother was compelled to send him to work in some of the jute mills in Calcutta, being advised to do so by many of her well-wishers some of whom were mill employees of this province." That "so many of his villagers were in the weaving [department]" aroused in Noormahamad the ambition to become a weaver. The final realization of this ambition was also something that he owed to his village connections. "[He] used to go in his leisure to the Weaving Department to help his villagers in their work . . . [and] thus acquired good practice in the art of weaving." Dar Basona, to give another example, came to Calcutta from Madras along with a covillager "who was a jute mill worker" and found, through his help, a "cooly's job" at Titaghur. Abdul Khan, another jute worker, was brought from Gaya to Calcutta by a cousin "who was a sirdar in the Champdany Jute Mills" and who "had him admitted in the said mill as a shifter boy in the Spinning Department."

Very similar were the stories of Biro, an Oriya "calendar cooly" at the Champdany Jute Mills, and those of Jumrathi Miah, Khedoo Miah, and Mohan Noonia, the first two being weavers and the last a worker in the machine sewing department of the Victoria Jute Mills. Biro came to Rishra from Cuttack "with one of his countrymen" who worked at Rishra and "through his help he secured a job as a drawing cooly in Rishra Jute Mills," Jumrathi came from Balia (U.P.) "with his brother who was a weaver in Victoria Mill . . . [and] at once obtained employment in the Spinning Department." Khedoo had been sent by his father "with some of his fellow villagers to look for work in a jute mill," and Noonia, another person from Balia, found employment at the Samnugger Jute Mill "by a relative who was a worker in that Mill." At the apex of the network of such relations stood the *sardar*, with his methods of recruitment and control that we have already described in chapter 3. "In some of the mills," the Royal Commission was informed by the Kankinarrah Labour Union, "if the Burra [Head] Sirdar (weaving supervisor) happens to be native of Chapra district, most of his men (weavers) under him are relatives of Chapra."[79]

[79] This and the preceding paragraphs are based on RCLI, vol. 5, pt. 1, p. 262; pt 2, pp. 26, 76, 78–79; vol. 11, pt. 2, pp. 355–356, 359–360, 362–364.

Apart from the question of employment, the insecurity of the jute worker's life—caused by poor wages and the absence of service rules—gave his village, racial, or religious ties a new economic significance in the city. Since the mills discouraged family migration (see chapters 1 and 3), most jute workers retained some links with their villages. Data collected for eleven jute-manufacturing concerns in 1929 showed that the "number of non-Bengali persons born in Jute Mill lines or neighbourhood who have been employed solely in Jute Mills and who do not normally leave the neighbourhood for a native village" to be about 2.57 percent of the total number employed by these concerns.[80] Moroever, in the absence of service rules, employment in the mills was rather irregular. The majority of the jute workers were, in the words of R. N. Gilchrist, "short service workers."[81] Dagmar Curjel was told by several mill managers during her investigations in 1922–23 that about one-third of the workers in any mill were always "on the move."[82] In 1929 the "length of service" of laborers in eleven mills was found to be short term: more than 60 percent of the workers had worked in their respective mills for less than five years, even though it was always believed that employment in the jute industry was the only source of livelihood for the majority of the mill hands, at least 90 percent (see Table 6.1).[83]

In a life characterized by poverty and insecurity of work, a laborer's need for economic and physical support from kin (real or putative) and linguistic or religious community naturally extended far beyond the stage of obtaining employment. These relationships impinged on several aspects of the worker's daily life. Two contrasting pieces of evidence go to show how crucial such support could be even to the question of sheer physical survival of the worker. The civil surgeon of Howrah made an enquiry in 1912 into the circumstances of the "100 or 150" people who died every year at the Howrah General Hospital of "dysentery, diarrhoea and other similar diseases which [could] be attributed . . . to starvation." The inquiry revealed that these men were "the flotsam and jetsam" of the labor market in Howrah, people who for some reason lacked the support of village or kinship connections in the city. Such laborers, the civil surgeon said,

> have great difficulty about cooking their food as they have not the means to provide themselves with suitable huts and have not the opportunity to cook their food properly; they live on parched

[80] W.B.S.A., Com. Dept. Com. Br., April 1930, A19–20.
[81] R. N.Gilchrist, *India Labour and the Land* (Calcutta, 1932), p. 10.
[82] See W.B.S.A.., Com Dept. Com. Br., April 1923, B77.
[83] RCLI., vol. 5, pt. 1, p. 279.

TABLE 6.1.
Length of service of jute-mill workers, 1929.

Name of Mill	(I) Proportion of total male employees working less than 5 years (%)	(II) Average of (I) (%)	(III) Proportion of total female employees working less than 5 years (%)	(IV) Average of (III) (%)
Gourepore	51.5		66.2	
Samnugger	61.8		68.7	
Titaghur	57.8		69.5	
Clive	65.8		75.6	
Victoria	68.1	62.2	73	71.6
Champdany	74.2		71.9	
Hastings	51.6		72	
Howrah	70.7		79.5	
Delta	69		62.7	
Lawrence	63.6		79.3	
Budge Budge	50		69.2	

SOURCE: W.B.S.A., Com. Dept. Com. Br., April 1930, A19–20.

grain or other indigestible diet with the result that they get bowel troubles which with ordinary suitable treatment and diet would be of little account. They become too weak and, their money exhausted, they then lie up in some corner of a hut or even in the open air and practically starve until . . . the police bring them to the hospital in a perfectly hopeless situation.[84]

In complete contrast was the case of Narsama Kurmi (a female jute worker interviewed during the proceedings of the Labour Commission), whose story of survival emphasized at every point the support she had received from members of her native "community." When she first arrived at Howrah from Madras, Narsama "could not speak . . . Hindustani." Someone "she had met on the train . . . put her on a tram car and told the driver to put her off at the Madrassi [coolie] lines."

The tramway man told her to get off about the place that she lives in now, and there she saw some people of her own country to whom she was able to speak. One of the Madrassis took her to a

[84] W.B.S.A., Medical Dept. Medical Br., January 1914, B287–95.

sirdar of the mill . . . [who] gave her work in his line in Howrah [Jute] Mills.[85]

The ties of language, religion, or village thus served the worker well in regard to his need for accommodation and shelter. A dismissed up-country worker, the Royal Commission was told, could live in working-class slums on credit provided by the *sardar* "till he got a job."[86] Such help could also be provided by "relatives." Mangari and her husband, both workers at the Titaghur Jute Mills, were "posted in the house of a relative" of theirs when they first arrived from Madras.[87] So was Gobardhan, another worker at the same mill who came to Titaghur from upcountry as a young man of twenty. He "stayed with a relative who secured for him a job as a cooly in the Preparing Department in the local jute mill."[88]

In ill health and bad times, too, the workers often fell back on their "traditional" relationships. "I had fever a year ago," said Gowri, a female worker of the Standard Jute Mills who was interviewed by the Royal Commission:

> I did not go to the doctor because I was too weak and unable to move, nor did the doctor come and see me. . . . I paid Rs. 3 to Rs. 5 to a man who came to my house and treated me. He is a man of my caste, but he is not a qualified doctor.[89]

Muthialu was another worker who "did not go to the doctor" when she had eye trouble. She said: "I put in my eyes the medicine other people gave me."[90] Curjel's investigations of 1922–23 into the condition of women workers brought to light the case of a Muslim woman called Mia whose existence depended to a large extent on the material assistance she received from her coreligionists. Mia was thirty-five and had three children to look after, having been deserted by her second husband; Curjel found her being "supported by the charity of a number of Mahomedan workers in the mill lines."[91]

One could use this entire body of evidence to "discover" the unfolding of a deep-seated "economic rationality" even in Hindu-Muslim riots, and argue that in choosing to emphasize (through violent feuds or otherwise) the bonds of race or religion, the jute-mill worker did

[85] R.C.L.I., vol. 11, pt. 2, p. 360.
[86] Ibid., vol. 5, pt. 2, p. 135.
[87] Ibid., vol. 11, pt. 2, p. 357.
[88] Ibid., p. 368.
[89] Ibid., vol. 5, pt. 2, p. 70.
[90] Ibid.
[91] See W.B.S.A., Com Dept. Com. Br., April 1923, B77.

not behave in an "irrational" manner. He may have imported a peasant culture into the industrial setting as he migrated from the countryside; but the retention of some of the key elements of this culture in his new environment was not a simple matter of nostalgic behavior on the part of the migrant peasant. The structure of the labor market was such that the ties of language, religion, or kinship—ties that are especially strong in precapitalist cultures—had a practical and economic utility to the worker in his struggle for survival in the face of poverty and insecurity. They helped him protect his standard of living. Is it surprising then, it will be asked, that these relationships should bulk large in his consciousness and undermine his sense of class solidarity? Indeed this is how the question has been put to us in a recent article:

> Are . . . these findings [about religious or racial riots among jute workers] very surprising? Look at the way the workers were recruited, the way they lived in the jute mill localities, the way their life cycles were shaped. They were recruited generally from villages several hundred miles away from Calcutta on the basis of ties with earlier recruits in the jute mills. They lived in abject poverty. . . . Most of them were illiterate and had little access to sources of information outside their own linguistic groups. . . . Their survival itself depended on keeping up their ties with villages and with their extended kin-groups defined in terms of community and language.

On another occasion in the same article a similar connection is made between "primordial loyalties" and people's need for survival: "the old society does impart a sense of community to the oppressed people because they need such a consciousness for survival."[92]

"Needs," that is, "utility," the celebrants of political economy will tell us, is the key to the secrets of consciousness. Yet it empties "culture" of all specific content. Serving the "needs of survival" is a function universal to all cultures in all historical settings. This functionalist understanding can never be a guide to the internal logic of a culture, the way it constructs and uses its "reason."

I DO NOT wish to dwell on the essentialist presuppositions regarding "human nature" on which this understanding rests. Suffice it to say that in a very fundamental way it misconstrues the jute worker's consciousness. The ties of kinship, religion, language, or race were of

[92] A. K. Bagchi, "The Ambiguity of Progress: Indian Society in Transition," *Social Scientist*, vol. 13, no. 3, March 1985, pp. 10–11. My own analysis in "Communal Riots and Labour" is based on arguments similar to Bagchi's.

course of much economic and material utility to the jute worker. But to see in this "utility" the workers' *reason* for valuing and retaining these bonds is to invest the jute worker with a bourgeois rationality, since it is only in such a system of rationality that the "economic utility" of an action (or an object, relationship, institution, etc.) defines its reasonableness.[93]

The jute workers, on the contrary, acted out of an understanding that was prebourgeois in its elements. It was not that they did not value things economic: poverty itself would have often brought home to the worker the value of money. Yet the "economic utility" and the "reasonableness" of an action were different categories, the former often subsumed under the latter. A very good example of this is the opinion that Behari Rai, a Bhumihar Brahman and upcountry spinner working at the Angus Jute Mill, expressed in an interview in 1929 regarding the problem of jute workers' indebtedness. Debt was incurred, said Rai, not through whimsical, thoughtless action on the part of the worker, but through "necessity." He himself would "never go into debt because he wanted to buy something beyond his means." Yet it is interesting to see what Rai saw as "necessity." "Caste, or fellow men," he said, "determine[d] how much an individual should spend . . . [since] caste itself [carried] an obligation as to spending." Being a Brahman, he was obliged "to spend far more than if he were less highly born."[94] To Rai then, it only stood to reason that one should go into debt, if necessary, in order to protect one's honor and position within one's caste even though the "economic utility" of such action could indeed be negative. The bourgeois notion of "utility" thus is not of much assistance in understanding a prebourgeois consciousness such as Rai's.[95]

[93] Cf. K. Marx and F. Engels, *The German Ideology* (Moscow, 1976), pp. 436–437: "Thanks to the Physiocrats, political economy for the first time was raised to the rank of a special science. . . . As a special branch of science it absorbed the other relations—political, juridical, etc.—to such an extent that it reduced them to economic relations. . . . The complete subordination of all existing relations to the relation of utility, and its unconditional elevation to the sole content of all other relations, occurs for the first time in Bentham's works, where, after the French Revolution and the development of large-scale industry, the bourgeoisie is no longer presented as a special class, but as the class whose conditions of existence are those of the whole society."

[94] R.C.L.I., vol. 11, pt. 2, p. 360.

[95] The opposition between "need" (utility) and "pleasure" (passion) is an old one in the philosophical traditions of modern social science. For a brief tracing of this in the works of Rousseau see Jacques Derrida, *Of Grammatology*, trans. Gayatri Chakravorty Spivak (Baltimore and London, 1984), p. 104. I have been much influenced by Bachelard's critique of James Frazer in *The Psychoanalysis of Fire* trans. Alan C. M. Ross (Boston, 1964).

There was another important aspect to this consciousness: the absence of individualism and individualistic identities that mark a bourgeois culture. The individual jute-mill worker never appeared "in the dot-like isolation" in which Marx placed the individual industrial worker belonging to a bourgeois society; the jute worker in Calcutta always conducted himself—to use Marx's words again—"only as a link, as a member" of a "community" defined, somewhat ambiguously, by the links of religion, language, habitat, and so on.[96]

The point can be illustrated by exploring the jute worker's sense of "honour," which, as seen in the last chapter, often informed working-class protest in the jute mills. "People of my district do not bring their families to these industrial areas here," said Abdul Hakim, a jute-mill worker from Darbhanga District in Bihar when he was interviewed by the Royal Commission on Labour. "If I brought my family," he added, "my people would laugh at me."[97] "My wife does not work [in mills]," explained another worker, a Bengali, "[since] in Bengal our wives do not work."[98] Indeed, so dishonorable, in Bengali eyes, was factory work for women that almost all of the Bengali women interviewed by the Factory Commission of 1890 declared that they would not let their daughters become mill workers unless they were desperate. Digambari, a woman working at the Howrah Jute Mill, said: "Unless Bengali women are widows, they do not come to work in mills."[99] Sookvaria, a woman from Chapra, however, was of a decidedly contrary opinion: "she [would] bring her daughter to work when she [was] sufficiently old."[100] It is clear that the sense of honor expressed in these statements referred back to a notion of "community" that the workers saw as the ultimate arbiter and dispenser of honor and shame. The worker's identity was merged in that of the "community."

In the examples given above, "community" was primarily defined by habitat and language. In addition to these two factors, religion was another, perhaps the strongest, source of a notion of "community" and, therefore, of a communal sense of identity and honor as well. In the statement of Behari Rai quoted earlier, his sense of honor was clearly a part of his overall sense of belonging to a community of "fellow men," the "community" being defined here by the ties of caste

[96] Karl Marx, *Grundrisse: Foundations of the Critique of Political Economy*, trans. Martin Nicolaus (Harmondsworth, 1974), pp. 472, 485.

[97] *RCLI*, vol. 5, pt. 2, p. 80.

[98] Ibid., p. 115.

[99] *Report of the Indian Factory Commission 1890* (Calcutta, 1890), pp. 76–77, 81, 84.

[100] Ibid., p. 85.

(hence kinship) and religion. Gopen Chakravarty, the Bolshevik leader mentioned in our chapter on organization, has left us a telling account of how important religion was in giving the jute workers a sense of "morality" and "honour." In 1928 Chakravarty and his comrades organized a historic march of industrial workers in the jute-mill areas. "The plan had a two-fold objective—the first was to rally support of the entire working class of Bengal behind this struggle [strikes of 1928] and secondly to rouse and organise the jute workers through the process." In Chakravarty's words:

> We took the marchers to the bank of the Ganges. There they rested while we went to the market to purchase [food]. . . . It was then that we received a shock. The marchers, who had remained firm in class battle and not flinched in the face of bullets, would not dine together—so deep was their prejudice of caste and religion. As they put it, "Jan dene sakta, lekin dharam nehi dene sakta" [We can give our lives but not sacrifice our religion].[101]

A worker, it would seem, would rather suffer than be put to shame in the eyes of his "community." Kamala, a drawing machine feeder at the Howrah Jute Mill, told the Royal Commission on Labour that her husband had been sick and unemployed for the past three months at the time of her interview. Kamala, therefore, had been "obliged to borrow the sum of Rs. 20 . . . [paying] interest at the rate of Rs. 2.8 per month." Living, as Kamala herself put it, was "very hard now." Yet her husband refused to "take medicine from the mill's dispensary" and the reason he gave is significant in the context of our present discussion: "[he] says it will break his caste."[102]

Being a "virtuous Muslim," similarly, was a matter of honor. It was to this communal sense of honor that the Muslim League trade unions appealed, for instance, as we have seen above. Noormahamad, the Titaghur Jute Mill weaver quoted earlier, prided himself on being a "virtuous Muslim." He drank tea "twice daily," smoked *biri*, and "at the weekends [was] in the habit of going to the cinema in Calcutta," but "being rather a virtuous Muhammadan himself, [he had] never indulged in any other vice."[103]

The question of honor (or shame or insult) of an individual was thus subsumed under the notion of communal honor. An insult inflicted on an individual member of the community, however defined at the time

[101] Chakravarty, "Interview," in Gautam Chattopadhyay, *Communism and Bengal's Freedom Movement*, vol. 1 (Delhi, 1970), p. 139.
[102] *RCLI*, vol. 11, pt. 2, p. 361.
[103] Ibid., p. 357.

in question, could be construed as an insult to the whole community. And conversely, the individual perpetrating the insult could easily be seen as acting on behalf of another community. This is why racial or religious conflicts could be sparked by events that historians often regard as "trivial." A "serious communal trouble" was "provoked" at Naihati in March 1934 (during the Id festival) by "a Muhammadan boy . . . running through the streets with hands covered with blood shouting and cheering, and secondly, [by] another Muhammadan . . . washing [sacrificial] meat at a public hydrant."[104] At Budge Budge the same year a Hindu-Muslim riot started "through [a] Muhammadan taking meat for his own consumption into the [coolie] lines of the Oriental Jute Mill."[105] At the time of the Holi festival in 1939, a riot broke out between Hindu and Muslim laborers at Metiabruj. According to the government, "the trouble started over a Hindu throwing red water on a Mahomedan without any warning . . . [then] the Mahomedans attacked the Hindu [coolie] lines in a body."[106]

Why were these individual acts, "trivial" by our judgment, capable of provoking such strong and collective reactions? Precisely because they were seen as gestures calculated to offend the sense of honor of a community. Such a communal sense of honor speaks of the non-individualistic, prebourgeois nature of the identity that the jute-mill worker had. And so innate to the worker's consciousness were the identities flowing from religion or race that some of the insults and counterinsults traded during "communal" conflicts attained highly codified, symbolic forms that were charged with an explosive potential. The playing of music by Hindu religious processions in front of mosques, debates over the routes by which the sacrifical cow would be taken during the Bakr Id festivities, "alleged desecration of the *Koran*," the singing of "objectionable songs" by Hindus while passing by mosques—these issues figure with monotonous and predictable regularity in all accounts of Hindu-Muslim riots among the jute-mill workers.[107]

Another issue was the question of women's *izzat* (honor). This was once again a question of the honor of the community, which is why the "molestation of women" of one community by men from another was considered a grave communal insult. A 1938 report on Hindu-

---

[104] W.B.S.A., Home Poll. Confdl. no. 117/1934.
[105] Ibid.
[106] Ibid., no. 324/1939.
[107] References on this point could be many. Some of the Bengal government files that I have consulted are W.B.S.A., Home Poll. Confdl. nos. 59/1900, 516(1–14)/1926, 51/1927, 51(11–25)/1927, 51/1927 K.W., 226/1927, 117/1934, 324/1939, 229/1940.

Muslim conflict at Kankinara mentioned attacks by Muslims on "Hindu houses and women."[108] A riot between Bengali and upcountry laborers at Bauria in November 1928 was caused by a piece of "false information" reaching the Bengalis that the upcountrymen "had entered [their] . . . villages . . . and had been molesting their women-folk."[109] Yet another riot in December 1938 between the Hindu workers of the National Jute Mill who had gone on strike and the "loyal" Muslim workers broke out when the strikers reportedly "started molesting the women and children in the [Muslim] coolie lines."[110] "Acute communal tension" was reported to exist among the workers of the Anglo-Indian Jute Mill in April 1937, where Hindu workers had gone on strike and "the Muhammadans [were] very unwilling" to join them. It is interesting to see how the communal construction of "women's honour" was used by workers in the war of insults. "In the Kankinara mill lines," the police said, "the Muhammadans have for some time . . . [been] in the habit of . . . exhibiting their private parts to the Hindu women of the same line." "This," the police added, "caused considerable ill-feeling which [had] been augmented by the strikes."[111]

ALL THIS should not lead us to imagine that the "communities" were separated into water-tight compartments by their irreconcilable differences, that the Hindus and the Muslims, for instance, were always out for each other's blood. Even though workers belonged to a culture that underplayed any idea of the individuality of the person, their notion of a "community" based on the loyalties of religion, language, habitat, kinship, and the like could only be ambiguous.[112] This was because a "community" defined by such loyalties was necessarily a self-contradictory entity. People sharing the same religion, for example, could be divided by language (or habitat) and vice versa. It needs to be emphasized that this both lessened and aggravated the danger of the outbreak of any particular type of "communal" conflict. For though in some cases a religious unity could be formed that cut across the language or ethnic barrier, this barrier itself could in other cases stop a religious conflict from spreading. In still other cases, the divisions of language and habitat could override those of religion, as in the case of conflict between Bengali workers and the upcountry people.

[108] Ibid., no. 260/1938.
[109] *Amrita Bazar Patrika*, 27 November 1928.
[110] W.B.S.A., Home Poll. Confdl. no. 403/1938.
[111] Ibid., 128/37, pt. 1.
[112] Ranajit Guha has made this point with regard to the Indian peasantry in his *Elementary Aspects of Peasant Insurgency in Colonial India* (Delhi, 1983).

The ambiguity inherent in the notion of "community," however, does not take away from our basic argument that the "distinctions based on birth"—religion, language, kinship—were central to the jute-mill worker's sense of identity. He conducted himself even in the "political" sphere of his life "only a a link, as a member" of mental "communities" based on these distinctions. He was never, in other words, the "bourgeois citizen" (even though the Indian constitution today defines him as such) that Marx described in his early essay *On the Jewish Question*. Unlike in the case of the "citizen," the jute worker's political culture, lacking any bourgeois notions of the equality of the individual, had not split him into his "public" and "private" selves; and he had not, unlike the citizen, relegated all "the distinctions based on birth" to the sphere of the "private," the nonpolitical. To quote Marx on this point:

> The *dissolution* of man into Jew and citizen, Protestant and citizen, religious man and citizen, is not a denial of citizenship or an avoidance of political emancipation: it is *political emancipation itself*, it is the *political* way of emancipating oneself from religion.[113]

In this sense, the jute-mill worker had never been "politically" emancipated from religion. Religion, therefore—or we could say, ethnicity or language or other similar loyalties—formed the stuff of his politics. This was so even at moments of confrontation between labor and capital. Mobilization for class battles (e.g. strikes) was often based on emotional appeals to the ethnic on religious ties of the workers and to their communal sense of honor and shame. During the 1929 general strike, it was publicized by the trade union organizers that Hindu and Muslim workers had sworn by their religions to support the strike. Strike breaking, it was said, would amount to beef eating for the Hindu and pork eating for the Muslim.[114] A group of Muslim weavers told the authorities of the Birla Jute Mill at the time of the strike that "if they resumed work they would be visited by bands of hooligans from other areas on strike and would have half their beards shaved off, which is a crowning insult to Mahomedans, the beard having religious significance."[115] Apparently, the threat of dishonoring the womenfolk of nonstriking men was also used during this strike.[116]

[113] Karl Marx, *On the Jewish Question*, in his *Early Writings* (Harmondsworth, 1975), p. 222. See also p. 219. Emphasis in original.
[114] K.C.R.P., Bengali diary no. 3, entry for 15 July 1929 to 26 August 1929.
[115] RCLI, vol. 5, pt. 1, p. 411.
[116] Ibid.

Thus the elements of solidarity that went into the making of "strikes" were not all that different from those that made up a case of racial or religious conflict. This was why, as the government had said, "there [was] always a possibility" of racial or religious violence breaking out in the middle of a strike by the workers. Whether or not the "possibility" would become an actuality was partly dependent, of course, on circumstances. But we cannot explain the logic of workers' consciousness by referring to these circumstances alone. In the jute worker's mind itself, the incipient awareness of belonging to a class remained a prisoner of his precapitalist culture; the class identity of the worker could never be distilled out of the precapitalist identities that arose from the relationships he had been born into.

My stress on the importance of language or religion in the jute worker's consciousness, however, is not intended to situate this working class in a web of immutable, unchanging loyalties that social scientists sometimes classify as "primordial." The so-called ties of birth did not carry the same political or social significance in the 1920s and 1930s as they did, say, in the 1800s or before. And for that reason the social meanings of these "ties" changed. Historians have argued for long—and with considerable justification—that the large-scale eruption of religious or racial violence with which India is often associated today is a phenomenon of "modern" Indian history. The proposition in this chapter does not in any way deny this perception, just as one could not deny the advent of Marxist and nationalist politics in the trade union scene of Bengal in the twentieth century. Also undeniable is the point that this politics would have introduced the workers to the notion of trade union and democratic "rights." Religion or language arose as an issue *within* this context. What is unsatisfactory, however, is the tendency—pervasive in Marxist constructions of working-class history—to add up these "changes" in terms of an overarching notion of "progress" or "development" within which the question of "consciousness" is placed. This is the problem I address in the next and final chapter.

· 7 ·

CONCLUSION:
RETHINKING WORKING-CLASS
HISTORY

The method of history—to slightly deflect the aim of a remark made by Michel Henry—is "the construction of the contrary which, in turn, is handed over to destruction."[1] In what does the contrariness of this book consist? And what would be its own critique?

My narrativization of jute workers' history takes issue with reductionist views of "subjectivity." I have endeavored to argue that the logic of a culture cannot be derived from a construction of "politics" or "economics" that looks on itself as something outside culture. The initial chapters of this book call into question the "objective" nature often ascribed to factors like "needs of capital," technology, "the nature of the industry," "working-class conditions," and so forth. The chapters on protest, organization, and solidarity seek to highlight the problems that the persistence of a prebourgeois culture poses to a Marxist reading of working-class history. The irreducible place that subjectivity occupies both inside and outside the relations of production has been a running theme of my exposition.

Fundamental to my text has also been an opposition drawn between the notion of a precapitalist "community"—distinguished by hierarchical, inegalitarian, and illiberal relationships—and the notion of individualism that has been with us since the rise of the bourgeois order in Europe, entailing ideas of citizenship, equal rights, equality before the law, and the like. The posing of this opposition raises a question. Since I analyze the issues in jute-mill workers' history in terms of a lack of the liberal code of power, do not I then—it may be legitimately asked—end up celebrating this code? Is it not from a liberal notion of "modernity," seen as the *telos* of history, that my narrative borrows its structure and movement?

The problem needs to be faced. For if the question of class consciousness and solidarity in working-class history raises by implication a whole series of issues related to bourgeois notions of equality, it also reveals the ambiguous legacy that the European Enlightenment be-

[1] Michel Henry, *Marx: A Philosophy of Human Reality*, trans. Kathleen McLaughlin (Bloomington, 1983), p. 81.

219

queathed to Marxist thought and its categories. The question of whether or not liberalism is to be privileged has to be placed within a critique of that legacy. When it does not self-consciously engage in this critique, labor history, especially the discussion of working-class consciousness, remains a prisoner of contradictions that arise from the gap between the universalistic claims of Marxist categories and their particular intellectual origins. A word of explanation is in order.

WE CAN BEGIN from certain empirical observations. An enduring feature of working-class and peasant movements in India (and elsewhere) is the ever-present possibility of fragmentation along lines of religion, language, ethnicity, and the like. This is widely acknowledged in the literature and the existence of the possibility as such is seldom a subject of scholarly debate. A problem arises the moment we try to set this observation in the context of a problematic of transition or change. Much to the disappointment of many radical historians, the working class does not show any obvious signs of progress toward a desired state of emancipation. (Whether we call this state class consciousness or proletarian revolution or anything else does not really matter in the context of this argument.) The point is of some consequence in labor history. For though a particular group of workers may or may not show straightforward signs of progress toward "class consciousness," a Marxist history of working-class consciousness cannot be written outside a problematic of emancipation (and hence of transition). It is, after all, from this problematic alone that there arise the questions that Marxist historians normally ask of workers' consciousness. Yet labor history is replete with instances of the class loyalties of workers being overridden by loyalties arising from the so-called distinctions of birth.

I raise the point in order to anticipate certain propositions that are often offered as solutions to the problem I have posed in this book. It will be said, for instance, that "class" and "class consciousness" are pure categories, analysts' constructs, never to be seen on the ground in a pure form anyway, and that it is even silly of me to look for them in concrete history. The solution, as it is often presented, is quite simple. If the workers evince both class and, say, caste loyalties, then they are both class and caste conscious, one form of consciousness being mediated by the other. Indeed this opinion is so widely held that it would be unfair to ascribe it to individual authors.

Empirically speaking, I see no particular difficulty with this claim. To the extent the observation is obvious—it is, in fact, only blindingly so—its "truth" is also an obvious one. The problem for the Marxist historian is, of course, that, taken by itself, the proposition does nothing to address the question of "transition" or "change" and hence does not address the question of the narrative either. Now I do believe that an atemporal understanding of the category "class" can indeed be sustained in philosophical readings of Marx. Michel Henry, for instance, writes: "The coherence of a class . . . is in all . . . cases the coherence of the individuals who constitute it, and this is why the class unceasingly makes and unmakes itself."[2] Henry indicates the atemporal nature of the category by using the word *unceasingly*—a process that obviously occurs in time but is not touched by it. On this reading, a "class" is, at one and the same time, always already, both in-itself and for-itself (contrary to the historian's reading of this opposition in purely temporal terms). The dynamics of "class," thus understood, escape narrativization and in that sense also escape history.

There is then an irreducible concern with "transition" in any effort that seeks to narrativize workers' history in terms of "class" and "class consciousness." And it is in this concern with transition that there is, I suggest, a source of constant awkwardness in labor history. To which better place could we turn for an illustration of the problem than E. P. Thompson's deservedly classic work, *The Making of the English Working Class*? Thompson's mistrust of determinism is well known, as is his advocacy of "the empirical idiom."[3] Moreover, it is not important for my argument to pursue the recent criticism that Thompson's narrative derives from a preconceived evolutionary schema.[4] I shall instead concentrate on a famous passage from his book, a passage that has been quoted too often in labor history for its implications to be really comprehended. Here then is Thompson at a brilliant moment in *The Making*:

> The making of the working class is a fact of political and cultural, as much as of economic, history. It was not the spontaneous generation of the factory system. Nor should we think of an external force—the "industrial revolution"—working upon some nondescript undifferentiated raw material of humanity, and turning it out at the other end as a "fresh race of beings." . . . The Industrial Revolution . . . [was] imposed, not upon raw material, but upon the free-born Englishman—and the free-born Englishman as Paine had left him or as the Methodists had moulded him. The factory hand or stockinger was also the inheritor of Bunyan, of

---

[2] Ibid., p. 104.

[3] See E. P. Thompson, *The Poverty of Theory and Other Essays* (London, 1979).

[4] See Hayden White, *Tropics of Discourse: Essays in Cultural Criticism* (Baltimore and London, 1985), pp. 15–18.

remembered village rights, of notions of equality before the law, of craft traditions. He was the object of massive religious indoctrination and the creator of political traditions. The working class made itself as much as it was made.[5]

Not being a historian of the English working class, I have no quarrel to pick with Thompson's "facts." But consider the wider problem that arises from the way he poses the question of culture. If the particular notions of "free-born Englishman," of "equality before the law," and so on were the most crucial heritages of the English working class in respect of its capacity for developing class consciousness, what about the working classes—for instance, the Indian one—whose heritages do not include such a liberal baggage? Are the latter condemned then forever to a state of "low classness" unless they develop some kind of cultural resemblance to the English?

The question itself reveals the absurdities of our dilemma. For if we were to answer it in the affirmative, which few today would risk doing in good conscience, we would end up privileging "the peculiarities of the English," and making "class consciousness" appear more an exception than the rule in concrete situations. On the other hand, if our liberalism moved us to reject the question and to argue that there was no one cultural route to class consciousness, that all cultures, in different ways, had the capacity to generate such consciousness, two conclusions would follow, both devastating for the argument at hand: (a) we would then make the question of "cultural specificity" redundant to the issue of class consciousness, and (b) Thompson's highlighting of certain particular elements in English popular culture as factors specially conducive to "class consciousness" would seem alarmingly arbitrary. For it is entirely possible that a contrary set of cultural elements could have also given rise to a similar consciousness (as indeed would be argued now for non-European working people without a liberal heritage).

A "universalist" mode of thinking, a reading that constantly produces out of Marxism a master narrative of history, is what defuses the dangerous potential of the "exceptionalist" argument of The Making.[6]

[5] E. P. Thompson, *The Making of the English Working Class* (Harmondsworth, 1968), p. 213.
[6] For an example of the problem that such claims of "exceptionalism" create in labor history, see Sean Wilentz, "Against Exceptionalism: Class Consciousness and the American Labor Movement, 1790–1928," and the response thereto by Nick Salvatore and Michael Hanagan, in *International Labor and Working Class History*, no. 26, Fall 1984, pp. 1–36. See also the discussion in Ira Katznelson and Aristide R. Zolberg, eds., *Work-*

The exceptional nature of the English case is not denied, but in many studies it is reduced, in spite of Thompson, to certain questions of political economy; the task then becomes one of explaining which "structural" features prevented the growth of a "class consciousness" elsewhere similar or comparable to the phenomenon studied by Thompson.

In the case of Indian labor history, this normally produces versions of two explanatory models. Either it is argued—as has been done recently[7]—that workers in India did not develop a full-fledged "class consciousness" because colonialism foreclosed the possibility of an industrial revolution; or we argue that Indian workers retained their religious, linguistic, or other ethnic ties because it was "rational" for them to do so, that is, the organization of the labor market made these ties essential to the workers' survival. The workers acted, in other words, from a deeply "rational" appreciation of their "material interests." The first proposition, in its implication, clashes violently with the position taken by E. P. Thompson and other like-minded scholars in European labor history.[8] The second is what we have criticized in the previous chapter: it assumes that the bourgeois notion of "utility" is the dominant form of "rationality" in all cultures.[9]

Both propositions share one assumption: that workers all over the world, irrespective of their specific cultural pasts, *experience* "capitalist production" in the same way. Since there cannot be any "experience" without a "subject" defining it as such, the propositions end up conferring on working classes in all historical situations a (potentially) uniform, homogenized, extrahistorical subjectivity. "Colonialism"— or differences between patterns of capitalist growth—only introduces variations on the surface of this original uniformity.

By thus constantly assuming into existence a desired subjectivity, the master narrative continues to run over and straighten out any breaches and dents that the awkward question of "consciousness" may make on the surface of particular narratives. The tenacity of its hold on the

---

ing-Class Formation: Nineteenth-Century Patterns in Western Europe and the United States* (Princeton, 1986).

[7] Ranajit Das Gupta, "Material Conditions and Behavioural Aspects of Calcutta Working Class, 1875–1899," Occasional Paper 22, Centre for Studies in Social Sciences, Calcutta, January 1979.

[8] Thompson, *The Making,* especially p. 213; William H. Sewell, Jr., *Work and Revolution in France: The Language of Labour from the Old Regime to 1848* (Cambridge, 1980).

[9] The argument of this paragraph is more fully developed in my "Class Consciousness and the Indian Working Class: Dilemmas of Marxist Historiography," *Journal of Asian and African Studies* forthcoming.

historical imagination is best shown in the dilemmas of those texts that expressly abandon all "unilinear" notions of progress in "popular consciousness" and yet cannot engage within themselves any possibility of a really radical, threatening rupture in the movement called "history." These texts, despite their sensitivity to empirical evidence and their conscious shying away from any simple-minded idea of progress, allow for a return of the master narrative through their conceptualization of "time" itself. In certain accounts of "popular consciousness," time, one of the ultimate constituents of the historical narrative, is allowed to stand in as a silent but unfailing guarantor of "progress" or "development," dissolving the effect of all discontinuities and assuming the role that once belonged to "material base" or "economic structure." This is how Sumit Sarkar, for instance, introduces "the question of variations over time" in a discussion of "the condition and nature of subaltern militancy" in Bengal in the early part of the twentieth century:

> Certainly any assumption of a unilinear development of popular consciousness in a "progressive" direction has to be abandoned. In labour history oscillation between class struggle and communal strife remains all too evident, while the united peasant actions of the Non-Co-operation-Khilafat period gave way by the mid-1920s to agrarian-communal riots very reminiscent of 1906–7. Yet certain shifts can be seen, *if we take a long enough time-span*, and the greatness of Satinath Bhaduri's novel [*Dhorai Charit Manas*] lies precisely in its comprehension of the complex development of popular consciousness *in and through* interruptions and retrogressions. The national movement had very far from a unilinear development, and yet the legitimacy of foreign rule was eroded *over time*.[10]

EXCEPTIONALISM and universalism—these "soul-torturing antitheses" reflect a problem that seems inescapable in all attempts at writing, from a Marxist point of view, the history of working-class (or popular) consciousness. The problem is this. What makes Marxist labor history possible are—apart from the fact of industrialization and the creation of an industrial labor force—the categories and concepts of Marxian thought including a notion of emancipation that defines a universal *telos* of history. It is for this reason that Marxist historical accounts,

---

[10] Sumit Sarkar, "The Conditions and Nature of Subaltern Militancy: Bengal from Swadeshi to Non-Co-operation, c. 1905–22," in Ranajit Guha, ed., *Subaltern Studies III: Writings on South Asian History and Society* (Delhi, 1984), p. 319. Emphasis added.

especially of the working class, are ultimately cast in the mold of an emancipatory narrative. But the notion of emancipation, though universal in its claim, arises from a body of thought whose immediate background, whatever the critical distance Marx might place between himself and his intellectual progenitors, is the Enlightenment and its pursuit of "liberty" and "freedom." The Enlightenment, it is true, has never been without its critics; the "modernity" it heralded has revealed many frailties, and the assurances once found in science and reason seem irretrievably lost.[11] "Modernity" fails even more miserably when we turn to a country like India where liberal thought was never strong and where the message of the Enlightenment and modernity was delivered only in an extremely travestied form by the mad and violent agency of imperialism.

Understandably, therefore, emancipatory narratives strain under the burden of their own conflicts: witness the dilemmas of Marxist labor history that I have outlined in the preceding section. On the one hand, the explicit privileging of a liberal heritage, which presents the question of "culture" in terms of an exceptionalist argument à la Thompson's; a universalism, on the other hand, where the question of cultural specificity is subordinated to an overarching idea of progress and modernity that emerges, paradoxically enough, from liberal thought itself.

The challenge of our reading of jute workers' history is precisely this: How do we pose the problem of culture and consciousness, and retain a notion of "working-class politics" (i.e. emancipatory politics) without giving ground to either the exceptionalist or the universalist argument in labor history? There is no elegant solution to this problem in Marx's thought, though there is, as is so often the case with Marx, the possibility of an answer. But an answer not without problems.

Marx places the question of subjectivity right at the heart of his category "capital" when he posits the conflict between "real labour" and "abstract labour" as one of its central contradictions. "Real labour" refers to the labor power of the actual individual, labor power "as it exists in the *personality* of the labourer"[12]—that is, as it exists in the "immediate exclusive individuality" of the individual.[13] Just as personalities differ, similarly the labor power of one individual is different from that of another. "Real labour" refers to the essential heteroge-

---

[11] See Jean-François Lyotard, *The Postmodern Condition: A Report on Knowledge*, trans. G. Bennington and B. Massumi (Manchester, 1984).

[12] Karl Marx, *Capital*, vol. 1 (Moscow, n.d.), p. 538. Emphasis added.

[13] Hegel uses these words in explaining "personality." See *Hegel's Philosophy of Right*, trans. T. M. Knox (London, 1967), p. 115.

neity of individual capacities. "Abstract" or general labor, on the other hand, refers to the idea of uniform, homogeneous labor that capitalism imposes on this heterogeneity, the notion of a general labor that underlies "exchange value." It is what makes labor measurable and makes possible the generalized exchange of commodities. It expresses itself, as we have seen before, in capitalist discipline, which has the sole objective of making every individual's concrete labor—by nature heterogeneous—"uniform and homogeneous" through supervision and technology employed in the labor process. We have discussed before (chapter 3) how the notion of the wage as "contract" underlies the ideal of capitalist discipline. Politically, then, the concept of "abstract labour" is an extension of the bourgeois notion of the "equal rights" of "abstract individuals," whose political life is reflected in the ideals and practice of "citizenship." The politics of "equal rights" is thus precisely the "politics" that one can read into the category "capital." All individual laborers, in conditions of generalized commodity production, have to be constantly disciplined into the ideals of "abstract labour." That is why labor, in Marx's analysis, always has a problematic presence in the process of production.[14]

From this one might reasonably conclude that the more individual workers internalize and live out the ideals of "equal rights" and citizenship, the more implicated they become in the rule of capital both inside and outside the factory. The absence of these notions from the culture of individual jute workers in Calcutta would then appear to be very much a point in their favor. The precapitalist "community" could easily be celebrated as a site of resistance against capital.

Historically, it is, of course, true that much resistance to capital has indeed arisen from precapitalist, communal forms of organization and consciousness. Marx's radical individualism, however, would not permit a romantic celebration of the precapitalist forms of "community." He never lost sight of the undemocratic character of the precapitalist community. These communities, as Marx said, "are founded either on the immature development of man individually, who has not severed the umbilical cord that unites him with his fellow men in a primitive tribal community, or upon direct relations of subjection."[15] As against this, Marx sees the coming of citizenship, the separation of the individual's private interests from his public rights, as creating at the same time "general interests" and bodies expressive of a unity based on the

[14] See chapter 3. Also Henry, *Marx*, pp. 202, 206, 244, 285, 297, discusses the issue extensively.
[15] *Capital*, vol. 1, p. 79. See also his *Grundrisse: Foundations of the Critique of Political Economy*, trans. Martin Nicolaus (Harmondsworth, 1974), pp. 487–494.

opposition of the private and the general. For the nation, this means the state; for the class, it refers to the class organization, such as the trade union. In *The German Ideology* we read:

> How is it that personal interests always develop . . . into class interests, into common interests which acquire independent existence in relation to the individual persons, and in their independence assume the forms of *general* interests?[16]

Marx answers:

> Communist theoreticians . . . have discovered that throughout history the "general interest" is created by individuals who are defined as "private persons." They know that this contradiction is only a *seeming* one because one side of it, what is called the "general interests," is constantly being produced by the other side, private interests, and in relation to the latter it is by no means an independent force with an independent history—so that this contradiction is in practice constantly destroyed and reproduced.[17]

But in Marx there is no absolute valorization of citizenship either. The "general interest" that citizenship creates points logically to the state as the only "universal" that can be posited against the particularities of competing private interests. (The trade union, as we have said in chapter 4, is only an image of the state.) The greater the emphasis on citizenship and equal rights as the ideal means of resolving conflicts arising from particular interests, distinctions of birth, and so on, the more the nation-state presents itself as the embodiment of universal attributes of freedom and emancipation, and indeed the limit to all politics and struggles. Needless to say, this exactly is the limit of all "practical" politics of our own times when even movements that find themselves fighting particular nation-states only end up reproducing the very same institution in some other particular form.

One has to recall that this was not Marx's vision of emancipation. The "proletariat" was born precisely in Marx's refusal to accept Hegel's celebration of the modern state as representing the most universal aspect of society.[18] From the outset the "proletariat" was defined in

---

[16] K. Marx and F. Engels, *The German Ideology* (Moscow, 1976), p. 262. Emphasis in original.

[17] Ibid., p. 264.

[18] K. Marx, "A Contribution to the Critique of Hegel's Philosophy of Right, Introduction," in *Early Writings*, trans. Rodney Livingstone and Gregor Benton (Harmondsworth, 1975), pp. 243–257. See also Marx's "Critique of Hegel's Doctrine of the State," in ibid., pp. 57–198.

opposition to the notion of the nation-state, and hence to the notion of citizenship. "The proletarian," says the *Communist Manifesto*, is "stripped . . . of every trace of national character"; "the working men have no country."[19] The point is also made in *The German Ideology*, where the proletariat is opposed to the idea of "national interests" (which is the universal that the state claims to represent)—"nationality is already dead" for the proletariat.[20]

This absolutely irreconcilable opposition between "the proletarian" and "the citizen" is never pursued far enough by Marx so as to usher in a fully developed critique of the nation-state itself.[21] Slippages in fact occur throughout the *Manifesto*, where the existing definition of a particular nation-state—that is, an oppressive, violent, and historically contingent social formation—is often offered as an unquestionable given: "The proletariat of *each country* must, of course, first of all settle matters with its *own* bourgeoisie."[22] In part, no doubt, this happens because of the revolutionary role the *Manifesto* ascribes to the bourgeoisie, which is pictured as breaking down not only the "Chinese Walls" of isolated precapitalist communities and customs but the barriers of national differences as well. The proletariat in this regard simply takes over the unfinished task of the bourgeoisie, at least as "the first step," "to win the battle of democracy," to raise itself "to the position of the ruling class," to "constitute itself *the* nation" (though not, Marx hastens to add, "in the bourgeois sense of the word").[23]

It is in this relatively uncritical use that Marx makes of words like *democracy* and *nation* that Enlightenment thought survives and the opposition between "the proletarian" and "the citizen" does not manifest its full, radical potential. Yet, as we have seen, Marx's vision of human emancipation, his thoroughgoing individualism, is predicated neither on bourgeois citizenship nor on the "archaic community."

An attempt to understand critically the problem of "working-class politics" in Indian history takes us back to a question we posed in the Preface: Where do we see this history going? What is the nature of the "emancipation" that we see as an integral part of our definition of

[19] K. Marx and F. Engels, *Manifesto of the Communist Party*, in their *Selected Works*, vol. 1 (Moscow, 1962), pp. 44, 51.

[20] *The German Ideology*, p. 82.

[21] Some, though by no means all, of the problems in this regard are discussed in Z. A. Pelczynski, "Nation, Civil Society, State: Hegelian Sources of the Marxian Non-theory of Nationality," in Z. A. Pelczynski, ed., *The State and Civil Society: Studies in Hegel's Political Philosophy* (Cambridge, 1984), pp. 262–278.

[22] *Manifesto*, p. 45. Emphasis added.

[23] Ibid., pp. 51, 53. Emphasis in original.

"modernity"? For that is the question that shapes the narrative we produce out of the myriad individual "changes" in society. Historians often debate "changes" and "continuities" in working-class history. The more fundamental question seems to be: From what teleological perspective do we even identify and name these "changes"?

It is in search of a teleology that I have used the opposition between the precapitalist, inegalitarian "community" and the bourgeois idea of "citizenship." It is not my intention, however, to use "citizenship" and the attendant notion of equality as defining a universal state of freedom and modernity to which working-class movements must aspire. The politics of the jute-mill workers of Calcutta, looked at in the 1940s or 1950s, could not be described in terms of a struggle for "citizenship." The power relations that made up their everyday life arose out of a culture that was hierarchical and inegalitarian, subordinating the individual to imagined communities of a distinctly precapitalist character.

It may be argued, of course, that the more the Indian state, its different organizations, and its trade unions come to be a part of this history, the more they present, by their practice, a discourse that indeed sees "citizenship" and the "universalistic" (the Indian word is *secular*) state as the goal of all history including that of the working class. Yet to select that as the theme of one's narrative is to make a choice in favor of the ideology of the nation-state. It is to mistake the dominant ideological discourse of our time for the real and contradictory process of history. To adopt this narrative strategy is, ultimately, to employ the nationalist problematic of "transition," which privileges liberalism and looks on the historical process as one that results, sooner or later, in a triumph of the universalistic "citizen" over the particularistic "community." Even if it speaks the language of Marxism, what we have here is the nationalist emancipatory narrative parading as radical philosophy.

But the concepts of citizenship, equal rights, and so on are still useful, not as ends in themselves, but for their negative critical value in highlighting the hierarchical and inegalitarian nature of the relationships of power within which workers such as the mill hands of Calcutta find themselves. The issues of consciousness, solidarity, organization, and protest in that history can be posed, within our framework, in terms of a tension between the undemocratic cultural codes of Indian society and the notion of "equality" that socialist politics both assume and seek to transcend. To some extent, this tension itself is now a part of the reality. But its resolution, I have argued here, cannot be had by recourse to economistic or narrowly political explanations.

Marxism, for that reason, cannot be reduced to a philosophy of social engineering; the course of history remains, ultimately, undecidable. Yet in choosing categories of analysis—such as "class consciousness," "equality," "democratic relationships," to which we relate positively, or "hierarchy," "inegalitarian relations," "oppression," "exploitation," to which our attitudes are negative—we reveal our own political choices, the future that is the object of the exercise of our desire and will. In the end, when the assurances given us by emancipatory narratives are gone, and we do not look in history, even in the history of the oppressed, for any objective guarantees for emancipatory politics, the only thing we can speak of with confidence is the struggle—of which this book is a part, as are the jute workers, seen through the prism of this book.

GLOSSARY

Akhara Gymnasium; society for physical culture

Arya Samaj Hindu-revivalist organization founded in 1875

Babu Bengali clerk in European-managed business

Badmash Scoundrel

Bakr Id Muslim festival commemorating the Patriarch Abraham's sacrifice of his son Isaac

Bakshish Gratuity; tip

Bande Mataram "Hail to the Mother" (nationalist slogan)

Batta Commission; discount

Bhadralok Lit. gentlefolk; respectable people of the middle class

Biri Traditional Indian cigarette rolled in a tree leaf

Brahmo Samaj Reformist Hindu religious sect started by Rammohun Roy in 1828–30

Burra Head; chief

Busti Slum

Chaukidar Watchman

Chota Haziri The Anglo-Indian institution of "little breakfast"

Dalal Agent

Dastoori Customary dues; derived from *dastoor* "custom"

Durga Puja The worship of the Hindu goddess Durga

Durwan(s) Gatekeepers; security men; armed

[Darwan] retainers

Fatka Lit. bubble; speculative market

Ghat Steps leading to river

Goonda Ruffian

Gora Lit. pale; European

Hartal Stoppage of work in protest

Holi Hindu religious festival originating from the myth of Krishna; involves the throwing of red powder and colored water by the participants

Izzat Honor

Jamadar See *durwan*

Kafir Unbeliever

Kanoon Law

Khilafat Lit. Caliphate. Refers to the pan-Islamic movement in India in support of the Turkish sultan after the First World War

Korbani Sacrificial killing of a beast; an Islamic practice

Ma-Baap Lit. mother-father; parents

Maiji/Mataji Mother

Maulana/Maulvi Title usually applied to Muslim priests or Muslims knowledgeable in the ways of Islam

Mazdur Laborer

231

Merua   A derogatory Bengali term for any native speaker of Hindi; derived
    from Marwari
Mufassil   Localities outside big towns or cities
Muharram   Muslim mourning ritual commemorating the death of Hossain
    on the battlefield of Karbala
Musjid [masjid]   Mosque
Nokri   Service; paid employment
Panchayat   Traditional Indian village council
Panwala (m)   Seller of the betel leaf
Panwali (f)
Parbani   Gifts related to religious festival (*parban*)
Rakhee   A piece of thread worn around the wrist as a mark of brotherhood;
    a traditional Hindu rite for tying the thread
Riwaz   Custom
Sahib   Boss; generally referred to the Europeans in colonial India
Salami   Gift given to a superior for favors received
Sardar/Sirdar   Lit. headman, chief; jobber in the jute mills
Swaraj   Self-rule
Swadeshi movement   Antipartition agitation in Bengal, 1905–1908, derived
    from *Swadesh* "one's native land"
Thana   Police station
Zamindar   Landlord

BIBLIOGRAPHY

A. GOVERNMENT RECORDS
  I. Unpublished
  II. Published

B. PAPERS OF ORGANIZATIONS
  I. Unpublished
  II. Published

C. PAPERS RELATING TO INDIVIDUALS
  I. Institutional collections
  II. Private collections

D. NEWSPAPERS AND PERIODICALS

E. INTERVIEWS

F. BOOKS, ARTICLES, AND THESES: A SELECT LIST

A. GOVERNMENT RECORDS

I. Unpublished

Government of India files held at the National Archives of India, Delhi:
  Department of Industries and Labour files, 1921–31.
  Home Department Political files, 1925–31.
Government of Bengal files held at the West Bengal State Archives, Calcutta:
  General Department Miscellaneous Branch files, 1882–1911.
  Judicial Department Police Branch files, 1890–1900.
  General Department Education Branch files, 1913–15.
  Medical Department Medical Branch files, 1914.
  Finance Department Commerce Branch files, 1915.
  Local Self-Government Department Public Health Branch files, 1927–32.
  Commerce Department Commerce Branch files, 1919–36.
  Commerce Department Labour Branch files, 1937–40.
  Home Department Political Branch Confidential files, 1900–1940.

II. Published

Report of the Indian Factory Commission 1890 (Calcutta, 1890).
Report of the Labour Enquiry Committee of 1895 (Calcutta, 1896).
Report of the Indian Factory Labour Commission (London, 1909), 2 vols.
B. Foley, *Report on Labour in Bengal* (Calcutta, 1906).

Census of India 1921 (Calcutta, 1923), vol. 5, pts. 1 and 2.

Report of the Royal Commission on Labour in India (London, 1931), vol. 1; vol. 5, pts. 1 and 2; vol. 11, pts. 1 and 2.

Report of the Bengal Jute Enquiry Committee (Calcutta, 1939), vols. 1 and 2.

S. R. Deshpande, *Report on an Enquiry into Conditions of Labour in the Jute Mill Industry in India* (Delhi, 1946).

[U.K.] Board of Trade, *Working Party Report on Jute* (London, 1948).

Indian Central Jute Committee, *Report on the Marketing of Jute and Jute Products* (Calcutta, 1941; reprint, Calcutta, 1952).

Report of the Central Wage Board for Jute Industry (Delhi, 1963).

B. PAPERS OF ORGANIZATIONS

I. Unpublished

(a) Archives of Thomas Duff and Co., Ltd., Jute Merchants, Dundee. The following papers have been consulted:
  1. Minute books of the Samnugger Jute Factory Company, Ltd., 1874–85.
  2. Minute books of Thomas Duff and Co., Ltd., 1883–99.
  3. Minute books of the Titaghur Jute Factory Co., Ltd., 1883–88.
  4. Minute books of the Victoria Jute Co., Ltd., 1892–98.
  5. Letters and telegrams from agents in India relating to business matters, 1887–90.
  6. Papers concerning Mr. James Robertson, manager of the Samnugger Jute Mill, 1865–87.
  7. Confidential monthly financial statements for the Samnugger, Titaghur, and Victoria mills, 1916–35.

(b) Dundee and District Union or Jute and Flax Workers, Dundee: Letterbook entitled "India" (contains copies of correspondence with Indian trade unionists, 1926–28).

(c) Archives of the Department of Modern History, the University of Dundee:
  Card collection on the records of Cox Brothers, jute merchants and manufactures, Dundee.

(d) Archives of the Dundee University Library:
  O. Graham, "The Dundee Jute Industry, 1830–1928," MS. 15/1.

(e) Indian Jute Mills Association, Calcutta:
  Confidential file of the Labour Office containing "Circular and Notes of the Committee," 1945–46.

II. Published

The annual and six-month reports of the Indian Jute Mills Association, 1886–1937. I have not been able to locate a few of these reports.

BIBLIOGRAPHY

C. Papers Relating to Individuals

I. Institutional Collections

India Office Library, London:
  Irwin Papers, MSS. Eur. C152.
  Hoare Papers, MSS. Eur. E240.
  T. G. H. Holman Papers, MSS. Eur. D884.
  Memoirs of P. D. Martyn, MSS. Eur. F180.
Centre for South Asian Studies, Cambridge:
  Papers of Sir Edward Benthall.
  Papers in the boxes with the following numbers were consulted: 1, 2, 7,
    10, 11, 12, 13, 14, 15, 16, 19, 24.
Nehru Memorial Museum and Library, New Delhi:
  Transcript of an interview with Prabhabati Mirza (née Das Gupta) held on
    24 April 1968. Acc. No. 275.
  B. C. Roy Papers, File No. 129.
Centre for Studies in Social Sciences, Calcutta:
  Transcript of an interview with Sibnath Banerjee held on 19 July 1975.

II. Private Collections

Papers of Sibnath Banerjee, Howrah (West Bengal).
  Mr. Banerjee was kind enough to let me consult his personal files of corre-
    spondence, memoirs, etc. These included an unpublished memoir written
    in Bengali, a lecture-note entitled "Jute Workers' Organisation" and a
    note entitled "Labour Problems in Jute Industry."
Papers of K.C. Roy Chowdhury.
  At present in my possession. These are mainly notes written in diary form
    (in English and Bengali) in eighteen exercise books. They also contain an
    autobiographical note and a printed copy of a play entitled *Dharmaghat
    or The Strike*, which Roy Chowdhury wrote in 1926.

D. Newspapers and Periodicals

I have made selective use of the following:
  Amrita Bazar Patrika, 1925–32.
  Capital, 1922–32.
  The Modern Review, 1909–39.
  The Englishman, 1893–97.

E. Interviews

With Mr. G. D. Butchart in Dundee, October 1979.
With Mr. Jyotish Ganguli in Calcutta, September 1979.

F. Books, Articles, and Theses: A Select List

Ahmed, Mohiuddin. *Essentials of Colloquial Hindustani for Jute Mills and Workshops*, 2d ed. (Calcutta, 1932).

Ahmed, Rakibuddin. *The Progress of the Jute Industry and Trade (1855–1966)* (Dacca, 1966).

Ali, Md Wazed. "Jute in the Agrarian History of Bengal, 1870–1914: A Study in Primary Production," M. Litt. thesis, University of Glasgow, 1975.

Althusser, Louis, and Balibar, Etienne. *Reading Capital*, trans. Ben Brewster (London, 1977).

Amin, Shahid. "Gandhi as Mahatma: Gorakhpur District, Eastern U.P., 1921–2," in Ranajit Guha, ed., *Subaltern Studies III: Writings on South Asian History and Society* (Delhi, 1984), pp. 1–61.

Ashby, Lillian Luker (with Whatley, Roger). *My India* (London, 1938).

Avineri, Shlomo. *The Social and Political Thought of Karl Marx* (Cambridge, 1970).

Bachelard, Gaston. *The Psychoanalysis of Fire*, trans. Alan C. M. Ross (Boston, 1964).

Bagchi, A. K. "The Ambiguity of Progress: Indian Society in Transition," *Social Scientist*, vol. 13, no. 3, March 1985, pp. 3–14.

———. *Private Investment in India 1900–1939* (Cambridge, 1972).

Banerjee, Sibnath. "Labour Problems in Jute Industry" (Calcutta, c. 1955), typescript.

Barker, S. G. *Report on the Scientific and Technical Development of the Jute Manufacturing Industry in Bengal with an Addenda on Jute, Its Scientific Nature and Information Relevant Thereto* (Calcutta, 1935).

———. "Scientific Research in Indian Jute Manufactures," *Journal of the Royal Society of Arts*, vol. 86, no. 4,454, April 1938, pp. 458–481.

Barthes, Roland. *Elements of Semiology* (New York, 1979).

———. *Image-Music-Text*, trans. S. Heath (Glasgow, 1979).

Bayly, C. A. *Rulers, Townsmen and Bazaars: North Indian Society in the Age of British Expansion 1770–1870* (Cambridge, 1983).

Bhatter, B. D., and Nemenyi, L. *The Jute Crisis* (Calcutta, 1936).

Birla, G. D. *In the Shadow of the Mahatma: Personal Memoirs* (Calcutta, 1953).

Breman, Jan. "The Bottom of the Urban Order in Asia: Impressions of Calcutta," *Development and Change*, vol. 14, no. 2, April 1983.

British Association, Dundee. *Handbook and Guide to Dundee and District* (Dundee, 1912).

Brock, R. W. "Bengal and Its Jute Industry," *Asian Review*, vol. 30, no. 103, July 1934, pp. 532–540.

Brown, Hilton, ed. *The Sahibs: The Life and Ways of the British in India as Recorded by Themselves* (London, 1948).

Buchanan, D. H. *The Development of Capitalistic Enterprise in India* (New York, 1934).

Buci-Glucksmann, Christine. *Gramsci and the State* (London, 1980).

"The Calcutta Jute Mills," *Dundee Year Book, 1894* (Dundee, 1895).

Carver, Terrell. "Marxism as Method," in Terrence Ball and James Farr, eds., *After Marx* (Cambridge, 1984), pp. 261–279.

Chakrabarty, Dipesh. "Class Consciousness and the Indian Working Class: Dilemmas of Marxist Historiography," *Journal of Asian and African Studies* (forthcoming).

──────. "Communal Riots and Labour: Bengal's Jute Mill-Hands in the 1890s," *Past and Present*, no. 91, May 1981, pp. 140–169.

──────. "Sasipada Banerjee: A Study in the Nature of the First Contact of the Bengali Bhadralok with the Working Classes of Bengal," *Indian Historical Review*, January 1976, pp. 339–364.

────── and Das Gupta, Ranajit. "Some Aspects of Labour History in Bengal in the Nineteenth Century: Two Views," Occasional Paper 40, Centre for Studies in Social Sciences, Calcutta, October 1981.

Chapman, Dennis. "The Establishment of the Jute Industry: A Problem in Location Theory?" *Review of Economic Studies*, vol. 6, no. 1, Oct. 1938, pp. 44–50.

Chatterjee, Partha. *Nationalist Thought and the Colonial World: A Derivative Discourse?* (London, 1986).

Chattopadhyay, Gautam. *Communism and Bengal's Freedom Movement*, vol. 1 (Delhi, 1970).

Chattopadhyay, K. P., and Chaturvedi, H. K. "How Jute Workers Live," *Science and Culture*, vol. 12, no. 8, Feb. 1947, pp. 376–379.

Chattopadhyay, Manju. *Sramik Netri Santoshkumari Debi* (Calcutta, 1984?).

Chaturvedi, H. K. "On Jute Industry in Bengal," *Marxist Miscellany*, vol. 7, April 1946, pp. 94–143.

Dasgupta, Ajit. "Jute Textile Industry," in V. B. Singh, ed., *Economic History of India 1857–1956* (Bombay, 1965), pp. 260–280.

Das Gupta, Ranajit. "Factory Labour in Eastern India: Sources of Supply, 1855–1946: Some Preliminary Findings," *IESHR*, vol. 8, no. 3, 1976, pp. 277–329.

──────. "Material Conditions and Behavioural Aspects of Calcutta Working Class, 1875–1899," Occasional Paper 22, Centre for Studies in Social Sciences, Calcutta, January 1979.

Day, J. P. "The Jute Industry in Scotland during the War," in D. T. Jones et al., eds., *Rural Scotland during the War* (London, 1926).

Dewey, Clive. "The Government of India's 'New Industrial Policy,' 1900–1925: Formation and Failure," in K. N. Chaudhuri and C. J. Dewey, eds., *Economy and Society: Essays in Indian Economic and Social History* (Delhi, 1979), pp. 215–257.

Dumont, Louis. "World Renunciation in Indian Religion," *Contributions to Indian Sociology*, no. 4, 1960, pp. 33–62.

The Dundee Year Book [1887–1909] (Dundee 1888–1910).

Firminger, W. K. *Thacker's Guide to Calcutta* (Calcutta, 1906).

Foucault, Michel. *The Birth of the Clinic: An Archaeology of Medical Perception*, trans. A. M. Sheridan Smith (New York, 1975).

———. *Discipline and Punish: The Birth of the Prison*, trans. Alan Sheridan (Harmondsworth, 1979).

———. *Power/Knowledge: Selected Interviews and Other Writings 1972–1977*, trans. Colin Gordon et al., ed. Colin Gordon (Brighton, 1980).

———. "Preface" to Gilles Deleuze and Felix Guattari, *Anti-Oedipus: Capitalism and Schizophrenia* (Minneapolis, 1983).

Gadamer, Hans-Georg. "The Hermeneutics of Suspicion," in J. N. Mohanty, ed., *Phenomenology and the Human Sciences* (Dordrecht, 1985), pp. 73–83.

Gadgil, D. R. *The Industrial Evolution of India in Recent Times 1860–1939* (Delhi, 1973; 1st ed., London, 1924).

Gangopadhyay, Mohanlal. *Asamapta Chatabda* [in Bengali] (Calcutta, 1963).

Genovese, Elizabeth Fox, and Genovese, Eugene D. *Fruits of Merchant Capital: Slavery and Bourgeois Property in the Rise and Expansion of Capitalism* (New York, 1983).

Ghosh, Parimal. "Emergence of an Industrial Labour Force in Bengal: A Study of the Conflicts of the Jute Mill-Hands with the State, 1880–1930," Ph.D. thesis, Jadavpur University, Calcutta, 1984.

Gibson, Colin. *The Story of Jute* (Dundee, 1959?).

Gibson, I. F. "The Revision of the Jute-Wages Structure," *Scottish Journal of Political Economy*, vol. 4, Feb. 1957.

Gilchrist, R. N. *Indian Labour and the Land* (Calcutta, 1932).

———. *The Payment of Wages and Profit-Sharing* (Calcutta, 1924).

Goswami, Omkar. "Collaboration and Conflict: European and Indian Capitalists and the Jute Economy of Bengal, 1919–1939," *Indian Economic and Social History Review*, vol. 29, no. 2, April–June 1982, pp. 141–179.

Gouldner, Alvin W. *The Two Marxisms: Contradictions and Anomalies in the Development of Theory* (London, 1980).

Gramsci, Antonio. *Selections from the Prison Notebooks*, trans. and ed. Q. Hoare and G. N. Smith (New York, 1973).

———. "The Turin Workers' Council" (trans. from the *Ordine Nuovo*, 1919–1920), in Robin Blackburn, ed., *Revolution and Class Struggle: A Reader in Marxist Politics* (Glasgow, 1977), pp. 307–409.

———. "Unions and Councils," in his *Selections from Political Writings 1910–1920*, ed. Quintin Hoare and trans. John Matthews (New York, 1977), pp. 98–113.

Guha, Ranajit. *Elementary Aspects of Peasant Insurgency in Colonial India* (Delhi, 1983).

Gupta, Indrajit. *Capital and Labour in the Jute Industry* (Bombay, 1953).

Haldar, Gopal, ed. *Communist* [in Bengali] (Calcutta, 1976?)

Harrison, Godfrey. *Bird and Company of Calcutta* (Calcutta, 1964).

Hatton, C. S. "The Situation and Prospects of the Jute Industry in India and Pakistan," Ph.D. thesis, University of California, 1952.

Hegel, G.F.W. *Logic*, trans. W. Wallace (London, 1975).

Hegel's Philosophy of Right, trans. T. M. Knox (London, 1967).

Helm, Elija. "The Growth of the Factory System in India," *Journal of the Royal Society of Arts*, vol. 23, no. 1, 172, 7 May 1875, pp. 547–555.

Henry, Michel. *Marx: A Philosophy of Human Reality*, trans. Kathleen McLaughlin (Bloomington, 1983).

Hobsbawm, E. J. *Industry and Empire* (Harmondsworth, 1972; 1st ed., 1968).

Huizinga, H. *The Waning of the Middle Ages* (London, 1949).

"The Indian Jute Industry," *Agricultural Gazette of New South Wales*, vol. 25, pt. 7, 2 July 1914.

Jackson, W. Turrentine. *The Enterprising Scot: Investors in the American West after 1873* (Edinburgh, 1968).

Johnston, Thomas, and Sime, John F. *Exploitation in India* (Dundee, 1926?).

Joshi, Chitra. "Kanpur Textile Labour: Some Structural Characteristics and Aspects of Labour Movement," Ph.D. thesis, Jawaharlal Nehru University, 1982.

The Jute Mills of Bengal (Dundee, 1880). This book is a collection of reports serialized in the *Dundee Advertiser* in 1880.

Katznelson, Ira, and Zolberg, Aristide R. *Working-class Formation: Nineteenth-century Patterns in Western Europe and the United States* (Princeton, 1986).

Kelman, J. H. *Labour in India* (London, 1923).

King, D. W. *Living East* (New York, 1929).

Kumar, Nita. "Popular Culture in Urban India: The Artisans of Banares, c. 1884–1984," Ph.D. thesis, University of Chicago, 1984.

Kydd, J. C. "Industrial Labour in Bengal," *Bengal Economic Journal*, 1918.

Labica, Georges. *Marxism and the Status of Philosophy* (Brighton, 1980).

Lal, Brij V. "Approaches to the Study of Indian Indentured Emigration with Special Reference to Fiji," *Journal of Pacific History*, vol. 15, pt. 1, Jan. 1980, pp. 52–70.

Leach, Edmund R. *Culture and Communication: The Logic by Which Symbols Are Connected* (Cambridge, 1976).

Leng, John. *Letters from India and Ceylon* (Dundee, 1896).

Lenman, Bruce, Lythe, Charlotte, and Gauldie, Enid. *Dundee and Its Textile Industry* (Dundee, 1969).

Lévi-Strauss, Claude. *Tristes Tropiques* (Harmondsworth, 1973).

Lokanathan, P. S. *Industrial Organization in India* (London, 1935).

Lukes, Steven. *Individualism* (Oxford, 1979).

Lyotard, Jean-François. *The Postmodern Condition: A Report on Knowledge*, trans. G. Bennington and B. Massumi (Manchester, 1984).

Macmillan, W. G. "Research in Jute Industry," *Jute and Gunny Review*, February-March 1950.

Mahalanobis, P. C. "A Sample Survey of the Acreage under Jute in Bengal," *Sankhya*, vol. 4, pt. 4, March 1940, pp. 511–531.

Marx, Karl. *Capital*, vol. 1 (Moscow, n.d.).

———. "A Contribution to the Critique of Hegel's Philosophy of Right, Introduction," in *Early Writings*, trans. Rodney Livingston and Gregor Benton (Harmondsworth, 1975), pp. 243–257.

———. "Critique of Hegel's Doctrine of the State," in *Early Writings* (Harmondsworth, 1975), pp. 57–198.

———. *The Eighteenth Brumaire of Louis Bonaparte*, in K. Marx and F. Engels, *Selected Works*, vol. 1 (Moscow, 1969).

———. *Grundrisse: Foundations of the Critique of Political Economy* (trans. Martin Nicolaus (Harmondsworth, 1974).

———. *On the Jewish Question*, in *Early Writings* (Harmondsworth, 1975), pp. 212–241.

———, and Engels, Frederick. *The German Ideology* (Moscow, 1976).

McPherson, Kenneth. "The Muslims of Calcutta, 1918 to 1935: A Study of the Society and Politics of an Urban Minority Group in India," Ph.D. thesis, Australian National University, 1972.

[? Meek, D. B.] "Trade Disputes in Bengal," *Journal of Indian Industries and Labour*, vol. 1, pt. 1, Feb. 1921, pp. 71–80.

Mehta, M. M. *Structure of Indian Industries* (Bombay, 1955).

Misra, Sridhar. *Bhojpuri Lokasahitya: Sanskritic Adhyayan* [in Hindi] (Allahabad, 1971).

Mitra, Ashok. *Calcutta Diary* (London, 1976).

Mohindra, C. L. *Die indische Jutindustrie und ihre Entwicklung* (Berlin, 1928).

Momen, Humaira. *Muslim Politics in Bengal: A Study of Krishak Praja Party and the Elections of 1937* (Dacca, 1972).

Momin, Abdul. *Bharater Communist Partir Bangla Pradesher Tritiya Sammelane Grihita Pradeshik Trade Union Front Report* [in Bengali] (Calcutta, 1943).

———. "Chatkal Sramiker Pratham Sadharan Dharmaghat," [in Bengali], *Kalantar*, 10–12 August 1970.

———. "Kolkatay Gadowan Dharmaghater Chardin" [in Bengali], *Mulyayan*, Pous-Magh (1977), pp. 11–12.

Mukherjee, Radhakamal. *The Indian Working Class* (Bombay, 1948).

Mukherjee, Saroj, ed. *Trade Unioner Godar Katha* [in Bengali] (Calcutta, 1934).

Mukherjee, Uma. *Two Great Indian Revolutionaries* (Calcutta, 1966).

Mukherji, Saugata. "Some Aspects of Commercialization of Agriculture in Eastern India 1891–1938," in Asok Sen, Partha Chatterjee, and Saugata Mukherji, *Three Studies on the Agrarian Structure of Bengal 1858–1947* (Calcutta, 1982).

Mullick, Kuladaprasad. *Nabajuger Sadhana* [in Bengali] (Calcutta, 1913).

Nandy, S. C. "Krisnakanta Nandy's Book of Monthly Accounts of 1195 B.S. (1787–88)," *Bengal Past and Present*, January-June 1980, pp. 3–11.

Oakley, C. A. *Scottish Industry* (Edinburgh, 1953).

Ollman, Bertell. *Alienation: Marx's Conception of Man in Capitalist Society* (Cambridge, 1977).

Pandey, Gyanendra. "Community Consciousness and Communal Strife in Colonial North India" (unpublished manuscript).

Pažanin, A. "Overcoming the Opposition between Idealism and Materialism in Husserl and Marx," in B. Waldenfels et al., eds., *Phenomenology and Marxism*, trans. J. Claude Evans, Jr. (London, 1984), pp. 82–101.

Pearson, R. *Eastern Interlude: A Social History of the European Community in Calcutta* (Calcutta, 1954).

Pelczynski, Z. A. "Nation, Civil Society, State: Hegelian Sources of the Marxian Non-theory of Nationality," in Z. A. Pelczynski, ed., *The State and Civil Society: Studies in Hegel's Political Philosophy* (Cambridge, 1984), pp. 262–278.

Perrot, Michelle. "The Three Ages of Industrial Discipline in Nineteenth Century France," in John M. Merriman, ed., *Consciousness and Class Experience in Nineteenth Century Europe* (New York, 1979).

Petrie, David. *Communism in India 1924–1927* (Delhi, 1927; reprint, Calcutta, 1972).

Pillai, P. P. *Economic Conditions in India* (London, 1925).

Ray, Rajat K. "The Crisis of Bengal Agriculture, 1870–1927: The Dynamics of Immobility," *IESHR*, vol. 8, no. 3, 1973, pp. 244–279.

——. *Industrialization in India: Growth and Conflict in the Private Corporate Sector 1914–1947* (New Delhi, 1979).

Rosdolsky, Roman. *The Making of Marx's "Capital"* (London, 1980).

Rousseau, Jean-Jacques. *A Discourse on Inequality (1755)*, trans. M. Cranston (Harmondsworth, 1984).

Roy Chowdhury, K. C. *Dharmaghat* (Calcutta, 1926).

——. "Some Thoughts on Indian Labour," *Journal of Indian Industries and Labour*, vol. 3, pt. 1, Feb. 1923, pp. 23–28.

Rubin, I. I. *Essays on Marx's Theory of Value* (Montreal, 1975).

Ryan, Michael. *Marxism and Deconstruction: A Critical Articulation* (Baltimore and London, 1982).

Saha, N. C. "Inside a Jute Mill," *Jute and Gunny Review*, February-March 1950, pp. 139–143.

Saha, P. *History of the Working Class Movement in Bengal* (Delhi, 1978).

Samuel, Raphael, ed. *People's History and Socialist Theory* (London, 1981).

Sarkar, Sumit. "The Conditions and Nature of Subaltern Militancy: Bengal from Swadeshi to Non-Co-operation, c. 1905–22," in Ranajit Guha, ed., *Subaltern Studies III: Writings on South Asian History and Society* (Delhi, 1984), pp. 271–320.

——. *The Swadeshi Movement in Bengal 1903–1908* (Delhi, 1973).

241

———. "Swadeshi Yuger Sramik Andolan: Kayekti Aprakashita Dalil" [in Bengali], *Itihas*, vol. 4, no. 2, Bhadra-Agrahayan 1376 (1969), pp. 113–115.

Sarkar, Tanika. "National Movement and Popular Protest in Bengal, 1928–1934," Ph.D. thesis, University of Delhi, 1980.

Saul, S. B. *Studies in British Overseas Trade 1870–1914* (Liverpool, 1960).

Sen, Amartya Kumar. "The Commodity Pattern of British Enterprise in Early Indian Industrialization," in *Deuxième Conférence Internationale d'Histoire Economique, Aix-en-Provence, 1962* (Paris, 1965).

Sen, Shila. *Muslim Politics in Bengal 1937–1947* (New Delhi, 1976).

Sen, Sukomal. *Working Class of India: History of Emergence and Movement, 1830–1970* (Calcutta, 1977).

Sen-Gupta, J. N. *Economics of Jute* (Calcutta, 1935).

Sharma, Tulsi Ram. *Location of Industries in India* (Bombay, 1954).

Singh, Raghuraj. *Movement of Industrial Wages in India* (Bombay, 1955).

Sinha, H. "Jute Futures in Calcutta," *Economica*, no. 27, Nov. 1929, pp. 330–337.

Stuart, Roger. "The Formation of the Communist Party of India, 1927–1937: The Dilemma of the Indian Left," Ph.D. thesis, Australian National University, 1978.

Thompson, E. P. *The Making of the English Working Class* (Harmondsworth, 1968).

Timberg, Thomas. *The Marwaris: From Traders to Industralists* (New Delhi, 1978).

Vakil, C. N., Bose, S. C., and Deolalkar, P. V. *Growth of Industry and Trade in Modern India* (Bombay, 1931).

Venkatasubbiah, H. *The Structural Basis of the Indian Economy: A Study in Interpretation* (London, 1940).

Vidyarnava, Ramanuja. *Kanthamala* [in Bengali] (Bhatpara, c. 1913).

Walker, W.A.M. "Growth of the Jute Industry in India and Pakistan," *Journal of the Royal Society of Arts*, vol. 97, no. 4,794, May 1949, pp. 409–420.

Wallace, D. R. *The Romance of Jute* (Calcutta, 1909; 2d ed., London, 1928).

White, Hayden. *Tropics of Discourse: Essays in Cultural Criticism* (Baltimore and London, 1985).

Wilentz, Sean. "Against Exceptionalism: Class Consciousness and the American Labor Movement, 1790–1928" [with response by Nick Salvatore and Michael Hanagan], *International Labor and Working Class History*, no. 26, Fall 1984, pp. 1–36.

Williams, Raymond. *Culture* (Glasgow, 1981).

Woodhouse, T., and Brand, A. *A Century's Progress in Jute Manufacture 1833-1933* (Dundee, 1934).

Zelený, Jindřich. *The Logic of Marx* (Oxford, 1980).

INDEX

All India Trade Union Congress, 116, 127, 150
Althusser, L., 11
Anderson, Sir John, 60
Arya Samaj, 199
Aziz, Abdul, 180

Bachelard, G., 212n
Bagchi, A. K., 50
Balibar, E., 11
Band, R. N., 41
Banerjee, A. C., 124, 139, 142, 184
Banerjee, Sasipada, 146–47, 154
Banerjee, Sibnath, 139, 141, 154, 176, 183; in 1937 elections, 150–52
Bangur, Magneeram, 58, 59
Barker, S. G., 38, 63, 86; on technological aspects of jute industry, 40–45
Barrie, J. J., 24, 26
Bengal Chamber of Commerce, 75
Bengal Chatkal Mazdoor Union, 116, 127
Bengal Jute Workers Union, 126, 134, 136, 140, 174. *See also* general strike *entries*
Benthall, Sir Edward, 52, 60, 62, 120, 122; on managerial authority, 161–65, 174, 184; on Marwari competition, 54–59; and Muslim League unions, 200, 202. *See also* Suhrawardy, H. S.
Bhattacharjee, Kalidas, 125, 129, 135–36
Birla, G. D., 54–59
Biswanand, Swami, 131
Brahmo Samaj, 147. *See also* Banerjee, Sasipada

Chakravarty, Gopen, 125, 149–50, 214
Cox, Thomas, 51
Curjel, D. F., 94, 208, 210

Das Gupta, Prabhabati, 121, 131, 136; and the nature of union leadership, 140–41, 145
Duff, Thomas, 24, 26–27
Dutt Majumdar, Niharendu, 184

Federation of Indian Chambers of Commerce, 56
Foucault, M., xii, xiv, 6, 68, 143n, 172, 181n

Gandhi, M. K., 152
general strike of 1929, 118, 155; economic basis of, 119–20, 125–26; managers' reaction to, 174–75; problems of leadership during, 136, 140–41; spread of, 130
general strike of 1937, 163–64, 173, 179; class solidarity and communal tension during, 186–96 passim; employers' reaction to, 163–64, 199; and the growth of trade unions, 125, 127
Ghosh, Kishorilal, 126
Gilchrist, R. N., 47–49, 106, 128, 208
Gourepore Labour Union, 129
Gramsci, A., xiv; on trade union organization, 132–33
Gupta, Indrajit, 116, 134–38, 154, 198, 203
Gupta, Santosh Kumari, 129, 136, 145

Hegel, G.F.W., 68, 141, 225n
Henry, Michel, 219, 221
Hindu-Muslim riots, 190–99, 204–5; and the question of women's honor, 215–16
Hobsbawm, E. J., 38
Holman, T. G., 168
Hossain, Latafat, 141
Huizinga, H., 143

Indian Jute Mills Association (IJMA), 14, 75–81, 97, 99, 102, 109, 126; attitude toward education and training of workers, 90–91; disunity in, 46–48, 57, 61–62; formation of, 28–29; labor policy of, 122, 199; pricing policy followed by, 41, 45; and short-time working movement, 101
Indian National Trade Union Congress, 138